Voice Acting

FOR

DUMMIES®

by Stephanie Ciccarelli and
David Ciccarelli

WILEY

John Wiley & Sons Canada, Ltd.

Voice Acting For Dummies®

Published by
John Wiley & Sons Canada, Ltd.
6045 Freemont Blvd.
Mississauga, ON L5R 4J3
www.wiley.com

Library and Archives Canada Cataloguing in Publication Data

Ciccarelli, David

    Voice Acting For Dummies / David Ciccarelli, Stephanie Ciccarelli.

Includes index.
ISBN 978-1-118-39958-3 (pbk); 978-1-118-41422-4 (ebk); 978-1-118-41423-1 (ebk); 978-1-118-41424-8 (ebk)

    1.Voice-overs. 2.Voice actors and actresses — Handbooks, manuals, etc.
I. Ciccarelli, Stephanie II. Title.
PN1995.9.V63C53 2013 791.4023 C2012-906677-X

Printed in the United States

1 2 3 4 5 RRD 17 16 15 14 13

WILEY

About the Authors

Stephanie Ciccarelli is co-founder and chief marketing officer of Voices.com. Immersed in the arts since infancy, Stephanie's formative years included classical training in voice, piano, violin, and musical theatre. A love for the written and spoken word and reverence for context and truth have prepared Stephanie well to lead within the industry and inspire many through her blog, VOX Daily. She graduated with a bachelor of musical arts degree from the Don Wright Faculty of Music at the University of Western Ontario and has found a unique way to apply her education to the field of voice acting, bringing a fresh perspective and voice to the industry. When she's not spending time with her husband David and their four children, Stephanie volunteers her time consulting local organizations on social media, singing, and connecting with other likeminded women who positively impact in meaningful ways their families, neighborhoods, work environments, and those around them.

David Ciccarelli is the co-founder and CEO of Voices.com, an award-winning online marketplace, connecting clients with voice-over talent. The unique blending of his audio engineering background with his self-taught business savvy and website development afforded David the creative freedom to pursue his passion for innovation during the first dot com boom, and the result catapulted him onto the scene as a pioneer in his field in the early 2000s. His areas of expertise include customer relationship management, search marketing, social media marketing, and e-commerce, and he speaks regularly on these topics at conferences in Canada and the United States. A number of case studies regarding Voices.com's growth and rebranding strategy have been published and are used on college and university campuses worldwide. David is an honors graduate of the Ontario Institute of Audio Recording Technology and an alumnus of the entrepreneurship program hosted by the Ivey School of Business. When he's not spending time with his wife and four children, David serves as a volunteer for a number of local organizations and manages his family's philanthropy and investment portfolio.

Dedication

To our family and the team at Voices.com.

Authors' Acknowledgments

Stephanie: I thank Bill and Brenda Zadorsky, Ted Gorski, Margaret Marentette, Teresa Vlasman, Nando Favaro, Michelle Iurman, Jennifer Moir, Karen Ann Schuessler, Susan Eichhorn Young, and Jackalyn Short. Each brought me to new realizations of my voice at different stages of my life and have nurtured me through their patience, artistry, empowerment, care, and sometimes brutal honesty as they served as my coach, mentor, and friend.

David: To my teachers: Ron Hartviksen for showing me how art and technology could be blended to create beautiful masterpieces, and Bob Breen and Ken Trevenna from the Ontario Institute of Audio Recording Technology for introducing me to sound for motion pictures.

Stephanie and David: Before we even knew what to write, the word was there and as such our words fell into place. The journey of writing *Voice Acting For Dummies* reminded of us of where we have come from and all the people who helped us along the way. We wish to thank those who have been with us through the thick and thin, and those who have blessed us with support, encouragement, and words of wisdom spoken at just the right time.

Thank you to our family and friends, specifically our parents, grandparents, and those dear ones who have always believed that we could achieve anything if we put our minds to it. Thank you for understanding us and for loving us, for open arms, and listening ears. Gratitude goes out to our staff at Voices.com with special thanks to Lin Parkin for her tireless work helping us to prepare our manuscript and for countless hours of editing.

We would like to thank our friends at John Wiley & Sons, Inc, specifically our Acquisitions Editor Anam Ahmed, Project and Copy Editor Chad Sievers, and our Technical Editor, audio producer Marc Graue.

We also acknowledge the contributions of the late great Don LaFontaine who had a big voice and an even bigger heart. Thank you Don for your generosity and for leaving a legacy that will live on in the hearts of voice actors around the world.

Thank you to our teachers during our formative years. So many plant seeds into the lives of others and rarely see the fruit firsthand. Know that the lives of those you teach are better because of your efforts and that many go on to blossom and yield fruit using the gifts you knew were deep within us.

We wouldn't be where we are without the friendships and fellowship of those in the voice-over industry. We hold a special place in our hearts for friends who have helped shape how we educate our customers. You know who you are. You've all provided insight and perspectives into the art and science of voice acting for which we are grateful. Thank you for walking alongside us and for your ongoing support. A big thank you goes out to our customers for motivating and inspiring us. Without your encouraging words and thirst for knowledge, we wouldn't have written this book.

Publisher's Acknowledgments

We're proud of this book; please send us your comments through our online registration form located at http://dummies.custhelp.com. For other comments, please contact our Customer Care Department within the U.S. at 877-762-2974, outside the U.S. at 317-572-3993, or fax 317-572-4002.

Some of the people who helped bring this book to market include the following:

Acquisitions and Editorial

Associate Acquisitions Editor: Anam Ahmed

Production Editor: Lindsay Humphreys

Project Editor: Chad R. Sievers

Copy Editor: Chad R. Sievers

Technical Editor: Marc Graue

Editorial Assistant: Kathy Deady

Cartoons: Rich Tennant (www.the5thwave.com)

Cover photo: © Chris Hutchison / iStock Images

Composition Services

Project Coordinator: Kristie Rees

Layout and Graphics: Jennifer Creasey, Joyce Haughey

Proofreader: Penny Lynn Stuart

Indexer: Valerie Haynes Perry

John Wiley & Sons Canada, Ltd.

> **Deborah Barton,** Vice President and Director of Operations
>
> **Jennifer Smith,** Vice-President and Publisher, Professional & Trade Division
>
> **Alison Maclean,** Managing Editor

Publishing and Editorial for Consumer Dummies

> **Kathleen Nebenhaus,** Vice President and Executive Publisher
>
> **David Palmer,** Associate Publisher
>
> **Kristin Ferguson-Wagstaffe,** Product Development Director

Publishing for Technology Dummies

> **Andy Cummings,** Vice President and Publisher

Composition Services

> **Debbie Stailey,** Director of Composition Services

Contents at a Glance

Table of Contents

Introduction

*W*hether people have told you your entire life that you have a great voice or you've recently discovered a hidden talent for creating characters, this book is for you. *Voice Acting For Dummies* is packed with helpful information that explains in plain English how to use your voice to make money, interpret scripts, audition like a pro, and build your own home recording studio. Everybody starts somewhere, and this book is the best place to begin when exploring your voice acting abilities and discovering more about your unique voiceprint.

Being a successful voice actor takes time to figure out how to use your voice. We repeat an important message through this book: It's not just about your voice, but also how you use it. Although you use your voice in voice acting, it's much more than just talking, and the craft can bring you a lifetime of enjoyment.

The guidance you find in this book is similar to what you may receive from a voice coach or hear at an industry conference. By employing the tips and ideas here, you can improve your voice acting skills and experience a dramatic difference in how you approach the written word.

Today most voice actors work from home recording studios, away from the glitz and glamour of Hollywood. Voice actors generally rely upon their skills honed from years of working with casting directors, voice directors, producers, and instructors. This book explains how you can assess your voice, look for clues in audition copy, and serve as your own director as often is required for the workaday voice actor.

About This Book

Voice Acting For Dummies has been literally years in the making. We always hoped (and expected) that we could share our experiences with more people than just those individuals we encountered in our business. *Voice Acting For Dummies* is the culmination of our education, practical experience, and industry expertise — basically everything we've learned about how you can use the human voice to communicate a message well, with purpose and capturing the spoken word in digital form.

Like all *For Dummies* books, this book is modular, so you can flip through and look for topics that interest you. Some may jump out more than others depending on where you are in your voice acting journey. You don't need to read this book in its entirety to improve your abilities as a voice actor; look for the topics you need and study them to develop your voice acting skills.

With step-by-step explanations and an abundance of examples, this guide clues you in on recording and producing voice-overs and promoting yourself as a voice actor with info on:

- Creating your *first demo,* a short audio recording used to promote yourself and demonstrate the types of voices you can perform

- Finding your *signature voice,* no matter whether you're young or old or have an accent or not, and then leveraging your previous life experiences into recording compelling, believable voice-overs that clients will love

- Interpreting scripts, deciphering characters, directing yourself, and delivering believable performances

- Getting the bare necessities (if you don't already have them), including a microphone, recording software, and an audio card

- Using audio-editing software and adding bed music and sound effects for a signature finishing touch

- Recording, understanding file formats, and capturing or minimizing ambient noise

The advice we present here is tried, tested, and true. We've been working with voice actors now for more than a decade and have been in the business of using our gifts for voice and audio production even longer. Having attended workshops with some of the finest teachers and actors working today in voice acting, we owe a great debt of gratitude to many wonderful people who have shared with us of their time, voices, and expertise. Now we share that information with you.

Conventions Used in This Book

To help you navigate this book with ease, we set the following conventions:

- We use **bold** text to highlight key words in bulleted lists.

- When we introduce industry jargon (a new term you may not be familiar with), we use *italics* and define the term within the text.

- Web addresses appear in `monofont` so you can easily find them. If you've purchased an ebook version, the URLs are interactive.

- When this book was printed, some URLS may be longer than the page will allow. Please note that we don't add any extra characters, such as hyphens, to indicate the break. So when using one of these web addresses, just type in exactly what you see in this book, as though the line break doesn't exist.

What You're Not to Read

You're a busy person, juggling the many balls of life. Your time is precious to you. So if you want to read just the essential, need-to-know information about voice acting, you can skip the sidebars, which are the gray-shaded boxes. The information in the sidebars is intriguing and fun, but not necessarily crucial for understanding voice acting. Feel free to read the sidebars when you have time.

Foolish Assumptions

When we wrote this book, we made a few assumptions about you, our dear reader. We assume the following:

- ✔ You want to know about the ins and outs of voice acting.
- ✔ You have an interest in voice acting and discovering how to use your voice to the best of your ability.
- ✔ You want to start your own voice acting business and begin to audition for work in the real world.
- ✔ You've already done some voice acting, and you're looking for tips and advice to elevate your abilities.

No matter where you're coming from, you don't need any prior knowledge of voice acting. You can find information for beginners and more experienced voice actors alike.

How This Book Is Organized

This book is organized into six parts, with each part containing specific types of information about voice acting. You explore the mechanics of voice acting before you work on your technique.

Part 1: Exploring Voice Acting Basics

In this part, we cover the basics of voice acting. You can use this information to get a strong start in voice acting. Chapter 2 helps you find your voice. Chapter 3 focuses on training your voice so you're ready for what voice acting throws at you. This chapter also explains the benefits of working with a voice acting coach. Chapter 4 discusses the different roles of a voice actor. Chapter 5 walks you through interpreting a script and creating and interpreting your character.

After reading this part, you may want to jot down some of these core ideas in a journal. You can revisit these ideas in a few weeks or months and see how much you've grown as you practice by reading aloud and experimenting with your voice each and every day.

Part II: Creating Your Audio Résumé

This part focuses on recording your very first voice-over demo. Your voice-over demo is like an audio resume that shows people what you're capable of doing. Demos help you promote yourself and help you get voice-over work. Chapter 6 explains what demos are and why they're important. Chapter 7 walks you through how to construct your own demo from the ground up, including how to plan for your demo, how to write your own scripts, and what to consider in terms of copyrights. When you're ready to actually record your demo, read Chapter 8, which also helps you figure out which recording approach to take and whether to include music in your demo. For voice actors who may already have demos, the chapters in this part include advice on how to take your demo to the next level and how to update your demos.

Part III: Auditioning and Finding Work

In this part, you move on to information that helps you apply your voice acting skills to auditioning in the voice-over marketplace. Chapter 9 focuses on where to find auditions, how to prepare for an audition, and how to best present oneself to the casting director or decision maker. Chapter 10 in particular is useful to market yourself and showcase your voice and upload demos for prospective clients to the Internet. This chapter covers a number of business topics, such as your brand and how to position yourself as a professional voice actor. We cover auditioning basics (a must for all beginners) in Chapter 11. Chapter 12 covers auditioning online, and Chapter 13 addresses auditioning in a traditional setting, such as a studio or an agent's office. This chapter gives insight for what the expectations of voice actors are and how to navigate relationships with people you meet at the casting call.

Part IV: Setting Up Your Voice Acting Business

When you've discovered all the amazing things your voice can do and have a clear understanding of how to interpret the written word, you can think about setting up a business and earning some money. Some people fail to realize in creative endeavors that they're also running a business. When you treat what you do as a real business, you can better develop your craft, build a proper studio, and invest in your career.

Chapter 14 discusses booking a voice-over job and all that this typically entails. We walk you through the hiring process and how to communicate with your client, making sure that you've reviewed the full and final script, and what to do if things don't go according to plan. Everyone gets sick or goes on vacation, so we also show you how to plan for contingencies. Chapter 15 focuses on getting paid for your work. You can find out how to quote for voice-overs and all the factors you need to consider when putting a price tag on your services. If you've ever had a business before, you know that it can become like one of the family, usually like another child. Chapter 16 includes tips for how to continuously nurture your business by developing relationships with your customers, getting an agent (or acting as your own), and building a winning team of professionals around your business to support you such as accountants, lawyers, and the like.

Part V: Establishing Your Home Recording Studio

The home recording studio is critical to working today as a voice actor. Equipment has significantly come down in price over the years, which makes creating your own studio that much easier and more affordable. You may be surprised at what you can create in terms of a professional and cost-effective recording environment, and how easy it is to master the basics of audio recording.

Chapter 17 covers the basics of the home recording studio, such as how to record on your computer, what to look for in a microphone, recording and editing software, and accessories for your studio, and how to create an awesome home studio environment. Chapter 18 shares information for recording your voice, deciphering studio terminology, using a microphone, and recording your first take. Chapter 19 is more advanced and instructs you on editing and mixing a voice-over recording. Chapter 20 explains how to record your final product. We include material relevant to review your recording before you send it to your client in Chapter 21.

Part VI: The Part of Tens

Every *For Dummies* book has this fun part that includes short chapters, chock-full of quick-and-easy tidbits. Here we include a chapter on ten reasons why regularly auditioning in voice-over work is important and a chapter on ten tips you can do to be prepared for voice acting.

Icons Used in This Book

We use the following icons in the margins to point out important information:

The Remember icon is a memory jog for those really important things you shouldn't forget.

This icon gives you a tip on the quickest, easiest way to perform a task or conquer a concept. This icon highlights stuff that's good to know and stuff that'll save you time and/or frustration.

We use this icon when we want you to avoid a potentially uncomfortable or dangerous situation.

Where to Go from Here

If you have no voice acting experience, start at Chapter 1 and work your way through the chapters in order. That being said, this book is modular, meaning that it's designed for you to jump in anywhere you want. Peruse the table of contents or index for different topics. If something piques your interest, by all means, read it first.

If you have some voice acting experience, choose whatever chapter appeals most to you. You may have to refer to other chapters from time to time, but otherwise choose your own adventure at your own pace and in any order. If you choose to go full out and take voice acting from the realm of hobby to that of a business, you can find that each part has useful information that you can apply almost immediately to help you turn your aspiration into a career.

Part I

Exploring Voice Acting Basics

The 5th Wave   By Rich Tennant

"Very nice audition, Vince. Let's talk a minute about that little thing you do at the end with the microphone."

In this part . . .

Welcome to *Voice Acting For Dummies.* Here you get an introduction to the basics of voice acting. You find out about your voice, how to use and care for your voice, and what it takes to be a voice actor. You also discover all kinds of interesting and wonderful ways you can fit your voice into voice acting, including training and education opportunities. This part also includes tips for meeting the voices in your head and taking on the different types of roles.

No matter whether you're a new voice actor or quite experienced, this part can help solidify your foundation of voice acting.

Chapter 1

An Overview of Voice Acting: Just the Basics

· ·

In This Chapter

▶ Understanding who a voice actor is

▶ Creating a demo

▶ Figuring your way through the maze of auditions

▶ Making a go in your home studio

· ·

*V*oice acting is an amazing way to put to use something you already have — your voice. Voice acting well is about knowing how to best use your voice and interpretive skills to deliver a well-crafted message. More than just mere talk, voice acting is the art of taking the written word and skillfully translating it into a persuasive spoken word message that encourages a listening audience to not only hear what you're saying, but also to act on it in some way. Voice acting is designed to educate, inform, or entertain.

This chapter serves as your catapult into this book and the world of voice acting. No matter if you're brand new and don't know anything about voice acting, you've dabbled a little bit in it and decided you want to pursue it more as a career, or you've worked in the voice acting field for several years and you want to take your abilities to the next level, this chapter can help you start your journey.

Being a Voice Actor: More Than You May Expect

Some people think that voice acting is simply getting paid to talk. In a way, that's true, although there is so much more to it! When you start as a voice actor, you need to remember that your voice is the instrument that helps achieve the script writer's goal, whether you're voicing a character in an animated film, reading for a company telephony script, or narrating an audiobook. You also need to take good care of your voice, which is your instrument that you literally take with you wherever you go. In the following sections, we explain your role in the creative process of voice acting and how this knowledge can help you to do your best as a voice actor.

Knowing what it really means

Being a voice actor isn't just about sounding pretty. Being a voice actor isn't just about the sound of your voice. Your voice is merely an instrument used to communicate effectively and breathe life into a story. Chapter 2 explains more about what voice acting is, shows what it takes to be a voice actor, and gives you a good idea of where your voice fits in.

Getting your voice ready

Preparing and taking care of your voice are essential keys to voice acting because you rely heavily on your voice to work. Anyone who comes from a background that includes public speaking, whether in public settings or professional settings, has an appreciation for the voice and how greatly it contributes to their ability to communicate successfully.

Preparing your voice includes everything from warming up to ensuring you don't abuse it by yelling, screaming, or smoking. Chapter 3 gives you the essentials for how you can take care of your voice, use your voice properly, and train it so you're ready for voice acting.

Figuring out your role as voice actor

As a voice actor, you play a unique role in a production. Those roles include the following:

- Real person
- Narrator
- Announcer
- Spokesperson
- Instructor

These different roles help get the message to the listener, and each has its own characteristics. In Chapter 4, we discuss these roles in greater depth and explain how you can engage your intended audience with each one.

Digging into the script

The script reveals the author's intent and contains a wealth of details that can help you to create interesting and unique characters. By reading the script, you can discover a lot about the characters you'll be voicing or portraying. When you read, you need to think like a detective and look for clues that will aid you in developing characters and creating unique voices for them.

Being able to differentiate characters as well as being able to create a solid character that you know like the back of your hand is essential. As a voice actor, your job is to bring characters and scripts to life. The more information you have, the more believable your reads and the greater your performance. In Chapter 5, you can figure out how to examine a script and find the clues to create characters based upon your findings.

Starting your own business

If you're going to take voice acting seriously, you need to approach it as a business. We mean that you need to invest properly in your business to make quality recordings, which means that you get some training as a voice actor and you also can produce quality work with a home recording studio. When you're working with clients, quoting the appropriate rates is also something you need to do to remain competitive. Even if you're just looking to do voice acting as a hobby, remember that you're entering into an arena of professional voice actors who have been working for years and make their living recording voice-overs.

We give you ideas for how to set up your business, manage your customers, and build a team of advisors, such as an agent if you want one, in Chapter 16. We discuss how you can market your business in Chapter 9. The other chapters in Part IV serve as a primer for running your own business — information you'll be grateful for when the time comes.

Making a Demo

A *demo* is to a voice actor as a portfolio is to an artist. Your demo shows people what you can do with your voice and is a tool used for marketing yourself. Most people start with a commercial demo to showcase their ability to read for commercials you would hear on television or radio. You can use demos as promotion vehicles on your website or to accompany your profile on a voice acting marketplace website. You can also send them to talent agents or clients you want to introduce yourself to.

Tapping into some helpful (and free) resources

Voice Acting For Dummies provides you plenty of great information about voice acting. However if you're itching for even more, you may want to check out one of the following resources. You may be amazed to find out that many more are available if you're willing to explore. Many of these are online communities where you can connect with and share knowledge with other voice actors.

✔ **Voice Over Universe:** This social network for voice actors is more affectionately referred to as VU. You can find it at www.voiceoveruniverse.com.

✔ **Voice Acting Hub:** The Voice Acting Hub is probably the fastest way to connect with other voice actors on Facebook. Close to 2,000 other people are in the group. The group has no topics or categories, but it has a stream of information that relates to voice acting. You can see updates for upcoming workshops, links to blog posts, polls, and general discussion at www.facebook.com/groups/2364217548.

✔ **Voice Acting Alliance:** The Voice Acting Alliance (http://voiceacting alliance.com) is an online forum with thousands of message boards on topics such as auditions and casting, completed works, and tutorials. Although the forum seemingly has a focus on animation and video games, it's still a great place to strike up a conversation on any topic. Be sure to check out the frequently asked questions, which can give you a feel for the expected behaviors and other etiquette guidelines.

✔ **Yahoo! Voiceover Group:** Probably one of the oldest groups of its kind, the Yahoo! Voiceover Group (http://groups.yahoo.com/group/voiceovers) is where people with a shared interest meet, get to know each other, and stay informed. This group gives you instant access to shared message archives, photos and photo albums, group event calendars, member polls, and shared links.

✔ **VOX Daily:** VOX Daily (http://blogs.voices.com/voxdaily) is the official Voices.com blog. VOX Daily keeps you in the loop with informative voice-over articles that encourage community involvement, conversation, and intelligent debate.

✔ **Voice Over Times:** Voice Over Times (www.voiceovertimes.com) is an industry news site and blog, providing feature stories, product reviews, tutorials, and opinion articles. Covering voice acting in all aspects, this website can help you find the news and stories that you need to hear now and connect you with media contacts who make your story happen.

✔ **Voice-OverXtra:** Voice-OverXtra (www.voiceoverxtra.com) is a news, education, and resource center. Both voice-over newcomers and seasoned pros can learn and share how to succeed in this vibrant industry, 24/7. The site gives you valuable tools, including an industry resource directory, and a comprehensive calendar of training opportunities.

✔ **Voice Over Experts:** The Voice Over Experts podcast (www.podcastdirectory.com/podcasts) allows you to hear from some of the top voice-over instructors, authors, and voice acting celebrities from around the world as they share some of their knowledge, available to you free of charge. Each podcast is about 10 to 15 minutes and features a special guest. The special guests are industry experts, often acting instructors, casting directors, agents, or vocal coaches who share a nugget of wisdom from their experience. You can also directly listen to more than 130 podcast episodes from the website or download them from iTunes.

✔ **Voices.com webinars:** Every week, Voices.com offers free webinars that walk you through how to use the website in detail. Sit back, watch, and learn as the presenter navigates through each section of the website. You can watch dozens of previously recorded webinars on www.youtube.com, where you can fast forward, rewind, or pause.

✔ **EdgeStudio teleseminars:** EdgeStudio is an education and training facility in New York City that offers in-person voice-over classes but also opportunities by telephone. Similar to webinars, a *teleseminar* occurs on a specific date and time where dozens if not hundreds of people call in to a conference line to learn about a new technology, service, or the basics of acting and performance. In some cases, you may find a teleseminar easier to join because it's literally just calling a phone number and then punching in an access code when prompted. The downside is that you miss the visuals, but often this is a moot point because you can just focus on the information offered by the expert.

In these sections, we explain what it means to decipher a script, how to know if a role is right for you, and the kinds of demos that you can make. We also discuss musical considerations. Something else you need to look at when recording a demo is whether you should record your own demo at home or you should work with a professional recording studio. We discuss the pros and cons at length in Part II.

Uncovering a script

Sometimes when reading through a script, you really need to be reading between the lines. Reading between the lines means that you can see beyond what's on the page. Your interpretation comprises more than just the text but also feelings and motivations behind what you're recording. Being able to do so is important to give a better read with more substance.

When making a demo, the scripts you choose are very important. You need to reflect both your vocal abilities and the roles you're willing to take on as a voice actor. You'll know if a script is right for you based upon whether or not you personally agree with its content. A coach or demo producer can help you if you want a second opinion. These professionals tend to have their ears on the pulse of what's trending in demos and will have a good grasp of the sort of material you should have on your demo to be competitive and stand out. Chapter 7 addresses finding scripts for your voice-over demo suitable to your voice and the work you want to do.

Hitting record

Stepping up to the microphone with the knowledge that a recording is in progress can be exciting! There's nothing quite like hearing your own voice played back to you.

Before you record your demo, you need to make sure you're ready before you hit the record button. During the recording process, you also need to consider these points to ensure your demo sounds professional and can get you work:

- ✔ You use the right music or sound effects.
- ✔ Your voice is warmed up and hydrated.
- ✔ You're well-rehearsed.

Chapter 8 gives you perspective about recording your own demo (DIY style) or going into a professional recording studio.

Finding Your Way through Audition Land

The audition process can be nerve-racking because you're showcasing prospective customers what your abilities and skills are. You want to stand out so you inevitably get hired. In today's voice acting world, auditions happen more and more in the virtual world, although sometimes you still do need to audition in person. The following sections give an overview to why the audition process is important and what you need to know to audition.

Touting yourself

The way you present yourself for opportunities is very important. Whether the audition is in person or online, putting your best voice forward is something you should aspire to for each and every audition.

To make a good first impression when voice acting, consider our suggestions:

- ✔ Only audition for roles you are able to do.
- ✔ Follow instructions.
- ✔ Greet the director or client warmly.
- ✔ Send in your best read.

Check out Chapter 11 for how you can stand out in your auditions.

Knowing how to audition

No matter whether you're auditioning online or in person, clients expect proper etiquette, which means you know how to do the following before your audition:

- ✔ Warm up your voice.
- ✔ Prepare your read.
- ✔ Follow directions.
- ✔ Be able to interpret copy.

Being able to navigate the audition waters, both online and in person, can serve you well. Chapter 12 explains how to audition online, which often requires you to record a custom sample of the client's script, prepare a quote, and submit a proposal. Chapter 13 walks you through some auditioning basics for real-person auditions.

Working in Your Home Studio

As the Internet becomes more and more a part of the business world, being a professional voice actor means that you can work with clients from your own home recording studio. Building a studio doesn't mean you have to take out a building permit and add on an extra room to your house. An in-home studio can be an affordable endeavor depending on what equipment you buy. If you're treating voice acting as a business, you'll be able to justify the cost of investing in some quality equipment to get you on your way.

These sections run you through the basics of what to include in your home recording studio, and how to record, edit, and mix your audio. Knowing how to record on your own is critical to being a successful voice actor in today's virtual age.

Identifying what you need

Your home recording studio needs to have the basic equipment to record a professional-sounding demo. Contrary to popular opinion, it doesn't have to cost a fortune to build a respectable home recording studio. It doesn't need to resemble a first-class audio production environment in New York or Los Angeles.

Your home studio does need the following equipment so your recordings don't sound amateur:

- ✔ Computer
- ✔ An external microphone
- ✔ Good quality microphone cable
- ✔ Pop filter

Chapter 17 runs you through everything you need to know about building a home recording studio, how much money you should budget, and the equipment you need, both hardware and software, to start.

Recording, editing, and mixing

When you record your voice, you may find that you make some mistakes here and there, leave too much space between words, or need to cough and clear your throat. The wonderful thing about digital audio is that you don't have to rerecord the entire read. You can edit rather painlessly by placing your cursor to select the area you want to remove and voilá! You can polish your recording in a matter of seconds.

Knowing how to record your voice, edit, and mix a recording is standard so far as professional voice actors go. Skills such as editing and mixing can turn a slightly marred take into a keeper, so you'll want to master how to edit because it can save you time having to rerecord every time you make a mistake or need to pause. You can find what you need about the basics of audio recording in Chapter 18. We cover more advanced topics, such as editing and mixing, in Chapter 19.

Getting your product to clients

After you record your voice, edit, and mix it, you want to make sure your prospective clients get their hands on it. You want to make sure you format the files and deliver them the way your client wants. Chapter 21 explains how to prepare and deliver the finished audio files.

Chapter 2

Finding Your Voice: How You Fit into Voice Acting

In This Chapter

▶ Uncovering what makes a good voice

▶ Seeing what is involved in voice acting

▶ Recognizing whether voice acting is a good match for you

▶ Discovering your signature voice

*P*eople have told you that you have a great voice, right? Someone has probably suggested that you should be on radio, be the voice on a movie trailer, or use your storytelling skills to narrate audiobooks. Even if you don't have an acting or broadcasting background, you're fairly confident that your voice has what it takes to do voice-overs.

What exactly though makes a voice right for voice acting? Everyone has a voice, but only some people have the necessary skills and traits needed for voice-over work. The good news: We're here to help explain what qualities make a good voice and how you can determine whether you possess the skills and traits to be a successful voice actor.

In order to do voice-overs, you need to be able to speak clearly, listen with objectivity, and know how to get the most out of your voice. Your voice is an instrument, and in order to play it well, you need to know what it's capable of doing. Something you can discover quickly is your vocal range. How high can your voice inflect? What's the lowest pitch you're able to make without feeling like you're hurting your voice? Discovering your vocal range is the first step to getting to know your voice.

In this chapter, we help you figure out how to assess your voice and whether you and your voice are right for voice acting. We also take a closer look at your skills and traits to gauge whether they match with what's needed from voice actors. We explain what a signature voice is and help you determine yours.

Eyeing the Characteristics of a Voice-Over Voice

Being successful in voice acting requires a lot more than just having a good voice. However, having a good voice can only help you. So how do you know whether your voice has what it takes? Although different voices are needed for different projects, the basic characteristics to a good voice are as follows:

- ✔ **Clarity:** Being able to speak clearly
- ✔ **Literacy:** Reading without stumbling
- ✔ **Fluctuation:** Using the range of your voice
- ✔ **Phrasing:** Shaping a phrase without running low on breath

Anyone who puts their mind to it can achieve these four characteristics. Speaking well enough to be understood while at the same time demonstrating understanding of what you're reading may take some work, but you can master these basics if you take the time to study the script, interpret its meaning, and practice. We go into greater detail with regard to interpreting scripts in Chapter 5.

Meanwhile, using the full range of your voice and phrasing with purpose can demonstrate your ability to use your voice as an instrument, not just as a vehicle for delivering the written word. You can read more about phrasing in Chapter 11.

Identifying What Goes into Being a Voice Actor

Just because you have been talking all your life doesn't mean that voice acting will come naturally to you. Voice acting is an art, and truly, it is acting. Although most voice work is recorded in the privacy of a studio away from the glare of the cameras, a voice-over can serve as a performance for the hundreds if not thousands of people who will receive the message you are giving voice to.

Before you can decide if being a voice actor is the right fit for you, you need a firm understanding of the important skills a successful voice actor has. In this section, we identify those important skills and also explain some of the cooler aspects of being a voice actor. Needless to say, although having a great voice is important, it by far isn't the only factor that builds a solid career in voice acting. You also need to have endless ambition, polished talent, and good business sense.

Naming the basic skills you need

Voice acting actually requires a well-rounded set of skills, skills that you may already have. In a nutshell, a successful voice actor needs three important skills:

- ✔ **Artistic performance:** These skills include fun stuff, like exploring your voice and creating characters. If your mother ever told you to stop being so dramatic, if you ever got into trouble at school for being the class clown, if you ever mimicked others around you with amusing success, or you've been told that your voice sounds like it should be on the radio, you're likely a good fit for voice acting. You can also tell if you have these skills by doing a few simple tests like recording yourself as you read aloud and hearing the playback or consulting a coach. Refer to the "Going over the important traits" section later in this chapter to help you.

- ✔ **Technical skills:** These skills include easy stuff, like knowing how to use the computer. If you know how to navigate on a computer, plug in a USB cable, and talk into a microphone, you're well on your way to producing your own audio recordings. Even if you don't have experience with recording software, no doubt a close friend or family member does. Technology is easier to use and acquire. You don't need to be a rocket scientist to record your voice, although rocket scientists certainly can try. Check out the chapters in Part V that deal more with the technical aspects of voice acting for more specific information.

- ✔ **Business know-how:** These skills include cool stuff, like using your voice to make money. If you've ever had to sell something, such as your home, you know a bit about what it takes to run a business. Showmanship is very important because it's about delivering an awesome recording at a reasonable price. Flip to Chapter 16 for more details about the business aspect of voice acting, including managing your clients, keeping records, marketing your services, and getting an agent.

Examining some benefits of being a voice actor

Being a voice actor has its perks. In fact, voice acting affords voice actors many advantages that traditional stage or on-camera acting don't have. If you don't have a burning desire to be on stage or to act on camera, or you prefer to take a back seat as the unsung hero of a production, working behind the scenes as a voice actor may suit you well.

Take a look at these facts about the voice acting industry in these sections. Can you thrive in this kind of environment? Knowing this information about yourself can help you determine whether you can see yourself doing voice acting.

Nobody sees you

Being off camera has many advantages, one of which being that no one sees you while you're recording a voice-over. The audience likewise never sees you. You can flail your arms about, and not a single person would know.

If you're sensitive to how you may appear when doing a character voice, you can feel free to "make the ugly face" as voice-over coach Deb Munro puts it without fear of scrutiny. Some of the greatest voices in the world use their hands to get their voices in gear. In fact, some voice actors have said that if they couldn't make use of their hands, they couldn't voice.

Comfort often dictates your attire

As much fun as dressing up can be, sometimes just knowing that what you wear doesn't matter to how the audience will receive the finished product is comforting. Wearing something comfy can also work in your favor where controlling noise is concerned. Certain fabrics tend to ruffle and make noise when you move. Furthermore, you can have a bad hair day and no one knows. Likewise, you can have no hair and no one knows.

Editing is your friend

One of the things most people love about voice acting is that you're able to make edits in the file in order to engineer the perfect take. You can edit out breaths, coughs, and the like, and you can even shave off sibilance. (*Sibilance* sounds like hissing. It's the "S" sound at the beginning or end of a word.) When editing your voice, you can use part of one word and put on another word that needs some touching up if a word didn't clearly come across. If need be, you can even speed up your voice a notch. Refer to Chapter 19 for more specifics about what tricks you can do with editing.

Assessing Your Talents to See Whether Voice Acting Is Right for You

If you have decided that you have the voice for voice-over work and would make a great voice actor, you need to think about some important considerations. Before you print business cards and start your voice-over business, you want to assess the following about yourself.

Whether you're a freelancer (and serve as your own agent) or work with an agent, a number of complementary skills and attributes can help ensure you're headed in the right direction. You can develop any of the skills you don't already possess by seeking out training in the industry.

Although voice acting is a popular career field to consider, remember that it's still a business; successful voice actors know that their career has everything to do with those specific factors. This section covers some important traits you need to have to make it as a voice actor and some questions to ask yourself to see whether voice acting is a good fit.

Going over the important traits

Your skills, abilities, interests, personality, and temperament all play a vital role in your success as a voice actor, but exactly what are the traits that you need? If you want to make it as a voice actor, you need to have the following traits.

If you have these traits, you can get started and begin your own line of work as a voice actor. To do this, make use of all the resources available to you that we provide you throughout this book.

Being vocal and reading aloud: Skills

In order to be successful as a voice actor, you need certain skills, such as the ability to speak and read clearly, interpret *copy* (the script), and use your voice effectively to communicate a message. Although these skills may sound easy, many people have difficulty doing so.

Reading well out loud is one of the most essential traits. Even some of the most enthusiastic bookworms have trouble articulating a well-phrased passage when asked to do so out loud. A skilled voice actor can read aloud with ease. If you stumble over your words and need to start over again, then you need more practice. Try reading books and newspaper and magazine articles aloud. Doing so is a great way to practice reading a variety of writing styles, which is something you'll encounter in the voice-over industry.

Read everything you can find and interpret it in various ways. Finding material or scripts doesn't have to be difficult. You can read the back of a cereal box or leaf through your favorite book and focus on a particular passage. You can record yourself and then listen to hear your performance. What did you like? What could you do better? How would you have phrased or said something differently given the chance? You can experiment in many different ways; take the opportunity to read aloud everyday to keep your skills sharp.

Other skills, such as interpreting text and using your voice to communicate a message, are equally important.

- ✔ Interpreting text is akin to being a detective. You have to analyze the who, what, when, where, why, and how of a script to gain a better understanding of what the copywriter expects of you performance-wise. You can uncover more about interpreting scripts in Chapter 5.

- ✔ Communicating a message means that you not only understand what you're reading, but you can also relate on some level with what you're talking about to give greater authenticity to your read. Chapter 7 gives you more about how to bring life to a message.

Adding notches to your belt: Experience

Another important trait you need in order to be a voice actor is to have experience. The question is how do you gain experience when you don't have any experience? You don't have to be a professional to gain experience.

Experience can range from reading aloud all the way through to creating characters in your spare time. Volunteering your voice to read for a charity, public service announcements (PSAs), or a spot for a local organization can go a long way in building your client list.

Feeling it in your soul: Ambition and passion

Having a drive to succeed and a desire to use your voice are essential. If you don't like doing voice-overs, what's the point? Make sure that you truly want to do this kind of work. As with any professional pursuit, being ambitious and passionate plays an important role in voice acting. For some people, voice acting is merely a hobby. For others, it's a passion that develops with each syllable and exploration of their voice. Many voice actors don't do it for the money. It's passion that drives them.

If you're passionate about voice acting, it won't ever seem like work. Voice acting can be a career that you're enthusiastic about, proud of, and are happy knowing that you've used your gifts to the best of your abilities.

Dedicating yourself to the craft: Persistence and commitment

In order to be successful with voice acting, you also need to possess some persistence and commitment to the craft, even when things aren't going well. You won't book every job that you audition for; you need to remember that the casting process is about selection, not rejection. Be committed to your art and the money will follow.

Always looking to improve: Study

Before you drive a car you need to learn how to drive. Voice acting is the same. Before you can start voice acting, you need to know how to use your voice. Although doing so may be obvious, starting out as a voice actor presents its own stipulations, such as studying the craft, discovering how to use the instrument (your voice), and maximizing the talents you were born with.

The best way to study the craft is to listen to professional voice-overs and read industry publications. Don't be afraid to seek out a teacher or resources online. Even the best actors have a coach, just as athletes train with someone each day. You can always continue to figure out new things about your voice and how to use it. (Refer to Chapter 3 for more help.)

Looking inward to see whether voice acting fits you

Before you make a decision to go into voice acting, you have to take a close look at yourself and determine whether the business is right for you. Decades ago, if you were to get into the business of voice acting, you either had to be born in a studio, raised behind a microphone, or have a relative in the business (that, or be very, very persistent, not unlike today). Times have changed. Now voice acting is all about the acting.

Your Mom may think you have a beautiful voice, but unless your Mom is the casting director or producer, she can't land you the job.

Ask yourself these questions to see whether this business is right for you:

- ✔ **Do you know how to use your voice for voice acting?** Although most people think that voice acting is all about the voice, the truth of the matter is that it's not about the voice but rather how it's used. For instance, you may be born with a booming, announcer voice, but if you don't know how to use it effectively or know how to act, your naturally sonorous voice won't get you anywhere.

    There's a voice for every job and a job for every voice. No two clients are the same and every business needs something different. The world of voice acting provides opportunities for all voice types, ages, and vocal characteristics — even if you think your voice is too creaky, childlike, or gravelly. Refer to the earlier section, "Eyeing the Characteristics of a Voice-Over Voice" for what makes a good voice.

- ✔ **Do you embrace technology?** This question is important, especially if you freelance. Being a freelance voice actor means that you need to have the skills to operate all the studio equipment as well as provide a convincing performance. Some people in the industry can help you get familiar with your equipment and show you how to put it to good use. The chapters in Part V delve deeper into the technical aspects of voice acting.

✔ **Do you have marketing know-how?** The voice acting industry, like all entertainment and media fields, is teeming with talented people. So how do you get noticed? Successful voice actors are savvy marketers. Marketing the services you provide as a voice actor is critical. People won't know what you do or why they should hire you unless you tell them. You can spread the word about your voice-over in hundreds of ways. Chapter 9 discusses some creative ways you can promote your talents and get noticed.

✔ **Do you think running your own business is risky?** Most entrepreneurs enjoy the thrill of risk. Whether you have an agent or you're freelancing, you are running your own business — you're an entrepreneur. Part of running your own business is accepting and being prepared to take some risks. Chapters 15 and 16 go into the basics of running a business.

So after asking yourself these questions, do you have what it takes? Your skills, abilities, interests, personality, and temperament all play a vital role in the career path you choose. The good news is that many career self-assessment tools are available in case you need some extra help. These tools test your compatibility with a variety of industries and potential career paths.

We suggest you check out our website, www.voices.com. It offers a free self-assessment tool in the help section. Other resources available include www.elance.com, www.guru.com, and www.odesk.com. If you're new to the industry, you may enjoy giving one of these sites a try. Remember that there are no wrong answers. By answering honestly, you can determine what areas you may need extra training in to establish a fulfilling career in voice acting.

You can also take this short self-assessment tool quiz at www.voices.com/tools/self_assessment to find out more about your talents as a voice actor.

Tuning Into Your Signature Voice

A *signature voice* is, at the very heart of it all, your money voice. It's the sound and kind of readings that people consistently ask and/or hire you to perform. Although some voice actors pride themselves in being able to be everything to everybody performance-wise, many choose to brand their voice and serve a particular market or niche within voice-over. In other words, your signature voice is the one you are most frequently hired to perform and make money with, not necessarily the one you think is the most fun to do.

The following sections help you figure out what your signature voice is and feel comfortable using your signature voice.

Some famous voice actors: Can you hear them now?

You've turned on the TV or radio and probably heard many memorable famous stars who also serve as voice actors for commercial advertisements. Some of the more memorable ones include the following:

✔ **Morgan Freeman:** Morgan Freeman's voice has become one of the most identifiable voices heard in film and commercial voice-over. His run as the voice of VISA and narrator of many documentaries and films, such as *March of the Penguins,* have positioned him as a trustworthy and authoritative storyteller.

✔ **James Earl Jones:** From the voice of Darth Vader in *Star Wars* to Mufasa in *The Lion King* and narrator of documentaries such as *Planet Earth,* James Earl Jones's voice is a deep, rich, grandfatherly voice whose unmistakable timber and delivery resonates with multiple generations.

✔ **Kelsey Grammer:** Best-known for playing Dr. Frasier Crane on the television shows *Cheers* and *Frasier,* Kelsey Grammer's baritone voice has been the voice chosen to help advertise some of the most commonly purchased products in the United States. Honey Nut Cheerios, Helzberg Diamonds, and more have all featured Grammer's voice in their commercials.

✔ **Carolyn Hopkins:** Although not a typical celebrity, Carolyn Hopkins's voice is heard all over the world by millions of people each day in airports, at train stations, and on subway systems. Hers is the most recognizable voice perhaps in the transportation industry.

✔ **Dame Judi Dench:** The voice of Dame Judi Dench has been defined by *The Guardian* and BBC News as embodying elements of what many consider to be the perfect female voice. Her voice is alluring, soft, and velvety using her richly textured instrument to the best of her ability in earlier comedic roles on television, via film as M in James Bond, and in narration on the Epcot Spaceship Earth ride at Disney World.

✔ **Don LaFontaine:** If you've ever been to the movies, you can relate to one of the most famous examples of a signature voice, which was Don LaFontaine's movie trailer voice. Whenever you heard the opening words "In a world . . . ", you were hearing his signature voice at work.

Finding your signature voice

Your signature voice is unique to you because everyone has a unique voice print. When getting to know your signature voice, you can gain understanding of how your voice works best in a commercial setting, such as paid work that you may do recording a voice-over for radio or television, and also become familiar with the sound or characteristics of your voice that resonate with those individuals doing a casting.

Zeroing in on a niche and distinctive read that makes you money is great, but it may take time to discover what other people feel your strong suits are and also what you continuously get hired to do.

Ask those people closest to you about what they think about your vocal characteristics and abilities to see if they can help you figure out your signature voice. Try reading different kinds of scripts to see if your vocal qualities lend themselves more to specific markets, character types, or applications of voice-over. For example, if you have a hard-hitting voice full of gravel, your voice may be more suited to the world of sports or radio imaging, whereas if you have a soothing, pleasant voice, your instrument may be better applied in telephony or narration. If you have a voice that doesn't seem to fit anywhere corporate and sounds rather unique or quirky, consider where you may go if you tried to voice characters as an animation voice-over artist.

Sometimes your signature voice and voice-over work runs parallel to your personality, disposition, and interests. For people who fit this mold, identifying and honing your signature voice may be easier for you, because it may come naturally.

Many voice actors find their signature voice through mimicry. Imitating the voice of someone you know — characters on television or a celebrity — can lead to work in voice matching, a relatively lucrative field. Some actors make a living sounding like other people and record for them in their absence. One such example is how Pat Fraley was the voice match for Tim Allen as Buzz Lightyear in *Toy Story II.* If Tim Allen couldn't rerecord something or come into the studio for whatever reason, Pat stepped in and supplied the voice for the character.

Seeing yourself in your signature voice

Although your signature voice can be a true reflection of your personality, according to many voice actors, their signature voices aren't always that way. In fact, sometimes the voice that you're hired for most contrasts with your natural self or what you consider to be your signature voice.

Sometimes your signature voice directly correlates with your own personality. You may be able to see yourself in your signature voice if you're particularly interested in something. The exuberance and confidence you pour into that read shines through with more brilliance because it's something you're already passionate about.

On the flipside, some signature voices rely more on the quality of your voice than on your general interest in the topic you're voicing. You may have a sunshiny personality but find that most of the time you're hired to record medical narrations or more subdued copy.

Honoring the past: A brief history of voice acting

Reginald Fessenden, a Canadian inventor, was a brilliant mathematician and excelled in academics. Being enamored with the invention of the telephone by Alexander Graham Bell, Fessenden set out on a quest to develop a means of remote communication without the restriction of wires — *wireless* as it was to be known later.

In 1900 Fessenden set out to work for the United States Weather Bureau. During this time, he test-recorded the first voice-over in 1900, while reporting on the weather.

The first radio recording

Fessenden became radio's first voice during Christmas of 1906 when he broadcast from a makeshift studio in Brant Rock, just outside Boston, a program of Christmas messages and spiritual music to ships at sea. The Christmas Eve program as recounted by Fessenden consisted of:

> "First a short speech by me saying what we were going to do, then some phonograph music . . . Then came a violin solo by me . . . which I sang one verse of, in addition to playing the violin, though the singing, of course, was not very good. Then came the Bible text, Glory to God in the highest and on earth peace to men of good will, and we finally wound up by wishing them a Merry Christmas and then saying that we proposed to broadcast again on New Year's Eve."

Walt Disney performed first cartoon voice

More familiar was the first cartoon voice-over in 1928 by Walt Disney as Mickey Mouse in *Steamboat Willie.* The following year, 1929, the first cartoon series produced, *Looney Tunes*, debuted in cinemas.

The first prominent voice actor in animation was former radio personality, voice actor, and comedian Mel Blanc. In 1936 he joined Leon Schlesinger Productions, a company that made animated cartoons, which were distributed by Warner Bros. Blanc was famous for his versatility and is still known today as *The Man of 1000 Voices.*

Recent history

In today's industry, one of the most famous people in voice acting is Don LaFontaine, who in 1964 recorded his first voice-over for a movie trailer. He was paid less than $100, a far cry from the premium rates that professional voice actors can command today. Throughout his long and successful career, he set the standard for how movie trailers were written and voiced, literally becoming the voice of the movies. Although his physical passing on September 1, 2008, left a great void, his spirit remains and legacy continues to grow and serve those in the voice acting community.

With any voice-over, be sure that the creation and delivery doesn't injure you or cause physical discomfort. If something doesn't feel right when you're performing, stop what you're doing and figure out why the pain is there and if you can create that sound without hurting yourself. There's nothing worse than having to record for long periods of time with a voice or delivery that hurts! Imagine if you were to book a job with a voice that hurt you to produce. Staying in good voice and maintaining a consistent performance would be difficult. You could also strain your vocal folds or injure yourself. Don't ever do an episodic role, such as being a character in a cartoon, video game, or long-form narration project, with a voice that hurts you to produce.

Voices.com provides contact customer service and support

Voices.com has a wonderful group of people dedicated to providing world-class customer service and support. To complement the personalized touch of a customer service representative, you can also access a wealth of resources at the website, which are sure to answer your question. Contact Voices.com via the following:

✔ **Telephone:** You can reach a customer service representative by phone by calling (888) 359-3472 toll-free in North America from Monday to Friday between 8 a.m. and 8 p.m. Eastern time. For international callers, you can get customer service and technical support by calling (519) 858-5660. Service is also available on Saturdays from 10 a.m. to 6 p.m. Eastern time.

✔ **Email:** Email support is available during the same hours. If you want to access online resources at your own convenience, the Help section of the Voices.com website is available to you at any time and includes resources such as a frequently asked questions knowledge base, user guides, blogs, podcasts, music and sound effects, videos, downloadable resources, and more.

✔ **Live chat:** Live chat is available from Monday to Friday between 8 a.m. and 8 p.m. Eastern time.

Ready to take the next step? Enjoy access to business and voice-over resources and create your very own website for free to showcase your voice and highlight your abilities. To launch your career, create your free account at www.voices.com.

Chapter 3

Training Your Voice

*B*efore you jump into recording your voice, looking for work, and calling agents for representation, you want to ensure that you're prepared for the rigors of voice acting. Making sure your voice is ready and trained is important because you need to be conditioned for whatever may come your way. Think of this from an athlete's perspective. Athletes know that they need to stretch and loosen up before exerting themselves to prepare for the best possible performance. Training is part of the game. Voice acting is no different. If you don't train, your voice won't be able to do what you want it to and will lack the elasticity it needs. You could even risk vocal injury!

When you've decided to take your passion for voice acting to the next level in preparation for actual projects, training is one of the most important steps you'll take on your journey to become a real voice actor. Reading everything you can get your hands on, attending workshops, and studying with a voice-over coach are all ways that you can train your voice.

Ongoing training is important for any voice-over actor, no matter whether you're a beginner wondering whether you can find a niche in this market or whether you're a veteran wanting to fine-tune certain skills. Training allows for comfortable use of the voice, facilitates continued growth, and provides important stamina that you'll need when working as a recording artist.

This chapter explores the benefits of training, ways that you can get training, and how you can find a voice-over coach. You can exercise your voice and practice interpretative skills in so many ways. You may be surprised by the sheer amount of free resources available to you online and in your library that can help you do this.

This chapter also takes a closer look at one-on-one instruction, education in a group setting, and the benefit of attending events such as conferences. We want you to get the best education you can, so be sure to entertain as many of these wonderful ideas as possible.

Caring for Your Voice

One of the main benefits from training that you, the aspiring voice actor, can get is that it helps you fully understand how important your voice is to you and how to treat your voice with respect. Think of your voice like a car. Cars need to be maintained and used in a certain way to ensure they work well. You ensure the fluids are topped, the tires are full of air, and the vehicle's interior and exterior are clean. If cars rely on maintenance to ensure they operate smoothly and efficiently, imagine how important taking care of your voice can be to you, especially if you rely on it as a way to make money. If you've never thought of your voice as an instrument and the means by which you make your livelihood, now is the time.

Focusing on the physical aspects

Training your voice gives you the tools to help you wisely utilize your voice. With training, physical aspects, such as making sure you have good posture and your support is well aligned, are important. Everything you do, including the way you stand, breathe, project your voice, and shape vowels, impacts the sound that you make.

Vocal exercises can help you concentrate on these physical aspects. A professional voice coach can give you guidance with what to do. Check out the later section, "Understanding how a coach can help you" for guidance.

Conserving your voice

Your voice is delicate. It's not something you can turn on or off by flicking a switch. It's also not something that you can carry in a bag or download on the Internet. Simply put, your voice is with you at all times and can't be put on hold or paused whenever it's convenient to do so.

When caring for your voice, be aware of just how sensitive your instrument is. Any number of external elements can affect the well-being of your voice and its performance, including sickness, what you eat, what you drink, and so on. Setting aside time for taking care of and conserving your voice is critical.

Taking time out for your voice is important for a variety of reasons, but for voice artists, observing set times for vocal rest can be nearly as important as using their voices to record. In today's day and age, clamming up isn't always easy. You have many potential distractions. As a voice artist, you never know when an audition will come your way that requires a custom read.

Carving silence into your schedule may need to be strategic and deliberate. Look for tasks that you do each day, such as audio editing, reading, writing, or production that are solitary activities and don't necessarily require your voice. If you like to exercise, make your morning jog a time to be quiet and rest your voice. Other people may need to schedule more frequent intervals in with a half hour of silence here or there every couple of hours. To give you some perspective, professional opera singers rest their voices for hours on end in preparation for a performance because of the demanding nature of their jobs and their heavy use of their voices. Although being quiet for hours during a day may not seem practical, make the time. You also want to get a good night's sleep and leverage those peaceful hours of slumber to benefit your voice.

So with that in mind, this section contains advice on how to handle these elements.

Avoiding sickness

Germs are everywhere, so avoiding them entirely is difficult, but you must try your best to stay healthy. In order to stay healthy, follow these tips:

- **Regularly wash your hands with soap and warm water.** Doing so can greatly reduce your chances of being sick.

- **Keep contact with sick people to a minimum.** Staying away from sick people can also reduce your chances of coming down with something.

- **Take vitamins.** Some recommendations include taking a multivitamin and ensuring you get adequate doses of vitamin C either in tablet form or through orange juice or citrus fruits.

- **Stay hydrated.** Drink plenty of water and always have a glass nearby to sip from. Limit your intake of caffeine. If you do drink caffeinated beverages, try balancing them by drinking a cup of water for each caffeinated beverage you consume.

- **Get adequate amounts of sleep.** A general guideline is that you get eight hours of sleep a day. If you're able to get more than that, for instance nine or ten hours, that's even better for you and your voice.

Being sick when you record changes the quality of your voice and its range. Voice acting when sick may also injure your voice. So when you're sick, let your voice rest and save recording for another day.

Eating healthy food

Eating healthy foods also keeps your voice at its best performance. When choosing what to eat, eat healthy foods, such as fruits, vegetables, lean meats, and calcium-rich foods, such as dairy products. A well-balanced diet goes a long way in keeping your body healthy.

Drinking fluids

Drinking alcoholic or caffeinated beverages can affect the quality of your voice by drying out your vocal folds. Stick to water as your beverage of choice.

Breathing healthy air

Smoking cigarettes and inhaling secondhand smoke can also injure your voice. Don't wear perfume or cologne before you warm up your voice and record because strong scents can affect your respiratory system and may also cause constriction of your throat. Consider an air purifier for your home or office.

Avoiding certain behaviors

Protecting your voice is also part of training and using it properly. In order to make sure you don't damage your voice, you want to avoid or at least take proactive steps to minimize certain activities, such as the following:

- ✔ **Screaming or yelling:** For example, attending a sporting event can cause more damage than you expect. You may not think about how cheering at a game affects the voice, but we assure you, voice actors do. If you're attending a game, whether it's your child's soccer match or a professional hockey game, you can protect your voice by not shouting and cheering. You may instead opt to clap, stomp your feet, or use a noise-making devise to support your team. One night of exuberant cheering isn't worth two or three days of hoarseness and lost (or subpar) productivity.

- ✔ **Smoking:** The carcinogens in cigarettes are hazardous to your health and also your voice. Smoking can change your voice's texture and can also affect your range. You also want to avoid secondhand smoke, which can also affect your voice.

- ✔ **Whispering:** When you whisper, your vocal folds don't vibrate as they normally do when you naturally speak. If your vocal folds are tightened in this way, they're strained, which can cause hoarseness and affect the way you sound.

Being realistic

Your voice has limits, and you need to respect them or you may grow tired quickly and find that your voice is underperforming or that your throat is in pain. Know your range and respect its natural boundaries.

If you know that your vocal range is limited to an octave or so, don't push harder to reach low, growly pitches or strain to speak too high, either. Don't force yourself because you'll not only sound bad but you'll also hurt your voice.

Your natural speaking voice sits in your comfort zone, also known as your *tessitura*. Tessitura is an Italian word that refers to a singer's comfortable range that presents its best sounding texture or timber.

Aligning Goals with Your Abilities and Working to Improve Your Skills

Knowing your voice type and its characteristics and timber can help you to better align your goals with your abilities. For example, do you want to be the booming voice of the movies but have a more genteel, higher pitched voice? You may have to revise your goals so they realistically match your abilities. At the same time, you can work to enhance your skills, which may alter your goals.

Certain roles fit your voice better depending on what is required. As you may have guessed, no one becomes a star overnight, so go slowly and progress at your own pace. Some of the best ways to improve your abilities are simple — just a little practice each day significantly can help build your skills. For example, try shorter reads and begin creating characters (see Chapter 5 about how to develop characters). The following sections are some basic areas that you can practice on a regular basis to develop your skills.

Breathing: Focus on your diaphragm

Of all the things you need to do when performing a voice-over, breathing should be at the top of your list. We mean *strategic breathing* that can yield the best performance possible while properly using your instrument.

We can't stress the importance of strategic breathing. Breath can make or break a performance. Figuring out how to breathe properly ensures that you can get through a sentence without taking more inhales than necessary, and it also serves as the fuel you need to be heard. For example, if you don't have gas in the car, the car won't go very far. The same is true for breath in a voice actor. Your intake of breath and how you manage your breath through diaphragmatic support determines how long you can speak without stopping. It also aids in creating more dramatic reads. Being able to budget your breath and use each one to your advantage can help you get more mileage out of your instrument.

As a voice actor, you want breathing to be comfortable. To figure out if you're breathing properly, try this exercise. Bend over and place your hands on your waist. If you can feel the air filling up like a tire around your waist, you're on the right track. You should feel your back expanding when you breathe in and contracting as the air is being released. You can feel more space open up in your chest, which helps you fuel your phrases.

Speaking clearly: Good diction

Seldom do you misinterpret what a professional actor says or miss words due to poor diction on a radio program; however, when it comes to speaking clearly, not everyone is a trained professional and aware of how he or she pronounces words, intones, or delivers his or her speech.

To practice your diction, enlist another person to listen to your recordings before you promote them. This person can be your second set of ears and help you with the following:

- ✔ Being conscious of how you sound
- ✔ Watching your diction
- ✔ Projecting your voice and not mumbling

Your voice speaks volumes about you. Your voice can define you, so how you use your voice directly impacts your audience. People expect to hear quality content and pleasant voices in your demos.

Voice acting is an audio medium, and the most important tool that you have to communicate your message is your voice. If you're recording for pleasure and aren't trying to make a business of it, people won't be as judgmental. But we assume that you're reading this because you want to voice act professionally for corporations or organizations, so the expectation exists that the voice acting is professional caliber.

Practicing breathing basics

When you were a little baby, breathing came naturally. Over time, you lose your ability to breathe properly and fall into some bad habits. When you're singing, speaking in public, or acting, you need access to as much supported breath as possible, and that may mean that you need to relearn how to breathe deeply, sustain the breath, and use it to buoy your phrases.

Try this exercise: Stand up and try to clear your head to concentrate only on breathing. Feel the air as you inhale and it fills your lungs, and then gently exhale and release. Put your hand on your stomach now as you breathe. When you breathe in, your rib cage should expand as your lungs fill with air. When you breathe out, let the air leave you slowly on a hiss.

Panting like a dog can help you to establish proper breathing technique in its earliest stages. Try it. You can't help but inhale and exhale properly when you're panting. Pant quickly at first to get the rhythm and then slow it down so you can dissect your breathing technique. When you breathe in, your stomach should expand. When you breathe out, or exhale, your stomach should return to its normal state.

Twisting your tongue

Aside from holding power speaking-wise, the tongue is also described as being the strongest muscle in your body. As such, the tongue plays a principal role in speech production and is one of the most critical parts of your articulating arsenal. Your tongue can either make you or break you in voice acting. This is why it's so important to loosen your tongue and get it working for you.

Many voice actors rely upon tongue twisters to be more nimble with their speech. Try the following to warm up:

- A big black bug bit a big black bear.
- Someone said something simple.
- A simple something said to me.
- Simply simple someone said.
- A simple something said to me.
- Swiss wristwatch.
- Unique New York.
- One smart fellow he felt smart, two smart fellows they felt smart, three smart fellows they all felt smart.
- How much oil can a gumboil boil if a gumboil can boil oil, if a gumboil can boil oil how much oil would a gumboil boil?

Narrating: Read books aloud

Audiobook narration basically covers the art of storytelling by assuming the role of narrator and providing unique voices to characters for dialogue between characters. Unlike shorter scripts for commercials or telephony, narration is all about the long distance run and is by no means a sprint to the finish. Vocal *endurance* (having a strong voice that can go on and on) as well as *artistic consistency* (being able to differentiate between character voices) are two necessary skills to complete a quality audiobook recording. Narrators need to have a special sensitivity when delivering copy because they play the role of someone who is all knowing and able to share what is going on without emoting too much.

Voice actors also need to have basic understanding of audio editing if working on a project like this from home. Here are a couple suggestions you can try to get used to narrating:

- ✔ Read books aloud to your family members. If you have children, grandchildren, nieces or nephews, or even a godchild, read the story to them and practice the voices.

- ✔ Consider volunteering to read for the blind or the dyslexic. Placing a call to a local nursing home to volunteer as a reader to their residents is also a good way to gain experience in this area and help you to build up your stamina as a narrator. You may even receive some excellent feedback, too.

Doing character work

Character work simply means that you're able to create distinct voices for characters in a script. Sometimes characters can be *archetypal,* meaning that you can base how they sound upon a standard character type, such as the superhero. Other situations require that you interpret the characteristics found in the script, either based on how the author presents them or how the artistic director instructs you. People often think that any old voice that sounds silly will do when it comes to characters and are unaware of the amount of thought that goes behind creating a character voice and understanding the character in general. Consistency is also important because you don't want to slip in and out of character while delivering the lines. Furthermore, you want to make sure you're clear about how the character relates to others, or you want to diversify many character voices so that people can easily distinguish them from each other.

One way you can staff up your character arsenal is to start with a few basic archetypes and build off each one, adding an accent here, a lisp there — the possibilities are endless! These characters can become like friends to you and help you diversify your stable of voices. Having a few key voices to draw upon as a starting point makes it simple to tweak or add to the voice when creating a new spin on an old friend.

Like in radio and on the stage not the same as voice-over work

If you have come to voice acting from broadcast radio or theater, you may think that voice acting should be easy because you have been paid for nearly your whole life to talk. A great number of people who started and built a career in radio find that voice acting has very different requirements when it comes to using their voices. Although some skills are transferable, oftentimes you need to develop and master new techniques to perform as a convincing voice actor.

Getting inside the head of a brand, an author, or a copywriter is one of the hardest things you do. Every voice actor, no matter how many skills they have mastered in terms of technical or artistic ability, needs to be able to intuit what the copy needs and be able to break it down to find clues and provide context. The good news: You can develop this special skill. Chapter 5 covers this topic as it relates to character development in greater detail.

Going With a Personal Voice Coach

Studying with a voice coach can help you assess your talent and develop your skills. Having a coach is the best preparation and nourishment that you can invest in to build a solid foundation for your voice acting career. A voice teacher can instruct, mentor, and prepare you for a lifetime of using your voice to make a living.

Training comes in different shapes and sounds. Although a professional coach can guide and train you and your voice, training also involves what you do during your own time to improve your skills. Refer to the later section, "Exploring Other Training Options," for what you can do in addition to using a voice coach.

Although studying with one coach to master the basics is to your benefit, each coach has his strengths in certain areas. In voice acting, you can choose to take lessons with a variety of coaches depending on what you want to study.

The following sections explain in greater depth the different ways a voice acting coach can help you develop, how different classes operate, what you can do to choose the right coach, how to hire a coach, and how to make sure your lessons are productive.

Understanding how a coach can help you

Voice coaches can teach you everything you need to know about technique and the ins and outs of the business. They can also provide much needed encouragement and help you to set goals that are possible, beneficial, and exciting.

A voice coach can provide you with objective guidance you wouldn't otherwise have. You can think of your coach as an additional set of eyes and ears with the added benefit of those eyes and ears being trained. Your coach can point out things to you that you may not be aware of, identify areas where you may be holding physical tension that affects your performance, and also instruct you on how to correct those things.

No matter your skill level, a coach can help you in the following areas. You may have strong skills in one area and don't need much assistance. If you hire the right coach, he can help you with them or just the areas you need assistance. Even if you decide not to use a coach for an extended period of time, you can use these same exercises to develop your skills.

✔ **Warm up your voice:** Before using your instrument in all kinds of wonderful and wacky ways, your voice needs some special attention. Warming up your voice is crucial to giving a performance that sounds good and feels pleasant. Your coach can show you a variety of vocal warm-ups that can engage your *resonators* (nasal passages, also known as the mask of the face) and *articulators* (tongue, teeth, and lips).

Some different vocal warm-ups you may do include the following:

- A soft, low hum spanning only a few notes at a time can kick in your resonators.

- A facial massage while humming can help loosen up your facial muscles and relax them.

- Yawning, believe it or not, is also a great way to prepare. Yawning helps to loosen your jaw and creates more space for you to breathe. After you have a nice loose feeling, you can start to expand the *range* (pitch) you're covering with your voice and try different, more elaborate exercises.

- Saying tongue twisters can release tension in your tongue. The tongue is the most powerful muscle in the human body, and it needs to be relaxed in order for you to articulate smoothly and without tripping on your words. Tongue twisters are a favorite of voice actors. You can find numerous tongue twisters online or recite nursery rhymes.

✔ **Breathe properly:** A good, deep breath can set you up to complete a phrase and allow you to be heard. In addition to breathing well, your breath needs to be supported, and you use your diaphragm to support your breath. Your coach can help you develop your breathing techniques with different exercises. As you master breathing techniques, you can deliver your lines more comfortably for longer durations with greater tonal consistency.

You can do breathing exercises that are as simple as breathing in for a few seconds, holding the breath for a few seconds, and then releasing the breath on a hiss, counting out the beats while snapping your fingers. Think of yourself like a full balloon. The hissing should feel slightly like you're deflating. Time yourself as the breath is released until no more breath is being expelled. After a while, you should be able to take a nice deep breath and let it out for a longer duration. Refer to the earlier section, "Breathing: Focus on your diaphragm" for advice on how to breathe.

✔ **Assume a proper posture for voicing:** Your coach also helps you maintain good posture, both when standing and sitting. You do most of your work as a voice actor from a standing position in proximity to a microphone, so you need to know how to stand in order to get the best possible performance from your voice.

When voice acting or singing, you're using your entire body to perform. You need to stand in a comfortable manner that properly aligns your vertebrae, with your feet shoulder-width apart. If you're in a sitting position, you may assume the posture of a chorister in rehearsal by sitting on the edge of your seat creating a 90-degree angle, feet touching the floor. A comfortable standing optimal position for voice acting means that you don't slouch, hold tension anywhere, or need to compensate in any way.

✔ **Develop these additional skills:** These are some more technical voice skills your coach can help you develop and perfect. He can provide an array of exercises to help with these skills.

 • **Intonation:** *Intonation* is how your voice sounds in terms of how it rises and falls as you speak. You can think of intonation as how your voice cadences at the end of a sentence, when you ask a question, and so on. As an example, most people's voices go up in pitch when they ask a question. Intonation can vary between cultures and may affect how the listener receives what the speaker is saying.

 • **Phrasing:** Having good *phrasing* means you're able to get through sentences in a script with ease, making the most of your breath, support, and tone in order to technically and artistically communicate the text well. A phrase can consist of an idea or fragment of a sentence or it can be an entire thought. Punctuation is important to consider as a guide to help you determine how you observe phrasing on a per phrase basis.

- **Fluctuation:** *Fluctuation* is how your voice can go up and down at will. This differs from intonation because fluctuation refers to the mastery of a vocal range and intonation refers to speaking in a certain manner, such as having your voice go up in pitch when asking a question. For example, fluctuating your voice means that you're able to bring your voice up or down in pitch, kind of like singing up and down a scale. If you have a wide vocal range, you can hit a wide range of tones. If your vocal range is limited to less than an octave (think of a musical scale representing one octave), you can practice to maximize your range and make it work for you.

  Fluctuating your voice adds interest and flair to a read. Think of how the use of *pitch,* meaning the relative position of a tone within a range of other tones, can affect how others pay attention to or perceive a message. The last thing you want is for your voice to sound flat or monotone — you would lose much of your audience! Adding color to your reads by fluctuating your voice can greatly improve your performance. We discuss adding color to your reads more in Chapter 5.

- **Elasticity:** *Elasticity* is in direct correlation with how well you have prepared your voice to perform and determines the ease in which your voice fluctuates or leaps around. That's why warming up your voice is so important, like we discussed earlier in this section. Warming up the full extent of your range provides you with confidence and the ability to experiment, play with, and shape your voice. This is a very important aspect of voicing for people who do character voice work. Keeping your voice well-hydrated by drinking plenty of water helps significantly in this area. Always have a bottle of water handy wherever you go and be sure that you're well-hydrated before attending a recording session or using your voice.

- **Versatility:** How far can your voice take you? *Versatility* refers to the different ways you can use your voice and your ability to change how it sounds. For our purposes, versatility takes into account your vocal range, *timber* (relates to the tone color or tone quality of your voice), tone, enunciation, and other vocal qualities. A voice actor who can read for a variety of applications or characters may be considered versatile. Some people, for example, are good at home recording commercials and can also do animation voice acting. Although these fields may seem polar opposites, a versatile voice actor can work in very different fields of voice acting and be very successful.

✔ **Explore the potential of your voice in a friendly and secure environment to find your groove:** Are you afraid to try something simply because of the way producing the voice makes you look? A lot of people in this business twist up their faces to achieve the desired outcome vocally. Others need to use their hands and gesture wildly to get the words to come out. If you're passionate about finding out what your voice can do, make sure you have a safe place to try things out where you won't be laughed at or considered odd. Your coach can help you feel at ease and try new things. Another safe place may be your bedroom or bathroom. Be sure to record your voice as you experiment and take note of what you did to create the voice or sound you made.

When you're ready, your coach can encourage you to record a professional voice-over demo. A *voice-over demo* is a brief sampling of your capabilities that demonstrates your personal style, brand, and highlights your natural talents. Chapter 6 explains what a demo is and Chapter 8 walks you through how to record your own demos.

Knowing your options for voice lessons

If you decide to hire a coach, you have several options for taking classes. Your classes may vary from once a week to every couple weeks to once a month. The class length depends on what you're able to commit to and whether or not you're traveling to see your coach. Most voice actors tend to schedule their lessons for one hour in duration, scheduled once a week. During this time, your coach can instruct you on how to use your voice and introduce new concepts and skills while polishing areas you're already skilled in.

 Because voice acting has many components, you may have lessons that are more technical in nature where you work on technique and other lesson that focus on the more fun, artistic side of things. Your coach can likely start with the basics that include fundamentals such as breathing, phrasing, diction, and so on. The voice is a versatile instrument and performs beautifully if the core skills are in place. Even though you may think all you're doing is talking, voice acting demands an entirely different level of commitment and attention to detail. Being a word painter requires work!

Some of these educational encounters are shorter in duration. Coaches who teach a very specific form of voice acting hold intensive weekend workshops drilling a particular skill or set of skills. You also may find that you have an affinity for a particular course of study in voice acting. A coach can help you specialize in certain areas, such as the following:

- ✔ **Accents:** If you want to master a particular accent or dialect and broaden your horizons as a voice actor, you can seek out training from someone who specializes in this area. Accents can be a lucrative piece of the pie, so mastering a few of the standard accents is a good idea, particularly a neutral accent (or unaccented) speech and a British accent. Your coach can introduce you to the International Phonetic Alphabet and accents in general.

- ✔ **Audiobook narration:** If you want to be an audiobook narrator, study with someone who has experience in that area and has narrated titles that you can purchase in stores.

- ✔ **Commercial work:** If you want to have your voice heard on television or radio commercials one day, taking lessons from someone who has built his or her career voicing broadcast television commercials and understands the ins and outs of advertising is to your advantage.

- ✔ **Video game voicing:** This kind of acting is different from voicing for animated cartoons.

Basically, if you have an interest in a field, make sure that you seek out a coach who has experience in that field.

Picking a coach

Your voice is your instrument and is also the main component of your business. That being said, selecting the right coach for you to study is a decision that will directly impact the outcome of your goals. We assume that you're a working professional or are on the brink of starting as a novice voice actor who wants to study with a coach to aid in the preparation of recording a voice-over demo and develop and improve your skills.

Although a great deal of your success is reliant upon your actions and level of dedication, studying with the right coach can play an equally important role in determining how successful you are in this field.

Considering individual or group instruction

Figure out whether you want one-on-one instruction or group instruction. Here's a quick overview of the pros and cons to these types of instruction:

- ✔ **Individual instruction:** When you study one-on-one, the pros include the following:

  • **You get more personalized attention.** Being in a class of one has its benefits, including that your coach can focus solely on you and your voice. You can accomplish more working privately with a coach than you would in a group setting.

- **You have an individual instruction plan.** When you study privately, your coach can plan lessons just for you that are specific to your needs and your goals. Each lesson will afford you the opportunity to learn, experiment, and improve as a voice actor, given the individual attention you're receiving.

- **You receive a custom experience.** Working with a coach one on one isn't only a wonderful way to accelerate your learning, but it's also the best way to receive a personalized education. You can ask all the questions you want about things you're most interested in and may also be able to choose scripts or texts to work from.

- **You get more microphone time.** Mic time is something that all voice actors crave when taking lessons or being coached. There is no better way to maximize your time at the microphone than to study privately with your coach.

- **Your coach can provide a personal consultation.** Being the only student in a class opens up opportunities for your coach to be honest with you about things you need to improve upon or celebrate areas that you have excelled in. You have time to consult with your coach and ask career-related questions, demo-related questions, or seek tips for how to book auditions that come your way.

Some cons include the following:

- **It's more expensive.** As the old saying goes, you get what you pay for. Studying with a coach privately will cost more than studying in a group setting. You're paying for the individual attention, which costs more.

- **You may have to travel.** Some of the best voice acting coaches are located in metropolitan centers, such as Los Angeles, New York, and Chicago. You may also find that a voice acting coach doesn't live near you. If you want to study in person, you may have to travel.

- **You have fewer people to obtain feedback from during a lesson.** Sometimes hearing the thoughts of others who have different perspectives is valuable. When you study one on one, you have only the coach's feedback to go from as opposed to multiple insights from a number of people.

- **You may feel isolated.** When it's only you and your coach, you may feel a bit isolated in the sense that the only voice you're hearing is that of your coach. You may also be someone who prefers to work in groups and likes to be part of a team.

- **You have nowhere to hide if you didn't do your homework.** If you want to truly succeed, you need to do your homework. A coach will know if you haven't practiced, which can reflect poorly on you as well as set you back in terms of progress.

✔ **Group instruction:** Studying in a group provides you with a unique setting to develop your skills. That being said, group instruction has its own pros and cons as well. Some pros of studying in a group are

- **You can give and receive more feedback.** Feedback is a helpful tool for improving your reads or performances. Giving feedback is a useful exercise because you need to be listening attentively and objectively to give good feedback. Listening is one of the chief skills you'll need as a voice actor because professional voice actors, believe it or not, do more listening than talking.

- **You can watch others perform.** Observing others perform or take direction is a great way to scoop up practical tips that you can then apply to your own performances or technique.

- **You potentially have a lower cost to participate.** If you're just exploring voice acting and want to invest only a modest amount at first, a group lesson may be a good fit as is auditing a class.

- **You're introduced to other voice actors in your area.** Meeting other voice actors is important because they understand you! Voice actors work in a very specialized area, so you can turn to each other for support and help.

- **You can get a feeling of community.** Being surrounded by people who know what you do and are encouraging of you is a must. Fellow voice actors are generally some of the most welcoming and helpful people you'll ever meet in a business setting. Get plugged in to your local voice acting community. (Refer to Chapter 10 for ways you can network inside and outside of class.)

The cons of studying in a group are as follows:

- **You get less personalized attention.** If you're looking for someone to hang on your every word and make the class all about you, a group class isn't right for you. Remember that the instructor needs to divide his or her time among other students to be fair to all in attendance who paid to take the class.

- **Other people can see you perform.** If you're shy and are worried about how you look and sound, this can be problematic.

- **You get less microphone time.** Mic time is very important for training sessions. You really can benefit from your performance with mic time. The more time you have at the microphone and the more work you have to review after the fact, the better.

- **Material may not be altogether at your skill level.** This issue can happen from time to time if who sign up for workshops geared toward a different level than you are. If you have any experience whatsoever, you may want to consider intermediate or advanced-level courses.

- **You may achieve less than you would if instructed privately.** When you're in a group setting, the instructor can't stray much from the curriculum to accommodate voice actors who are at different skill levels because the instructor needs to focus on teaching what he advertised.

Your choice is ultimately yours. Starting out with group coaching or attending a weekend workshop for beginners and aspiring voice actors is a great way to test the waters before committing to private lessons or lessons of any kind.

Knowing what to look for

When you start to look for a voice acting coach, you want someone who leaves an imprint on your perspectives, goals, and potentially the direction you take in your voice acting career. Coaches have the ability to inspire or to deter, depending on how you interpret their methodology, or bedside manner if you will. As a result, you need to select the best fit for you as a student for voice acting to succeed.

When you start your search, you need to consider a few important points about your potential coach:

- ✔ **Experience level:** When looking for a coach, look for someone who has been working in the industry for more than a decade and has a wide array of clients. Some coaches may have enjoyed a successful voice acting career for a long time and have decided to turn their attention to teaching in their golden years. If the coach has a website, look at it to see a partial client list or roles that the coach has performed. Do what you can to research the coach's educational background.

- ✔ **Fee:** The fees that coaches charge vary depending on their level of experience and the amount of time you will be spending with them on a per lesson basis. If you're studying to learn something very specific, you'll likely pay a premium for that information and guidance. If you're studying in a group versus one-on-one setting, group lessons may cost less than if you were having a private lesson. Each coach reserves the right to charge what she feels her services are worth and will bundle lessons in either a curriculum or month-to-month basis. Ask the coach if you can study once or gain an evaluation period with her before you commit to ongoing study.

- ✔ **Your niche:** Figuring out what you want to study or improve upon is half the battle when finding a coach. Coaches who work in the niche you are focusing on will be a better fit than working with someone who is an amazing voice coach but specializes in a different area of voice acting. When you can, find a coach who has been acknowledged as a top performer by his or her peers and other industry players, perhaps even award-winning. If you want to work in audiobook narration, for instance, try to find a working narrator who has received awards such as an Audie or a Golden Earphone. If you want to work in commercials, look for coaches who served as the voice of an award-winning campaign and can lay claim to an Addy, per se.

- ✔ **Personality:** Life can be a lot easier if you get along with and respect the person who is coaching you. You need to be able to take constructive criticism from the coach without feeling threatened or discouraged. Finding an encouraging coach is a must. Make sure the coach is able to encourage and still be objective and honest.

- ✔ **A coach's voice demos:** When considering whether you want to study with someone, listen to his or her current voice samples. Many coaches are still working voice actors and have a few demos on their websites that you can hear. Their demos can tell you a lot about what you can expect of their talent and also how they may direct you in producing a demo at some point. Studying with a coach who has voice samples in the area you wish to work in also can give you a greater appreciation for the work she has done and validate her abilities in this niche of voice acting.

- ✔ **Close to your home:** If you want to study with someone in person, location is a significant consideration when choosing a coach. If you live in a metropolitan city, you're in a better position geographically to study with a coach who leads a peer group. Centers with a wide array of voice acting coaches to choose from include cities like New York, Los Angeles, Chicago, Toronto, Vancouver, and Montreal. Keep in mind that if you want to study in person with a coach who lives far away, you may need to travel unless the coach offers services over the phone or by Skype. Some people are willing to travel a fair distance (sometimes up to eight hours) to train, but doing so isn't practical for everyone nor is it desirable at times.

Finding the right coach

A coach who can open you up, develop, and refine your skills is available for every person. Finding these individuals and having the ambition and humility to become a student of voice acting is the real challenge. If you know your criteria (we help you figure out what you want in a coach in the previous section), you can actually start your search.

To uncover the coach that's right for you, use these tips:

✔ **Ask your colleagues about their experiences with a particular coach (one with whom they study on a regular basis).** Get the inside scoop from them on why they love studying with their coach. They'll have specific reasons why they chose and continue to work with that individual.

Don't just ask one of the coach's students; ask several. Each person has his or her own unique reasons for studying with that coach, and you may also find that students in a given studio share similar thoughts on why studying with a particular coach has improved their performance.

✔ **Read written reviews or testimonials from past students.** Nothing is more telling than feedback, whether good or bad, from people who have actually studied with a coach you're considering. You can find this information by visiting the coach's website, doing a search for the coach's name, or visiting a chat room or forum.

✔ **Find out whether the coach's students are booking jobs.** One sign that a coach is helping his or her students is if those students are booking voice acting jobs, landing agents, or continuously crediting part of their success to a particular coach. Good coaches also keep their eyes and ears open for opportunities that can suit their students. People who study with these sorts of coaches are quick to share that information and often do so via social media.

✔ **Listen to podcasts or watch videos of their work.** You can easily find information online that can serve as a soft introduction to a voice acting coach before reaching out to connect. Many coaches participate on the Voice Over Experts podcast (which you can find in iTunes) or donate articles and expertise to the community.

After you narrow down your search to a couple, have a phone consultation or interview with each one to see if you get along. You can also ask any questions that you may have about the coach's teaching style and whether or not the coach feels she would be a good teacher for you. If auditing is an option, attend one of the coach's workshops and sit in to observe how she interacts with students. Above all, make sure you feel comfortable in the presence of your coach and that you trust her. Your voice is a very personal thing and not just anybody should be shaping it. Be selective in this regard and use all the information you have gathered before making a decision.

Starting off on the right foot with your coach

You find a coach, and you're excited about starting this relationship with the hopes of developing your voice acting skills. When you hire the coach, keep these points in mind as you start your official relationship:

- ✔ **Be true to your commitment.** Treat this relationship as you would the same professionalism shown to your doctor, accountant, and so on. Make sure that you clearly understand the structure of your lessons, set reachable goals, and if applicable, determine how long you will be studying with the coach. Will this be a long-term relationship or are you planning on studying with him for a set period of time? If you're unable to make it to a class or need to reschedule, be sure that you understand your coach's policies and how he treats absences and how he compensates you for lost time if he is late or ill. Knowing what your coach expects of you professionally is very important.

- ✔ **Be a good student.** If you want this relationship to prosper, you need to put in some effort and give your coach reason to look forward to each class. Show up on time and be prepared to work. In between sessions, review what your coach has taught you and work on specific things you discussed in previous lessons. Applying your coach's advice and demonstrating your ability to follow instructions can go a long way in maintaining a good rapport with your teacher in addition to improving your skill and talent as a voice actor.

Getting the Most from Your Training Sessions

You want to make sure you consistently apply what your coach has instructed you if you want to improve your skills. Take what your coach has presented and find a way to interpret it and make it your own. In this section, we look at ways to maximize your lessons and ideally improve your chances of getting hired for work in voice acting.

Doing your homework

Remember what it felt like in school to have your teacher walk by to check the previous night's homework assignment only to find that it wasn't completed, perhaps not even started? The same thing happens in the arts when you don't practice. A voice acting coach will know if you've been working on what he assigned by your performance and skill, so make sure you dedicate time to do your homework. Review your lessons and apply what your coach taught. To help you, many teachers will make an audio or video recording of your lessons for you to refer to when practicing at home.

Practicing is always a good idea. When you're studying one on one with a coach, you need to have done your homework. Practicing allows your coach more freedom to move ahead with introducing new concepts and pieces of copy for you to try.

Being open to trying new things

The key to getting the most from your voice lessons is to discover your own voice and not to mimic someone else. What you bring to the table is special and unique, and no two voices are exactly the same. In your classes and in your free time, be open to new experiences. You may feel uncomfortable at first, but you can't grow your voice acting skills without doing something new. If your coach suggests new exercises, don't resist. Trust that she knows what she is doing.

In doing so, experiment. You can work with different scripts and characters and allow your coach to share ideas with you. Don't get pigeon-holed into one style or one type of character. Although not everything you try will suit you or work, the more you exercise your voice, the more knowledge you'll have of your voice.

Accepting constructive criticism

You don't want to pay a coach to tell you how great you are or pat you on the back. You want insight, so when your coach or classmates offer you feedback, be open to what they're saying. Many times people don't take to heart what objective outsiders have to say about their work. When you get feedback, take away what you need from the experience and toss what you don't.

Exploring Other Training Options

Studying with a coach is just one way that you can develop your voice acting skills. Fortunately for you, training options for voice acting are as varied as they are plentiful! Everything from industry conferences, voice acting workout groups, and free resources online are at your disposal. In this section, we overview what you can do to grow as a voice actor and how you can do it.

Attending industry conferences

Going to conferences related specifically to voice acting is a great way to inspire you and discover new developments and skills needed for a voice acting career. Furthermore, conferences are a great way to meet and network with other voice actors. By going to a conference, you can attend sessions on how to stay ahead of the curve in the industry and chat with others about what works and doesn't work for them.

When determining whether to go to a conference, look at how much it costs. The price of conference tickets should be equal to the perceived value of what you are going to receive. From a business point of view, investing several hundred dollars, even for a day, to be in the same room as industry leaders, experts, and people you wouldn't be able to meet with, network, and learn firsthand from is worth the price of admission. Before you register for any workshop, talk to other people who have attended in the past to see if it's worth attending.

Putting on a conference costs money, and part of the fee you pay to attend goes toward costs associated with the venue, food, speakers, and any materials that are being provided to you. It isn't uncommon for a conference to cost $500 or more to attend. Generally, conferences that cost several hundred dollars also provide food and drink throughout the day.

Participating in workshops or peer groups

Attending workshops and participating in small groups of your peers are great ways to improve your skill set and network. No matter whether you're new to the field or you have decades of experience, you still need to brush up on your skills every so often or get referral business from others in the field.

- ✔ Workshops give you opportunities to discover something new in a group environment. For instance, you can attend a workshop on voice acting in animation or a workshop on how to read commercial scripts for television and radio.

- ✔ A *peer group* is great for developing new skills, figuring out voice acting in general, and gaining support and encouragement from others in your field.

  You can find workshops and peer groups by searching online for keywords related to the type of group you want. For example, you may search for "voice acting workshops, New York City" or "voice-over group in Toronto." Most workshops are advertised well, but peer groups are harder to find. You may have more success finding peer groups by asking other voice actors for referrals.

Taking classes via phone, Skype, or webinar

If you live outside a large city, such as New York, Los Angeles, or Toronto, where many voice acting coaches hold classes, you may be able to take classes via the phone, webinars, or Skype.

Coaches may teach telephone classes on a weekly basis with a curriculum that they want to teach for a matter of weeks. These classes can be short or can run for more than an hour. You can go with private coaching sessions or group lessons taught in an ongoing educational course format.

Other coaches may provide webinars that allow you to listen to special guest instructors. At the end of the webinar, participants can ask questions and receive immediate answers from the featured presenters and experts. Webinars offer an alternative to simply hearing what is being shared by sharing material in real time. Check out the resources section at www.voices.com for some different types of webinars.

Listening to podcasts

Podcasts are radio-style shows that you can listen to either on a website or by downloading your podcast of choice from a podcast directory, such as Apple's iTunes. You can listen to podcasts to enhance your voice acting skills and discover new skills. Most episodes contain pearls of wisdom and tricks of the trade to improve your voice-over career. *Voice Over Experts* is the No. 1 educational podcast featuring renowned voice-over coaches from the United States, Canada, and abroad.

Watching YouTube videos

You can find videos online that give you a greater appreciation for the art of voice acting and touch on a variety of industry topics, including home studios, recording, audio editing, vocal technique, performance, auditioning, and voice acting. Many of the most successful voice actors have uploaded videos to YouTube that share tips and let you into their studios for a sneak peek. Some voice acting coaches also share tips that can help you grow in both knowledge and skill.

For example, plopping down on the couch to watch a YouTube video of Kevin Conroy in session being directed by Andrea Romano won't suddenly make your Batman voice or interpretation any better. Watching what Conroy does, studying his choices, interpreting them, and rehearsing those choices on your own as the Caped Crusader will.

Chapter 4

Understanding Your Role

· ·

In This Chapter

▶ Getting to know the "real" person

▶ Finding your voice as a narrator

▶ Releasing your inner announcer

▶ Acting as a spokesperson

▶ Being an instructor

· ·

*T*he art of communication — the most powerful, persuasive, and distinctly human tool in any marketer's arsenal — has evolved to the degree that you don't have to be in the same room to get a message across, even the same country for that matter. Despite this advancement, making sure the audience receives, understands, believes, and acts upon a message is so important. Voice acting skills (as well as the copywriting) can ensure you achieve this audience response, which is where the voice actor's role plays out. As a voice actor, you can play different character roles to get the message of your client across in a direct and effective way.

Voice actors play many different roles. In fact, voice actors can find themselves voicing for five main categories of roles, each one representing a different purpose and segment of voice-over work. Think of all the situations in which you've heard voice-over work. Commercials, entertainment, or educational purposes all use voice-over work. That being said, no matter what the voice-over is, it still falls within one of those five areas.

In this chapter, we introduce you to these five categories: the real person, the announcer, the narrator, the spokesperson, and the instructor. These roles apply to any and all voice acting, depending on the goal the voice-over wants to achieve and the direction you receive.

We also explore subtle differences between these roles and provide instruction on how to give each sort of role your best shot with insider tips to help in your preparation for practicing, auditions, or jobs you have booked.

Saying Hello to the Real Person

Projects requiring a more casual approach often benefit from relatable, genuine voice-overs. These voice-overs are referred to as *real-person* voice-overs, commonly known as "the regular guy" or "the girl next door." The character is homegrown, sensible, and friendly with a touch of familiarity, and it provides a more intimate interpretation that instills trust. You probably have heard the real person in commercials, podcasts, explainer videos, or any application where the voice actor needs to speak as though he or she is having a conversation with the listener.

By their very design, these types of reads sound natural. This naturalness ideally connects with the audience in a more direct and affable way. Think of the real-person read as a form of *permission marketing* where the listener is welcoming the advertisement. It carries a greater currency in a relational sense. An example of permission marketing is if you catch someone's attention and she continues to listen, this person has allowed you into her world and is more likely to consider or value what you're saying.

With this type of read, the audience must relate to you as a real person. Sounding like you're speaking to an audience of one, when in reality you're speaking to hundreds or thousands if not millions of people, is a skill that takes time and practice to develop.

The following sections delve into the characteristics of the real-person character and give you some pointers when using these characters in your voice-over work.

Becoming more conversational

In order for your read to sound like a real person, you want to make sure you sound informal and genuine. Just like walking a dog, you have to train your read to stay authentic, which takes discipline.

Furthermore, these tips can help your real-person read sound more conversational:

- ✔ **Speak slowly.** Reads come across with greater sincerity when spoken at a slightly slower pace. When people rush through their words, they can either sound like they're hiding something or that what they have to say is more of a sales pitch. Although this is true, you may find that commercials don't afford you the luxury of reading slower because they contain too much copy to read at a slower pace. Commercials require that the voice actor reads the copy within the time allotted for the spot.

When you're nervous, you may react by speeding up in order to finish more quickly. Quickening the pace can get your read all out of sorts, potentially resulting in stumbling over words, slurring words, or sounding like you're out of breath. Keeping a steady metronome-like tempo gives you the freedom to massage each and every word and give it the proper attention it deserves while observing punctuation and places to breathe.

✔ **Speak naturally.** Reads also sound more conversational when they don't sound as if you're reading the words or that the dialogue is contrived, meaning that it's deliberately created instead of arising naturally.

✔ **Speak with conviction.** Sounding genuine also implies that you believe what you're saying. Authenticity and being able to relate to your audience are very important for this type of read. (Refer to the later section, "Extending authenticity" for more information.)

✔ **Speak conversationally.** Other factors that can make you sound more conversational are pitch, tone, phrasing, intonation, and fluctuation. Being able to control your voice helps to shape how your voice comes across from a tone perspective and also how effectively you're able to use your instrument to deliver a message. Chapter 5 is full of great information specific to using your instrument and goes over elements such as tone, pitch, and so on.

Coming across as real

A real-person read requires you to put aside your professional voice-over voice and just be real. Even though your trained voice usually serves as a benefit, sometimes the client wants you to sound less polished with a real-person read.

To help deliver a read as a real person, you can picture the person you're talking to. You may even go as far as pinning a picture up in your studio and speaking to a photograph of a loved one as if that person is the audience. Perhaps you even need to gesture with your hands or pretend that someone is seated beside you. If you find that looking at a friend or family member helps to inspire a more conversational, genuine read, go for it!

One of the beauties of voice acting is that the audience doesn't have a front row seat to your recording session nor does anyone else. You don't need to be embarrassed because no one can see you when recording at home. Setting yourself at ease is critical when performing a real-person read.

Extending authenticity

Sounding authentic is an important aspect of delivering a real-person read, although doing so isn't easy, especially when you're recording a commercial or a piece that involves persuasion or the selling of an idea. *Authenticity* is very important in voice acting because listening audience members need to feel that what you're telling them is true and that you're in agreement with what you're reading 100 percent. To be authentic, you need to make sure the listener feels as though you, as the voice actor, match the role and who the listener expects you to be. People who come with a broadcast radio background in particular often struggle with sounding like a real person. They often fall back into the default announcer or on-air persona when interpreting a script.

You may hear someone say that if you can fake authenticity in this business, you've got it made, but that isn't necessarily the case. If your heart isn't in sync with a piece of copy or your role, or a conflict of interest comes into play, you won't sound authentic. Voice acting requires that you immerse yourself in the role you're being asked to perform, which may require that you leave certain aspects of your voice or speaking style behind, such as a radio voice, a regional accent, or a shift in intonation.

If you really want to sound like you mean something, believing it to be true helps! If you don't believe or agree with what you're saying, passing on the audition or job is a good idea. (Chapter 9 discusses questions you can ask yourself to determine whether you want to audition for a job.)

Meeting the Narrator

Storytelling is where the *narrator* is most at home. Omniscient, courteous, and honest, a narrator's job is to provide an audio landscape for the listener, briefing the listener on background information, posing questions, telling a story, and providing solutions as he or she guides the audience through a program or documentary. Narrators can be male or female, and the most important factors are that they can communicate clearly and engagingly. These sections explain what an effective narrator looks like.

Suspending the audience's disbelief

Although the listener is quite aware that the narrator is only telling a story, no matter how fantastical it is, the listener can suspend his or her belief and decides to enjoy the story. The listener embraces the narrator's world and the author's intended different reality to be entertained.

As a narrator, you can help the audience suspend its disbelief. These sections give you some pointers to make your reads believable, no matter what.

Knowing how to make your read believable

Your primary role as a narrator is to draw your audience into the story you're telling and to get your audience to temporarily let go of preconceived notions for the duration of the commercial, audiobook, or animation. You need to believe what you're saying. In order to do so, place yourself in the time, place, and minds of the voices you provide, which can help your audience follow suit and become more invested in the story you're telling.

For example, one of the greatest storytellers today, Pat Fraley, teaches voice actors how to create an environment wherein the audience signs a contract so to speak with the narrator to temporarily suspend their disbelief.

If you, as the narrator, slip in and out of character or overdo it, the listener will notice and lose faith in you, which breaks the suspension of disbelief. By maintaining your presence and keeping to the contract you signed as narrator with the audience (as Fraley suggests), meaning that your read is consistent and unbiased, you can keep the listener engaged and earn the listener's trust.

Focusing on the narrator and audiobooks

Narrating audiobooks is a marathon that requires the ultimate balancing act of artistic and technical endurance coupled with the ability to continuously suspend the audience's disbelief. Because some audiobooks are so long, they may take up to three weeks to record. As a result, you need to be able to pace yourself and preserve your voice.

If you're narrating an audiobook, you can utilize these suggestions to help suspend the audience's disbelief:

- ✔ **Engage the listener.** Give the listener a reason to listen to what you have to say. Be a solid voice that they can rely on to share information as it unfolds.

- ✔ **Make and keep a contract with the listener to suspend their disbelief.** Do everything in your power to ensure that you don't break the illusion that you have transported the listener to a different time, place, or season of life. When recording, remember that you need to know everything about the world the story inhabits, lending the omniscient perspective of someone who is looking in.

✔ **Give a consistent performance.** Stay consistent with the narrator's voice and anything else that requires consistency throughout the recording, such as character voices, accents, voice ages, and so on.

✔ **Have intuitive timing.** Develop a feel for how you pace your read as well as how much time you give to punctuation marks, such as periods or commas. You may find that the text sometimes sounds better when timed differently than what the printed page may present in terms of punctuation.

✔ **Develop multiple convincing and separate character voices.** If a book you're working on has many characters, you need to give them each distinct voices. You may want to keep track of each character's vocal attributes in a document for reference or record how each character sounds to remind yourself of how to voice them. Giving each character its own identity can help you to clearly differentiate which character is speaking for your benefit and the benefit of the listener. (Refer to Chapter 5 for more assistance.)

✔ **Be an authentic narrator with an independent voice.** A narrator's voice needs to be distinct and set apart from the characters' voices in the story. You may find that the narrator's voice most closely resembles your own natural speaking voice with a touch of authoritativeness. When shaping your narrator voice, make sure that you're comfortable with voicing it and that you can perform using this voice for long stretches of time.

✔ **Interpret the author's intent.** Try to understand why the author has positioned things the way she has. What are her motivations? What means the most to her and how can you follow through with her intentions? Good narrators are able to grasp an author's concept or vision. You can achieve it by reading the full manuscript before recording, and if possible, having a chat with the author. If the author isn't living or is unavailable, the person who commissioned the audiobook may have an understanding of how the story should be told.

✔ **Transport the listener to a different time and place.** Use your voice and the tools provided to you in the text to take the listening audience to the landscape, soundscape, and time period the book was written in. Accents, manners of speaking, and production elements, such as sound effects and music (if appropriate), can help with this.

✔ **Maintain a solid presence.** Consistency is key for narrators. Audiobooks are more of a marathon than a sprint. Be sure to keep the contract (suspension of disbelief), keep your voices consistent, and stay true to the author's intent.

✔ **Bring the story to life.** Here you get to have a lot of fun! Establishing all the voices, creating the characters, and setting the scene for a story well told is an exciting experience for actors. You get to play all the roles in this book, so have fun with it.

When you meet these criteria, you can feel great about your work and can also be assured that your audience will connect with the story, relate to the characters, and have full confidence in your ability as the narrator to captivate, amuse, and delight.

Telling a story

As a narrator you're a storyteller, which isn't always as easy as it looks or sounds. You have to consider the who, what, when, where, why, and how as they pertain to the story in general, the characters, the context, and so on. In a way, you may find that you're just as much a researcher as you are a storyteller. Knowing everything there is to know about the story you are telling provides a solid foundation for every word that you speak.

Think of yourself as a detective of sorts and use the text as your guide when seeking clues about the author's intent and how you can best communicate what the author prepared for you and the intended audience. Although punctuation is important as you communicate to the audience, don't let punctuation dictate all that your voice must do. Use inflection to color words in order to authentically express what the author has in mind.

As you tell a story, consider how you will design unique character voices that suit each role and give your characters diverse vocal traits that set them apart so the listening audience can distinguish them. This task can be fun, especially if you have several characters to voice. The author tends to help you with the clues presented in the book. The author is your greatest ally when it comes to creating believable characters. Creating a variety of characters is easier when you know what you can do to differentiate them from each other, especially vocally.

Keeping the voices as separate as possible can help you to more clearly remember what each character sounds like and why they sound the way they do. Great narrators consider the following criteria to shape and differentiate the voices of their characters in a book:

✔ **Gender:** Before you hit record, you need to consider what the gender of each character is so that you can shape how they all sound. If you're reading for characters who are the opposite gender, consider how you would speak. If you're a man, how would you voice female characters? If you're a woman, how would you voice male characters? Good narrators are able to utilize their vocal range. Men sometimes need to speak slightly higher when voicing females and women generally deepen their voices by using the lower end of their range to voice male characters. The falsetto voice (think the Beach Boys) isn't necessarily the best way to go for men voicing women, although using the upper register with a lighter tone and different vocal placement may do the trick.

- ✓ **Pitch:** Everyone has a natural *vocal range* where they normally speak, sometimes referred to in singing as *tessitura.* Think about where your character's speaking voice rests and where it's more comfortable. You can use pitch to differentiate characters. Just make sure that you're comfortable performing in the vocal range that you have assigned to each character. You can also use pitch to express emotion. The higher the pitch is, the more emotional the audience may perceive a read.

- ✓ **Accent:** Giving characters accents is a wonderful way to make them stand out and inform the character's identity. Make sure that the accent is believable and consistent throughout the audiobook. Many voice actors work with accent and dialect coaches to master new accents to add to their repertoire.

- ✓ **Qualities:** Believable characters are important. In order to be believable, you need to know the characters inside out. Give each character his or her own set of qualities. List those qualities and use them as tools to shape how you read for each particular character. For example, if one of your characters has a kind temperament, speak kindly and with care. You'll also want to consider physical qualities. If your character has dentures for instance, you'll need to learn how to speak as one who has a set of dentures.

Look for clues about the characters that may tell you how they talk. How old are they? Do they have anything specific about their physicality that determines how they speak? Are they from a place that has a regional dialect you can tap into? If you want, you can also consider borrowing vocal traits from friends and family.

Knowing how the story ends

A good narrator also knows how the story will end. To do so, the narrator reads the script before recording to have a good idea of how everything plays out before the audience does. As the narrator, you don't want the ending to surprise you. The more you know, especially about how things turn out, the more convincing your read will be.

The more comfortable you are with telling a story, the greater the likelihood that your listeners will come along for the ride because they trust your knowledge as the narrator and are secure in where you're headed. By starting your work with the end in sight, you can lead your listeners through the peaks and valleys of a well-woven tale and truly function as the omniscient narrator you are meant to be.

Going online for help with plot and character development

A number of tools online can help you succeed in your quest to narrate to the best of your ability, enabling you to know more while saying less. Even if you have read the book, you may find these resources to be helpful when researching because they can provide additional context for your read and analysis to aid in developing character voices.

Many free online resources break down books in terms of plot, characters, and so on. Some even go chapter by chapter. When time is of the essence or you want to deepen your understanding of the book, its characters, and your role as narrator, the following are great resources to discover and invest some of your time in:

✔ **JiffyNotes:** One of the reasons why we really like JiffyNotes, which focuses on literary analysis, is because of the chapter summaries they provide, which can come in handy if you want to get some context at the chapter level. Other features of JiffyNotes include access to a book's historical context, main characters, points to ponder, and the plot summary.

✔ **SparkNotes:** What appealed to us about SparkNotes was that you can learn so much for so little. Context, summary, characters, and analysis are available for free by navigating through the section devoted to each book. You can also purchase to download the SparkNote as a PDF or an ebook for under $5. Being able to do so comes in handy when you're in a bind and need to take the material with you in places where you can't connect to the Internet. You can even print and read it on a plane or anywhere else.

✔ **CliffsNotes:** Did you know that CliffsNotes offers free audio summaries of some of the books in podcast form? In addition, you can also download iPhone and iPod apps for certain books to take them with you on the go. Most are available for about $1.

You never know when you might get caught off guard by something in the book that throws you for a loop. If you haven't read through the book before creating a character voice, midway through the story, the author may give you a hint about that character, and suddenly you realize that the character you thought sounded one way is actually quite opposite.

Typically, narrators read through the book if the material is new to them given that they have time to do so. Sometimes a narrator doesn't have to read the book before recording it, particularly when he or she is reading books in a series. After the narrator has read one or two of the books, he or she will have a good idea of the plot and characters.

Although reading the book before recording is the most obvious way to gain pertinent information, you can also acquire this information in other ways if you're unable to dedicate sufficient time to read the book in full or conduct an in-depth analysis. Refer to the nearby sidebar for some excellent online resources that provide summaries of books with detailed character sketches and more.

Listening to the Announcer

The *announcer,* often heard live at events, on commercials or promos, and as segment introductions for podcasts, is a product of the broadcast age, most celebrated at its height in the Golden Age of Radio and early television broadcasts. Announcers can introduce an idea and assertively make a call for action at the conclusion of a commercial advertisement or short video.

One common misconception is that an announcer has to sound like an announcer from decades ago; however, modern announcers act more like narrators, and in many cases, adopt the real-person approach.

These sections walk you through the forms an announcer can take and how you can give an effective announcer read.

Identifying the two types of announcers

When announcing, you can announce in two different ways:

- ✔ You can be a live announcer.
- ✔ You can record announcements in advance that are played at the appropriate time.

Announcing lends itself to both, and in some instances, a live announcer also pre-records some of what is said during a live event. You technically can be announcing some parts of a program live while other, nonchanging aspects are cued up for just the right moment.

Announcers have the exciting job and responsibility of sharing the news or providing commentary, often without much time to review what has been handed to them to read. To be a professional announcer, you have to be quick on your verbal feet to clearly deliver a message.

Measuring your announcer abilities

The Announcer's Test, as it is commonly referred to, originated in the 1940s at Radio Central New York as a cold reading test given to aspiring radio talent to demonstrate their reading ability. Today most voice actors and announcers use this test as a warm-up for their voice to get their articulators going.

The Announcer's Test involves:

- ✔ **Retention:** Being able to retain information is important, especially if you have to refer to it later or as you're building on what has already happened. Having the capacity to remember what you've said is important, especially when trying to recite something by heart.

- ✔ **Memory:** Doing the test helps to increase the length or extent of your memory span as you'll need to repeat each line numerous times.

- ✔ **Repetition:** Repetition can help you to remember more, follow and identify patterns, and become more comfortable speaking your way through difficult passages, phrasing, and most importantly, with budgeting of your breath! If you know how repetition works in the *12 Days of Christmas* carol, you get the idea.

- ✔ **Enunciation:** Speaking clearly and coherently is important. You want people to know what you're saying, right? Recording yourself while you recite the test and then listening back afterwards can give you an indication of how clearly you're speaking.

- ✔ **Diction:** Spitting out consonants helps dramatically with the shaping of words and how your audience receives your voice. Be particularly sensitive with consonants, such as *t, k, p, b, f,* and *v.*

- ✔ **Ten factors that use every letter in the alphabet a variety of times:** This test incorporates literally every letter in the alphabet and will give you a great workout. You'll likely encounter words and combinations of words that you've never seen before, which will happen often in the course of announcing.

You can find recordings of announcers reciting the famous test online. Here's an especially wonderful example of Jerry Lewis showing how it's done at `www.youtube.com/watch?v=06D1F5-4Atc`.

Although you can rehearse some aspects of announcing, such as in the cases of award shows, game shows, and special events, you'll always have surprises along the way that you need to be mentally prepared for in order to articulate on the go. The best way to prepare for cold copy live to air is to train. One of the best ways to train is with the fun Announcer's Test (see the nearby sidebar for details). You can take this test for your own benefit (more of a warm-up). Taking the test isn't required of you at a job interview or for becoming a professional announcer; it's more just a fun way to gauge your skills and abilities.

Grasping the message

As an announcer, you need to be, in effect, all knowing or omniscient, which is different from the narrator role. Sometimes announcers have to work with what they have at the moment and be prepared for new information to come their way as a story unfolds or if something changes unexpectedly. Regardless of whether you're announcing live or recording for something to be used at a later date, be diligent in your work to highlight the central plot, pivotal moments, and underlying themes so that you don't get lost in the midst of it all. A voice actor's comprehension and knowledge of the story helps drive key points home so that the listener is able to fully understand the core message and enjoy following alongside.

Pacing your read

If you're reading as an announcer, you have a set amount of time that you need to deliver the copy. Because you have a limited amount of time to read, you want to pace yourself appropriately so that the copy fits within the time frame and doesn't go long. Pacing yourself is important for commercials as well as any other application where voice-over is only one component of a storyboard.

To help keep within the time limit, use a stopwatch and measure your read. For example, if you have only 30 seconds to deliver the copy, practice so you can fit it all in 30 seconds without rushing or finishing early.

When narrating audiobooks, you have a little more freedom with pacing your read. When voicing for animation, the artists often animate to what your voice has already done. If you're dubbing, however, you need to be able to match what a character is doing on the screen in keeping with the original performance.

Selling without sounding like a salesperson

The more conversational your speech is when you're an announcer, the more likely your listeners will believe you're engaging them in a dialogue that is safe and has their best interests at heart. On the other hand, if you speak quickly or appear too aggressive, they will think you're only trying to sell them something instead of building a relationship. Audiences these days don't fall for much. They seek relationships and need to know why what you're presenting to them matters in their lives.

Just think about it: Have you ever listened to an advertisement where the actor is talking at you rather than speaking to you? If the actor's tone of voice and approach to the script sounded like a sales pitch, you probably were turned off. People have built-in radar for this sort of technique nowadays.

Knowing How to Be a Spokesperson

The fourth kind of character you can play as a voice actor is the spokesperson. A *spokesperson* can be on or off camera, depending on the medium you're using. A confident, charismatic person able to promote a cause, product, or service with ease and authority usually plays a spokesperson. This type of voice-over needs to be driven, optimistic, and assured.

The spokesperson represents a brand and is associated with that brand. If the spokesperson is on camera, his or her physical image is more aligned with the brand, but if the spokesperson is off camera, the voice resonates more closely with the brand.

The next sections provide more detailed information about what a spokesperson does and what you can do to be an effective spokesperson.

Representing the brand

When you record a voice-over, you're representing a company and its brand. Being an organization's vocal ambassador can be an amazing opportunity with enormous responsibility. Knowing the brand and understanding how the company wants its brand projected to the public is very important. In this capacity, your voice isn't merely a representative of the brand, it also must embody the brand and advocate for the company while exuding the essence of the brand and its core objectives.

The bigger the brand, the greater the likelihood that it requires some form of exclusivity regarding the use of your voice in the industry. In fact, a number of larger companies pay significantly higher fees to their voice actors to secure insurance for a brand and ensure that a competitor or another company doesn't use the voice actor. If such an agreement is in place, you may need to turn down opportunities.

Working with a brand may also mean that you not disclose that you're the company voice or that you have done work for them. The industry refers to this as a *nondisclosure agreement (NDA)*. These sorts of agreements can last for a very short time, or they can be in place for as long as the voice-over is used, perhaps even longer.

Feeling comfortable

As a spokesperson, being fully comfortable with a script and the director's expectations of you is paramount. Are there certain words that you won't say, and are there particular kinds of roles or concepts that you steer clear of or don't identify with? If you find instances in a script that you don't feel comfortable with, let the director know. Perhaps the writer can change the copy to make you feel more at ease.

At the end of the day, you have to think of what the story is that you want to tell in your own life, not just what the stories other people are telling through voice-over. If a project doesn't sit well with you or goes against every fiber in your body, leave it on the table.

Endorsing with confidence

Endorsing something that you don't believe in or subscribe to can make you feel like a fraud, and that will come across in your read. As a result, make sure when you're playing a spokesperson role that you know the brand well, are familiar with the product or service being promoted, and understand all that you can about what is being asked of you.

If you can't stand behind and endorse it 100 percent as a spokesperson, you should pass on the opportunity rather than compromise what you stand for. Although most voice acting, including spokesperson roles, goes without credit (where your name generally isn't associated with the final product nor are you recognized publicly in most cases as the voice artist), if you don't feel as though you can put your name on something publicly, don't do the work. Recording the job in private doesn't make a difference; you're still doing the job, even if other people don't know you did it.

Learning from the Instructor

A straightforward, didactic, and encouraging voice is the voice-over best suited for teaching someone how to do something, such as a corporate training video or a children's game. The role of this particular voice talent, called the *instructor,* is to provide information to fulfill a specific goal or purpose. Everyone learns better when they feel that the person teaching comes from a place of authority, knowledge, and a genuine desire to see them succeed. We describe the instructor role in more detail in these sections.

Becoming the expert

As an instructor, you read as though you're knowledgeable. In fact, the script can enrich your understanding of the topic and thereby your read, which can allow you to sound like an expert. Experts typically sound formal, didactic, and confident.

Doing a little extra research to help you understand the script is always a good idea. Knowing more about what you're talking about is a critical piece for sounding like you're in a position to teach. You can do research in other ways too, including the following:

- Use a dictionary to look up words.
- Search online for the topic or profession for more information.
- Ask the director for advice.
- Go online if you're unsure how a word is pronounced. Many online dictionaries have a listen feature where you can hear how a word is pronounced in North American English.

  If for whatever reason you're working in a different accent, you can go to the International Dialects of English Archive (IDEA) to hear native speakers from different parts of the English-speaking world and appreciate how they sound when speaking. People who are studying a different dialect of English often use this resource.

Speaking with authority

When you're recording an instructor role, your voice and how you use it can tell an audience a lot about how informative and prepared you are to teach listeners with your voice-over. Tone, pacing, and comprehension all play into how authoritative and confident you can sound. Speaking with authority means that you understand what you are saying, that you believe what you are saying, and also that you feel the information is of value to other people.

Communicating objectives

Communicating clearly the objectives set before you can give your audience a good idea of where the value lies and how they can best apply the teachings presented. When you're able to identify what is most important in a script, you can zero in on those objectives and place greater emphasis on them with your voice and manner of speech. If you feel something is important, use your voice to let people know by varying pitch, tone, pacing, or the weight you give to a particular word or concept. Check out Chapter 5 for information on breaking down a script.

Chapter 5

Interpreting a Script and Finding Your Character

*O*ne of the primary responsibilities of a voice actor is that of a story-teller. Instead of passively reading a story, the voice actor has an opportunity to actively tell the story by being directly involved in how the story is told.

Although being a storyteller can be fun, you, as the voice actor, have been entrusted with this significant responsibility. You have the power to shape how someone may receive what you're saying, so you carefully need to exercise that power without robbing the audience of its experience or imposing your own views. You're also responsible for how well the author or copywriter's intent is being delivered.

Because you get to read the story before the listener hears it, you can decide how to bring it to life, which allows you to construct a safe place for the story to unfold.

In this chapter, you discover how to find clues from the author, create believable characters, use your voice (tone and so on) to shape a message, and get buy-in from the target audience.

Analyzing a Script: The Five Ws and How

When figuring out how to read a piece of copy, you need to first analyze the script. Think of yourself as a detective, sorting out the most important pieces of the puzzle, such as the who, what, when, why, and how of a script. When answering these questions, you're looking for clues that can help determine who your character is in the script, why you're saying what you're saying, and who you are speaking to. Doing so is important because you need everything you can get your fingers on to help you create a believable and effective read.

You can dissect from all kinds of angles when you know what to look for. The more you know about the script, the better you can interpret your script, thus giving a richer performance.

Use these exercises to examine the script as a whole and more specifically your character. You want to know every detail possible about the script you're voicing, who the intended audience is, and how you need to convey the information or story being shared.

Who you are playing

When reading the script, look to see who you are in the script and what role you play. Are you a narrator who is supposed to be all knowing? Are you a character in need of a back story? When trying to figure out who you are in the script, you also need to read between the lines to gain a better appreciation for who your character is, why your character is relevant, and how your character relates to other characters in the script.

The "who" question also refers to other characters in the script. Make a list of all the characters you come into contact with and write down bits of information about them to see how they relate to each other. This information can help you to understand the story or script better as a whole and make your interpretation more fluid and believable. Each character is there for a reason, so you need to know who your character is in relation to you and everyone else before you pick up that script and hit record!

What you want to communicate

You also need to answer the "what" question regarding the plot, including what is going on, what needs to be communicated, and what the theme or the subtheme of the script is.

Answering the "what" question gives you a firm place to stand and sets the expectations. When you're reading from a place of confidence and have laid a firm foundation, your read can be more believable simply because there are no unknowns or ambiguities. You know what you're talking about because you have all the facts and can therefore set the mood and listener expectations by communicating to your audience with authority.

When the story happens

The third "W" question you answer when reviewing the script is "when." Figure out when the story takes place, including the time period. What is the time frame for the story unfolding (does it cover an hour or cover many years before reaching a conclusion)? Answering this question can help you to establish a timeline and gain historical context.

Where the story takes place

One of our favorite questions to ask is "where." Where allows you to create a physical environment for yourself or a stage to set your players on in the theater of the mind.

Having an idea of your physical location, based upon a place that could be either fictitious or real, can help you to visualize your surroundings and understand the world that the characters live in. An understanding of this particular element can help you to suspend your audience's disbelief as you paint word pictures and soundscapes. (Refer to Chapter 4 for more about suspending the audience's disbelief.)

Why?

Answering the "why" question helps you better understand the story's *context,* which tells you what's going on, how it affects the characters, and why it matters. (Refer to the later section, "Understanding Context" for why you need to know the context of a script.)

When you answer these why questions, you're able to more fully comprehend the author's intent with the characters, plot, theme, and so on. On a deeper level, you can also discover the purpose for a character or gain an understanding of the reason for a particular situation by answering "why." An appreciation for these answers allows you to picture beyond what the audience would see.

How?

"How" is a problem-solving question. When you ask how, you instinctively need to find a solution. How does this factor into the story? How should you interpret this phrase? How can you best deliver your lines? Studying the script reveals the answers to these different questions. A good author or text provides you with many clues.

Developing Your Character

Knowing the ins and outs of your character is essential for any voice actor in order to give a believable performance. You can develop a character in many ways, including writing a character sketch and understanding how your character relates to other characters in the script. You also want to take note of any physical characteristics each character has. The following sections explain the different ways you can identify your character and understand the role you're playing.

Understanding your role: Back to basics

The author (or copywriter, depending on what you're reading) has provided you with some clues in the text about who your character really is. Authors tend to have more to share regarding how characters behave, what motivates them, how they relate to others, and why they do the things they do. You, as the voice actor, need to find out who your character is and what makes him tick.

A copywriter may only have a paragraph at most to share her vision for voice roles in the script. As a result, making the determination about your character may not be easy. Even if the details are handed to you on a silver platter, you still have to create a distinct voice that fits your given character description.

Break the copy down by asking yourself simple questions. The answers to these questions can help you get in your character's skin and what makes him breathe. You can delve deeper into the script and ask yourself more who, what, why, where, when, and how questions as we explain here. (These questions focus on helping you figure out your character, while the previous discussion on questions deals more with breaking down the script as a whole.)

> ✓ **Who:** Decide who your character is and give him a life history. What makes him tick, what does he like, and what kind of person is he? Is your character an influential person?

To help, write a *character sketch,* which is a detailed description of your character, including everything known about his personality and any physical attributes. In your sketch, include physical attributes and personality traits. You may even want to draw a picture of what you envision your character looking like to help you get a complete grasp of who he is. By setting the stage for your character and developing a persona for him, you can slide into the role and create a more authentic, organic performance. You may also consider how your character sounds. Does he have an accent? Does he have a speech impediment of any kind? How does he speak?

✔ **What:** What is your character trying to say? Whose attention is he trying to get? What makes his message important and worth listening to?

If you can distill what your character's main objective is in relation to whom he is trying to reach or persuade, you have more purpose and authority behind your words.

✔ **Why:** Why should people listen to your character? Why does your character need to share his message?

You really need to get inside the head of your intended audience for this question. Make your audience members care about you and help them to grab hold of your cause by way of artfully communicating the message.

✔ **Where:** Where is your character when delivering his lines?

You may not think this question is all that important, but you need to know where your character is in terms of physical location while he's delivering his message. This knowledge can affect your read and also make it easier for you to create an ambiance if you're using sound effects or including music in your recording to complement the voice. Having music in the background can do much to support your read.

For example, if your character is in a restaurant, you may want to include some soft music in the background, the sound of utensils on plates, glasses clinking, and so on. Building the scene through audio design can be fun and make it easier for the listener to feel as though he or she is in the scene with you, thereby making the recording more believable as a whole.

✔ **How:** How is your character relevant to the people he is speaking to? How is your character motivated?

Revisit the character sketch you created earlier in this list. Now identify the target market or audience (A *target market* represents the people an author or advertiser wants to reach with the message.) For example, the audience for a popular laundry detergent is generally women of a certain age with families who have lots of laundry to do. What inspires your character to speak to this audience in particular? How much does he have invested in successfully delivering the message to those people and what is the desired outcome?

Reading between the lines

When developing your character, you want to look at what the author's message is that he doesn't come out and clearly state. Finding the unspoken words in a script and conveying them through your voice demands not only attention to tone but also to the choices you make when interpreting the text and use of inflection, timing, and punctuation.

Each script that you read, whether for an audition or a booked gig, demands that you make distinct and motivated choices in order to do proper service to the words. Knowing the script and your characters well gives you what you need to read between the lines. When *reading between the lines*, you're able to infer important elements, such as motivation and tone.

The legendary late, great Don LaFontaine once said that your voice is merely a vehicle for the written word. The words take center stage, and your responsibility is to convey them in a respectful and meaningful manner. In fact, Don had even been quoted as saying that you should specifically "devote yourself to the service of the words," which means interpreting the written word to make informed choices.

To do so, you need to be not only sensitive to the copy, but you also need to create a character as we explain in the previous section. Each job that you do as a voice-over professional requires you to take on the persona of the character in the advertisement, narration, or cartoon to deliver a message as someone other than yourself.

Understanding Context

Context gives you a 360-degree view of the story and your character, and how your character and his story relates to others and his surroundings. Knowing everything you can about the production can aid you in building a plausible back story from which you can draw upon to flesh out your character.

In addition to providing a solid foundation for your choices, context supports your back story and helps direct how your character would react in any given situation.

Building a back story can be a lot of fun. Each character you voice for, and even ones you don't, require a back story in order to deliver a thoughtful, well-engineered performance. These sections explore what a back story is and how a good back story can set you up for a successful read and an informed acting experience.

Building a back story

A *back story* is all the information about a character that an actor creates, based upon clues the author has given the actor, and through character development and details the actor infers from his own imagination from the text. Essentially, having a comprehensive back story allows you to make solid choices about how to be the character you're assigned. The choices you make concerning your character are very important and need sound reasoning to support them.

The back story can include details such as where your character grew up, what his family was like, what he likes to do, what types of people he associates with (basically who his friends are), what his political leanings and religious beliefs are, and any experiences he has had that shaped who he is up to the point he is presented within the confines of the script.

In order to truly understand your character and present him well, you need to know the lens through which your character sees the world. How a person sees the world determines how he views himself, what's most important to him, how he makes decisions, and how he relates to other people.

Every person sees the world a certain way, based upon his or her life experiences. You can refer to this as a *worldview*. You have one of your own, and if you're trying to create an authentic personality for your character, your character has one as well. This worldview is why you want to know about your character and why creating a history for him gives you insight for why your character may do the things that he does or feels the way he feels about people or events in the script.

When you make a choice as your character, such as choosing what to say, how to say it, or when to flesh out your character's back story, make sure you commit to the choice or otherwise it won't come across with authenticity. Then physically play the character in your voice and act on those choices with conviction. For people to believe you, you need to first believe in yourself and the choices you've made for your character.

Gaining an appreciation for your character in its relation to other roles

Another aspect of character development includes making sure you know in great detail how your character relates to other characters in the script. Look at this experience as an adventure and have fun exploring.

Understanding relationships between characters isn't only important in longer scripts and productions; it can also be critical for giving a believable performance in shorter projects like commercials.

Relationships fascinate people. Stories are interesting mainly because they involve people and how they relate to each other. Just think of all dramas, sit-coms, and reality TV shows. Although the show's genre or plot may initially pique your interest, the characters and their relationships with each other pull you in and keep you interested.

When you first receive a script, we suggest you do the following to help you figure out as much as you can about the characters:

✔ **Take note of who the characters are and jot down a little bit about them.** You may want to know, for instance, if certain characters are related to each other. Whose lives are interwoven? What do these people have in common with each other? Are they part of each others' lives for a reason, a season, or a lifetime?

✔ **Create a mini character sketch for each one.** (Look at the earlier section, "Understanding your role: Back to basics" for how to create a character sketch.)

✔ **After you know who the characters are, categorize each one in terms of their significance to your character.** By categorizing, we mean that you identify which characters are most important to your character and also note whom your character interacts with most. This ordering can tell you whom your character has loyalties to or feels strongly about. Relationships between your character and those characters listed near the top of your list will be different than relationships your character has with characters who are lower on the list.

If you're a narrator, consider how each character impacts the story and other characters as well.

✔ **Draw a family tree.** Doing so can help you visualize how the characters are connected to each other.

Be careful and don't overthink the script or who your character is. Overthinking can make it difficult for you to change your read if you've studied it one way. Keeping an open mind until you get the go-ahead from a director is important because your first attempt at the character may not be what has been asked for or what is expected.

Identifying the takeaway

Identifying the *takeaway* message, or premise, of a project can help you to better deliver on what the author's intent was and give your read a richer, more informed interpretation. A *premise* is a statement that is assumed to be true and from which a conclusion can be drawn. This exercise is important regardless of project type or length of copy.

By focusing in on the premise, you can also find that getting where you need to go in terms of direction where plot is concerned is easier. Some examples of premises you may find in scripts are

- ✔ Good triumphs over evil.
- ✔ Love conquers death.
- ✔ Pride comes before the fall.
- ✔ Honesty is the best policy.
- ✔ Beauty is in the eye of the beholder.

In our research online and via published works, we discovered a number of traditional literary genres, including but not limited to the following. Although voice-over scripts are very short, they often have some of these same elements:

- ✔ **Mythic:** The triumph of God or gods; triumph of a hero because of an act of God.
- ✔ **Heroic:** The hero is triumphant because of his own strength.
- ✔ **High ironic:** The hero triumphs because of a twist of fate.
- ✔ **Low ironic:** The hero fails because of a twist of fate.
- ✔ **Demonic:** The hero is overcome by evil forces or uses evil to defeat evil forces.

Considering the plot

All stories have a basic plot. A *plot* consists of the main events of a work that the author devises and presents as an interrelated sequence. A well-devised plot is critical to telling a great story and helps you understand what happens to your character. Characters need a challenge or an obstacle to overcome and are often presented with this challenge at the beginning of the story.

These four basic plots include

- ✔ Man against man
- ✔ Man against nature
- ✔ Man against himself
- ✔ Man against the supernatural or the sub-natural

When doing research on anything you read, consider what the plot is and if there are any subplots. If there are subplots, consider what their purpose is and if they strengthen or weaken the principal plot.

Marking Up a Script

Have you ever looked at an actor's script or peered at a musician's score? No doubt you noticed as many pencil markings as ink! Although the effort may seem over the top, those thoughtful markings can help you better navigate your script, color your read, and keep it consistent. Following a well-marked-up script is like reading a well-written map.

When marking up a script, consider a number of factors:

✔ Where to breathe or pause

✔ What tone of voice and inflections to use

✔ The volume of your voice

Some voice actors prefer to print off a script and mark it with a pencil, making sure that their erasers are handy should their interpretation change during the process. Others read directly off a screen and find ways to mark up copy using italics, bold, different colored font, and so on.

Don't be married to your markings before you've voiced them aloud and know how they come across. Feel free to experiment before setting your markings in stone. Sometimes, plans for how you deliver the copy may change!

Although markings should act as boundaries for how your interpretation of a script comes across, you don't need to be legalistic about them. This artistic freedom, when guided by markings, can blend together to create a purposeful and believable performance.

In this section, you discover how to choose and mark where to breathe and also how the volume level you speak contributes to a great performance.

Choosing where to breathe

Knowing where to breathe can depend on a few things. You want to observe punctuation marks in particular. For singers, it's often permissible to breathe wherever there is a comma, colon, semicolon, or a period. In voice-over, you may need to be more selective with where you breathe.

You can definitely breathe after a period, but may need to be more choosy with what commas you can breathe after or sail right through. Another good place to breathe is when a new idea or concept is introduced. If breath support is something you are working on, you may need to structure your breaths accordingly so you can get through a phrase without losing tonality or speeding up. Check out Chapter 3 for more specific how-to information about breathing.

Adding dynamic markings

You will need to determine the volume level you're speaking at and any variation on how your voice is being heard. For instance, sometimes you may need to be a bit quieter. If so, mark it on the script. You can even use the musical decrescendo ">" symbol. Other times, you may find that there's a movement building that leads to a climax in the script. Mark it in! Try the crescendo "<" symbol. Perhaps you're simply reading comfortably and setting a relaxed, conversational tone for the script. You still need to know how you'll be speaking, so get that pencil and start jotting your dynamic markings down!

Playing with Mood: The Tone

Every good actor and professional speaker knows how to use her voice to her advantage. Getting to know your voice, being able to use different tones of voice to set the mood, and understanding how your voice can come across to others can help you to communicate more clearly and effectively. The tone of voice you choose impacts your audience and may also determine how your audience receives what you're saying.

If you grew up watching cartoons produced by Warner Bros., Hanna-Barbera, and so on that employed smaller voice casts with a sizable number of characters, you've probably seen just how versatile a voice actor can be when using her instrument to the fullest. Legendary voice actors like Mel Blanc and Daws Butler manipulated their voices to make full use of their range and tonality, and implemented creative decisions for spot-on inflections and comedic deliveries.

These sections explain what tone is, identify elements that can affect the tone of your voice, and characteristics that are related to tone and attribute to vocal performance. You can use this information when you interpret a script and get the absolute most out of each character and piece of copy you encounter.

Understanding what tone is

Have you ever heard that it's not what you say, but it's how you say it? Anyone who uses her voice to communicate needs to be aware of tone. *Tone* refers to the overall quality of a voice and also how the sound of a voice comes across to others. Tone can express a particular feeling or a mood in addition to its sound in general.

When you're communicating something important and have a solid argument behind you, the tone of your voice has a way of shaping how other people receive what you're saying.

Identifying elements that affect tone

Certain elements that you can control affect your voice's tone. These five elements include the following:

- ✔ **Attitude:** Something as simple as your *attitude* or *state of mind* can dramatically impact how your voice sounds when delivering a script. Everyone leads busy lives and faces daily challenges, so not letting what is going on at home, at work, and in the world affects your mood, and how you sound isn't easy. As an actor, you need to get to a place where you can put those other things out of your mind and focus on the task at hand.

- ✔ **Breath support:** You'd be surprised by how greatly the lack of breathing techniques and poor support can affect the overall quality of voice. Proper breathing techniques and support from the diaphragm help set you up for success, both in terms of producing a desirable, consistent tone and getting through a phrase comfortably. Refer to Chapter 3 where we discuss how to breathe.

- ✔ **Artistic choices you make:** A little planning can go a long way when shaping the tone of your voice. Because the voice is a versatile instrument, you want to experiment and play with different segments of your voice by varying its *pitch* (where your voice sits, whether high or low), *inflection* (how you say something), and the *gravity* of the words you're saying (where you place emphasis).

   Use a pencil to mark your script and include directions reflecting the mood, where your voice may go up or down, and also factor in where you can take breaths. Doing so can help you to remember your good ideas, solidify choices, and create more consistent performances. (Check out the earlier section, "Analyzing a Script: The Five Ws and How" for what to do when reviewing a script.)

✔ **Your voice's health:** Yelling, screaming, crying, vomiting, and sickness (think cold and flu) can also change how you sound. If you're sick or you overuse your voice, you can give your voice a different quality that may or may not prevent you from creating the sounds you're accustomed to.

✔ **How you treat your voice:** How you take care of your voice is also important. You may have noticed how certain foods, drinks, or substances can change the quality of your voice. Some people find that caffeinated beverages or alcohol dries their vocal folds. Others claim that dairy products produce more mucous and consequently make them sound phlegmy. Being near smoke of any kind can also dry out and impact the quality of your voice. (Check out Chapter 3 for how to take care of your voice.)

To counteract these vocal hazards, you can drink lots of water to hydrate your voice. You can also avoid yelling or screaming and resist anything that negatively affects how your voice sounds.

Coloring your words

When talking about tone, you can also think of it in terms of color. *Coloring* means adding another dimension to your read with tone and inflection. A read that stands out often has been thoughtfully constructed to include flourishes of color on words that elicit a response. Coloring words helps you to paint a picture with words that gives feeling to individual words and phrases. Coloring your words well can also help you to authentically sell a product or service with your voice.

When you choose to inflect somewhere, be sure to mark it by using adjectives to describe how you're going to paint a particular word. Infusing your read with emotion and believability helps to better paint the picture for your audience who may or may not have the luxury of a visual image to go along with your voice-over. Your voice can set the scene. (Refer to the earlier section, "Marking Up a Script" for more information about how to make notes in your script.)

Some of the easiest words to color are adjectives, such as hot, cold, big, small, delicate, strong, young, old, interesting, beautiful, glorious, and wise. You can make your voice audibly express or sound like its definition. For instance, you can put a little shiver in your voice if you're talking about something that is cold, whether it's a biting storm or cool fall breeze.

You can color other words too. When coloring nouns, you may want to look for clues in the text to see how the author treats particular nouns or how your character perceives them. What your character thinks of those nouns adds to how you say them. For example, if your character likes ice cream, she will favorably refer to it, which may sound like a smile in her voice. If your character dislikes ice cream, likewise you have the artistic license to determine whether that perception creeps into how she refers to ice cream.

Nouns often come after adjectives. The noun that follows an adjective you have colored with your voice may enjoy that same sentiment. To illustrate, your character may say: "I love ice cream." The color you've assigned to the verb "love" can also apply to "ice cream." If you add an adjective to say "I love soft ice cream," you can make the color different on "soft" than what you chose to do with "love" to add more depth and variety, transforming what could be a relatively dull statement into an interesting, captivating — even salivating — statement.

You can also color pronouns and verbs. Coloring words requires thought and purpose. When you have decided what you want to do, mark up your script to reflect which words you want to color and how you are going to say them to remind yourself of your creative choices.

Seeing the connection between your voice's tone and musical instruments

Think of your voice like an instrument, and we like to consider stringed instruments, such as the violin, viola, cello, and bass, as similar to the human voice. Stringed instruments can mimic the human voice in many ways, primarily through use of tone.

The tone of a voice is endless; it can come across as shrill, squeaky, soft, harsh, or raspy; you name it. Stringed instruments, when played a certain way, can also imitate those tonalities and inflections to communicate with other instruments or the audience. Just as a skilled musician can utilize tone in a variety of ways, so can a skilled voice artist change the tone of her voice to suit a role or fulfill a vocal requirement from a director.

Some voices like the violin, comparable to a soprano voice, have a lighter, airier tone whereas others, such as the viola, compare to an alto voice. The cello compares to a tenor and has a darker, warmer tone. The bass compares to a bass voice and is deeper.

Even instruments that don't use words to communicate a message can do so effectively using tonality. Think of tone as the vocal equivalent of body language. What someone may not be telling you with her words may be fully evident in the tone of her voice. Tone dictates how people receive a message, and the voice is often all a voice actor has to give when recording for a project. That being said, voice actors in particular need to be more vocally expressive with their interpretations than actors (like on stage or TV) who have the benefit of using their physicality to communicate in addition to their voice.

Try playing with your voice to see where you can take it and see how similar it can be to a musical instrument. Speak intentionally using moods, colors, shapes, and feelings as your palette. If you can read music, take a piece of music and look at the dynamic markings on it. By using the sound "ah," speak the musical markings (notes, rests, staccato, and so on) to experiment what different tones your voice can form.

Selling with Your Voice

In voice acting, your voice is one of the most persuasive tools you could ask for to drive home a message and demonstrate who your character is. You can use your voice in the following three ways to help someone believe your character and entice the audience to buy into what you're saying, which may include having them buy a product, service, concept, or idea.

Staying soft

The *soft approach* is suggestive and persuasive without directly asking for the business. This soft or gentle approach presents the *ask* as more of an invitation than a direct order. The soft sell often targets women, although it can also be used in advertisements directed to men. Soft sells don't push the listener and often appeal more to the intellect and emotions. These are the commercials that pull at your heart strings. You can consider the soft sell to be more like an option, but a smart option.

A soft sell empowers people to make a decision without hitting them over the head. Musical selections used in commercials with a soft sell are generally pleasant, depending on the content of the script. A friendly, conversational tone works best for the majority of soft sells. That being said, authoritative reads can also be used. Examples making use of the soft sell approach are commercials for soap, diapers, and yogurt.

Going halfway: The medium sell

When reading for a *medium sell,* you're asking for the business but not in a forceful or abrupt way. These commercials have a more upbeat, lively, and entertaining composition. Excitement, discovery, and family themes permeate this category of sell. Music varies but is invariably fun. The medium sell often targets families, but it also reaches out to young adults and kids.

A medium sell may remind people of why they love a brand and sell new people on the feeling it brings. Speaking in a conversational manner and using humor are elements of this sell. Remember that you're talking to someone in a comfortable way but still asking for the business. The medium sell can often be heard in commercials for restaurants promoting a special or new item or hotels inviting you to book your vacation with them.

Hitting hard

The *hard sell* takes no prisoners and demands the business. The hard sell has a sense of urgency unlike any of the other sells. It's go-big or go-home time. The hard sell is generally associated with limited-time offers, and the target market is typically, but not exclusively, male. The music is upbeat if not rocking and helps take the *ask* (the company's pitch) up to another level. Your voice may take on hard hitting attributes, such as a different tone of voice (think gruff, booming), although you're always full of confidence.

Although not entirely pushy, the hard sell needs to be aggressive and assertive. Hard sells are frequently employed in television infomercials, pitches by big box stores, beer commercials for or at sporting events, and marketing for car dealerships.

Part II

Creating Your Audio Résumé

The 5th Wave — By Rich Tennant

"I think your demo tape's going to be more effective if you don't begin every sentence with a long 'Rrrrrrr.'"

In this part . . .

In this part, you get an introduction to demos, that is, a sampling or demonstrative recording of your vocal abilities for prospective customers to listen to. You can go about getting your demo made in a couple different ways such as doing it yourself (DIY) or working with a professional recording studio.

Every good demo starts with a good plan. Be sure to focus in on the chapters relating to planning your demo, picking copy to include in your demo, and knowing how to select appropriate music and production elements to complement your reads. If you've been voice acting for a while, we also give you some pointers to help you determine whether you demo is ready for a tune-up.

Chapter 6

Deciding What Demos Are Essential

*I*n hopes of being hired for a job, many voice actors and musicians started out by giving live performances to give prospective customers a taste of what they can do. A pre-recorded demo serves as that taste. Thanks to modern technology, you can submit your demo to prospective clients, and they can access it and listen to it without your having to be present.

In this chapter, we explain what voice-over demos are, show you why you need one, express what a demo can do for you, determine how long a demo should be, and help you plan on how many demos you should have.

Discovering Voice-Over Demos

In order to get voice-over work, you need a voice-over demo. Your *demo* needs to be your best work you can do at the present time to show prospective clients and potential agents what you can do. Furthermore, it also needs to be something you feel comfortable assigning your name to and marketing to the public.

Your prospective clients can listen to the demo and evaluate your services firsthand. Creating a variety of voice-over demos rounds out your portfolio, showcasing the styles of voice acting that you can perform.

Voice-over is ubiquitous, meaning that it's everywhere. You can listen to professional voice-over demos online at www.voices.com to get a taste for what actors are using to promote themselves online to get work.

These sections explain the importance of voice-over demos and how they can help increase the chances of your getting work.

Knowing why you need one

A voice-over demo is like your business card and résumé all wrapped into one. Your demo gives listeners an appreciation for what you're able to do vocally and also provides a glimpse into how you can sound as the voice of their job.

Having at least one voice-over demo is essential to promoting yourself as a voice actor. How will people know if they want to work with you unless they can hear your voice?

In today's digital world, a demo is typically hosted online these days with little reason to have a hard copy on a compact disc. Demos also tend to run shorter and narrower in scope. Having some copies on disc isn't a bad idea because you may have some opportunities to hand out or send them to agents or casting directors that still accept CDs.

Serving potential customers at all times

When you feature your voice-over demo online, your prospective clients can listen to it at their convenience, no matter what you're doing. Listening to the demo doesn't require any effort on your part after they download the file. Technology has definitely helped voice actors get their demos to potential clients. Before the digital age and the Internet, people handed out CDs or gave live reads at a studio or an agent's office.

Having your demos available online provides a great amount of value to you. Not only are those demos working for you in your absence, they could be getting you bookings! How do you make this a reality? Produce a handful of one-minute demos that highlight your best work, each of which focuses on one application of voice-over. Keep reading for help in how to record demos that can do this for you. Chapter 8 can help you when you're ready to actually record your demo and where to place it online.

Determining How Many Demos You Need

Having a variety of demos for prospective clients to hear is beneficial to you in many ways, not the least of which is that your voice-overs can appear in more searches when those clients are seeking a very specific sound or kind of voice sample when working on an online marketplace site (such as www. elance.com or www.voices.com).

Even though you may have a few different types of voice-over demos online that represent the type of work you can do, you also need to realize that a client may have a certain need, and just because the client is picky, doesn't necessarily mean the client isn't interested in you or doesn't appreciate a good selection for future reference. The client is looking for something specific to cast a voice for his project.

For example, if you go shopping for a loaf of multigrain bread, would you pay much attention to pumpernickel, sourdough, or raisin bread? Not likely. You're decidedly going for something very specific and only want the multigrain bread. Everything else is a distraction, no matter how good or healthy it appears to be. That's exactly what clients go through when they're looking to cast a voice.

 If you post your demos on a voice acting marketplace site (refer to Chapter 8 for more guidance), what you can do to help attract customers to your demo is use as many accurate, descriptive words as possible in your text to explain what your voice-over demo is about. We suggest you start with three or four demos that best highlight your skills. As a beginner, you may only have tried a couple different styles of voice acting and may be most comfortable making a few short sample reads of material you found in the public domain or wrote yourself. If you post on your own website, you still need to make sure you include a detailed description.

These sections can help you to discover your unique abilities and leverage opportunities for your voice to shine. The voice is a flexible instrument that lends itself to many purposes and applications. Being able to release yourself from preconceived notions or pigeonholes can only be good for you and your business if you choose to run one.

Releasing yourself from self-imposed limitations

As a voice actor, you have the ability to create a variety of different reads and interpretations, and you're able to fluctuate your voice to achieve a desired effect. As a result, you should exhibit your abilities and talent and offer your clients demonstrations of your abilities by uploading several different types of voice-over demos that show your range of ability.

Many voice actors don't record or promote more than one voice-over demo, which is a detriment to being hired. In most cases they only present a commercial demo. By offering several samples of work, you set yourself apart from others.

Failing to offer something = lost potential

If you don't have at least one voice-over demo (we suggest you start with multiple demos) online showing your abilities, you lose out on prospective jobs and ultimately money. Some people don't have demos, at least demos produced by someone other than themselves, because they consider recording the demos too expensive. Although demos do cost some money to have someone else produce, the expense is relative to what your return on investment (ROI) will be from each demo you have produced.

If you talk to producers, they'll certainly point you in the direction of recording a demo in a professional recording studio, which does cost money. If you do have a demo professionally recorded and produced (we discuss in Chapter 8), you need to be able to replicate the voices you did and the production values, such as music, sound effects, and so on.

An alternative is recording your own demo if you have the skills and technology. This option is limited by your abilities as an engineer. The time, creativity, and energy you invest don't cost much, but you don't have the benefit of a producer or voice director to coach you like you would if you professionally recorded your demo. If you decide to self-record your demo, you need to know a thing or two about production elements, such as music and sound effects, copywriting (or sourcing royalty-free or public domain material), and artistic direction. (Refer to the chapters in Part V for setting up your own in-home recording studio.)

Setting the Ideal Duration of a Voice-Over Demo

The voice-over demo can range between 60 to 90 seconds to five minutes, depending on the type of demo. For example, commercial demos that promote your skills doing radio and television ads should be around 60 seconds. An audiobook or narration demo needs to last about five minutes in order to demonstrate your ability to stay in character for long passages in a story or possibly even to provide voices from different characters in a dialogue passage.

The optimum time for a demo to run with multiple spots is about 60 to 90 seconds so the listener has ample time to appreciate your voice and what you can do. Anything shorter than 30 seconds runs the risk of not being long enough to demonstrate your abilities. You may record a shorter demo if you're not recording a compilation of spots but instead featuring a full 30-second commercial that you produced.

If you plan on uploading your demo to a marketplace website, you should keep your demo to 60 seconds, which equates to 1 megabyte (MB) in size. A 1MB file loads quickly for a listener, while still sounding great.

We want as many people as possible to listen to you what you can do. To help with that, in these sections we include a number of tips for how to keep someone's attention when listening to your demo and ways you can present your demo material for the best possible results.

Cooking up a sample demo recipe

A standard demo should include five spots, which are between 5 to 15 seconds in length, give or take. Here's a breakdown blueprint for a standard 60-second demo:

- **Intro monologue, known as a *slate* (who you are and the subject of your voice-over demo.)** Skip to Chapter 11 for more info about what to include in a slate**:** 5 seconds
- **Spot 1:** 15 seconds
- **Spot 2:** 15 seconds
- **Spot 3:** 10 seconds
- **Spot 4:** 10 seconds
- **Spot 5:** 5 seconds

> ✓ **Closing remarks (including your contact information and a plug for your website):** 5 seconds
>
> ✓ **Closing music jingle (optional):** 5 to 8 seconds

Always put your best spot at the beginning of the demo and choose to end your demo on a high note, leaving your audience pleased with what they heard but wanting to hear more. Not everyone has time to listen to an entire demo, so start off with your money voice. Your *money voice* is basically your signature voice, a concept we cover in Chapter 2. Your money voice shines the most brightly, and is more than likely the one that gets you hired most frequently. Your money voice is the strongest read you can muster and deserves first billing on your demo.

Be sure to leave at least two seconds between tracks if you have multiple tracks. Keep in mind that you can include as many tracks on a demo as you want, but be sure to send people only the tracks that they ask for. For instance, don't send an audio publisher who works strictly with narrators a sample of your voice that isn't audiobook narration.

A demo isn't just a bunch of spots thrown together, and you definitely don't want to skimp or cut corners in producing. Your demo reflects your level of professionalism, your range, and the value you have to offer the client. It should provide just enough of a sampling to whet your clients' appetites, draw them in, and leave them wanting more. It should showcase your range and versatility.

Working with short attention spans

So why should most demos be around 60 seconds long? People, including your prospective clients, have short attention spans. Marketers now face a generation of people who are unable to budget more than a matter of seconds to advertisements. If something doesn't grab a person immediately, the opportunity is lost.

You want to capture your prospective clients' attention and keep it, while at the same time demonstrating what you're capable of doing. If you ramble on for a long time, they'll quickly lose interest. As a result, you lose out on being noticed. Being able to communicate in such a way that the listener cares about what you're saying (as well as being able to retain the information and act upon it!) is the primary goal of a voice actor. You're battling for space in their minds. If you want to get a piece of their attention, perhaps even their undivided attention (and their desire to hire you), what you're saying and how you're saying it need to be worth their while.

Conventional demos and methods don't always work today on the Internet

Decades ago, it was popular to have an all-in-one demo that ran five minutes, give or take, demonstrating all that a voice artist could do on something called a *demo reel.* They were called demo reels because they were recorded using analog technology, and the demos were saved on cassette tapes. This kind of demo is also often referred to as a *montage.*

Although technology may have changed from analog to digital, some producers continued to cling to the one-size-fits-all procedure for crafting demos, albeit the montages were noticeably shorter. The montage, however, still offered its listeners a full-course meal to digest whether they wanted to hear the whole gamut or not.

Even though the montage was effective years ago, technology and consumer expectations have changed, making it necessary to cater to individuals who have unique needs that a combo demo, at first blush, fails to meet.

Breaking up demos into bite-sized pieces

Today's market and business place is hectic, and everyone is busy with little free time. You don't get a second chance to impress. As a result, you have to be ready to show your skills when prompted. One of the ways of showing your abilities is to be armed with a good selection of your strongest work featured in bite-sized demos, organized by application or style of read.

Presenting your demo in small pieces allows your prospective clients to pick and choose from what best applies to their needs. Opportunity is knocking for you here because people are looking for quick and simple solutions! If you create a number of short demos in a variety of styles, you stand a better chance of those demos being heard and listened to. Featuring those demos online and properly describing them for the search engines is paramount to achieving your goal. If you specialize in a given area, say narration for audiobooks, you may want to have a demo for each genre you read in (such as children's literature, young adult, business, and so on).

Avoid recording montage demos because a montage usually includes many styles in one demo, which may turn off clients or fail to engage them as intensely. Some producers still do *montage demos* (compilation demos that present a variety of different reads for a number of applications, sometimes including bits of commercials, narration, character work, corporate work, and so on). These montages, by virtue of the vast material they cover, must by necessity run longer than the present standard time for demos (the standard demo time is 60 to 90 seconds) because talent and producers try to squeeze in as many relevant bits as possible to show versatility. Clients are busy, and they don't have time to listen to a long montage to see if you can do a certain style.

The essence of the montage doesn't need to go out of the window entirely. If your producer wants to use a montage, make sure the montage is more targeted to meet the individual client's needs.

Inspiring Ideas for Demo Subjects

You don't have to look far for a project in need of voice-over. A voice can be used in so many different ways, which means that you can create unique demos that zero in on a specialized niche or application of voice-over and voice acting.

If you stop to think of all the voice-overs you hear in a day, most likely in the hundreds, and list the different applications of voice-over that you heard, a shocking number of possibilities arise in terms of opportunities for your voice and voice acting in general.

We once asked people how many voice-overs they thought they had heard in a day. Some were thinking 50 or so, and others estimated more than 250. The number you do hear depends on how closely you're listening and how much media you encounter.

Considering how vast voice acting is, you may be more attracted to or interested in a certain area of voice-over. The types of demos you record are endless. Here we look at the most popular categories for demos used online today.

Commercial

The *commercial* demo has been a standard for decades despite the fact that there is substantially more work for voice actors in other areas of the business. Commercial demos are typically used for broadcast; however, they can also be used on the web in advertisements that roll before videos on platforms, such as on YouTube, on Internet radio, or on mobile devices.

Commercial demos used to have a characteristic announcer sound, but the trend has been for a number of years to give more of a real-person read with more emphasis on building relationships with the listener and target market than going in for the hard sell. (Refer to Chapter 4 for the characteristics of an announcer and real-person reads.)

Telephony

One of the most popular demos to have is a *telephony* or *telephone* demo. Every business has a phone system, and most at least invest in a voicemail recording for their company. The telephone demo can consist of segments such as the auto attendant, interactive voice response (IVR), messaging-on-hold (MOH), and voicemail. You can make each of these segments its own demo.

If you have a full telephone demo, make sure it's labeled properly and let people know what they'll be listening to. If the recording is simply an auto attendant, be sure to call it an auto attendant. The recording technically falls under telephone, but serves a specific purpose within that umbrella, which is to greet people when they first call in. If you also break those segments into multiple demos, you can potentially bring traffic directly to your voice samples and this can often result in delivering a more qualified prospect in need of your services. To discover more about featuring your voice samples online and proper labeling, refer to Chapter 10.

Business or corporate narration

The largest category of voice-over work worldwide is business. If you think about it, the corporate world needs voice-overs recorded for a variety of purposes. In fact, more and more businesses need voice-overs than in any other market. Your demos for business work can range from corporate narration projects to e-learning modules, product videos, explainer videos, workplace training videos, and voice-overs on company websites.

From telephony to training videos, corporate messages and programming, voice-over in this niche can be exciting because a big brand or the shop down the street may need your services. This area of voice-over is often referred to as the bread-and-butter work of the industry and is generally the kind of work that most voice actors make the majority of their money doing.

Audiobook narration

Audiobooks is one of the fastest growing and broadest areas of work for narrators and voice actors. This market is exploding because of how digital technology and downloads have decreased the amount of money it takes to produce, distribute, and promote audiobooks.

Using auditions on your demo for self-promotion: A big no-no

From time to time, we come across recordings on voice actors' websites or profiles that are in fact auditions that were recorded for clients posting jobs online.

Is this a problem? Yes. As a best practice, you should never use audition material on a demo, unless the client has consented to its use in that capacity, because of these reasons:

✔ The audition copy is usually part of a client's actual script, and the copyright generally belongs to that client.

✔ The client may plan to use the copy in an advertising campaign, or it's from an internal corporate document that the company doesn't want its competitors to hear prematurely or have access to.

You can have multiple audiobook demos, each one featuring an excerpt from a different book. Creating several demos (which typically each lasts five minutes) for each genre of literature you're interested in narrating is well worth your time. The more demos you have, the greater the likelihood that a prospective client can find you and that your voice samples will appeal to more people and audio publishers.

Character voices or animation

Just when you thought character voice acting was only required for animation purposes, more work exists than you may have imagined! Think about all the forms of entertainment that require a character voice: cartoons, animated films, dubbing for foreign cartoons, interactive, video gaming, talking toys, computer games, apps, audiobooks, and much more.

Many people like to leverage their vocal creativity by designing characters in their demos that feature accents, different voice ages, and even physical mannerisms. This area of work is perfect for voice actors who have vivid imaginations and want to put the voices in their heads to work.

Trailers

A *trailer* demo is meant to grab someone's attention and make him want to see, hear, or take part in the upcoming event. Trailers often include the element of suspense given that they're supposed to draw people in without revealing the entire story or its outcome.

Whenever you hear the word *trailer,* you probably think of movie trailer voice-overs and the field pioneered by Don LaFontaine. Trailers in reality can refer to any voice-over that promotes something that is coming soon and can extend to everything from the launch of an upcoming video game, a published book, or even a save-the-date promotional piece for weddings.

The voicing style for trailers, movie trailers specifically, is still characteristic of the way the great movie trailer voices of the last 20 to 30 years have been voicing.

Interactive

Voices can come at you from nearly anywhere, can't they? Maybe you've heard a voice in an elevator announcing the floor you were on or when commuting on a city bus, train, or airplane. These voices interact and guide people in practical terms at kiosks, self-checkouts in stores, and online. Work in this area can be quite diverse.

A demo geared for this category can include interactive voice response or a menu of choices that need to be selected from. Work in this area is educational or helpful, and sometimes, purely entertaining. Your voice can lead someone through a survey or tutorial online, or engage someone at the pump while filling the car with gas.

Other types

The following list contains a wealth of ideas for the other kinds of work available that can warrant having their own demos.

- ✔ Announcing
- ✔ Bilingual demo if you speak two languages
- ✔ Celebrity impressions
- ✔ Emotion-based demos
- ✔ Husband and wife or multiple talent spots
- ✔ Jingles
- ✔ Play-by-play or color commentary
- ✔ Promo

✔ Real person

✔ Tour guide

✔ Voice age demos (senior, adult, young adult, teen, child, toddler, and so on)

If you're interested in one of these areas, search for demos that other voice actors have done that fit in the category of demo you want to record. After you do your research, start planning for your new demo and locate scripts that you can record.

Chapter 7

Getting Your Script Ready for Your Demo

In This Chapter

▶ Writing your own script

▶ Utilizing preexisting material for your script

▶ Practicing your scripts

Making a voice-over demo is a personal, artistic, and technical process. Your voice-over demo can be your ticket to success and often serves as the first impression of your voice a prospective client will hear. As a result, you want to make sure that the material on the demo not only suits your voice, but that it also flows well and gives you the ability to showcase your range.

The demo represents your best possible work and gives people a way to quickly hear your ability and skill to assist them in making a hiring or casting decision. Because a demo plays such an important role, you want to plan and ensure that what you're recording best suits your voice.

As a result, the script you use for the demo is utterly important. When compiling material for your demo, you can write your own material, license the works of others, or find copy that is in the public domain. This chapter takes a closer look at these script options for your demo. After your script is ready, we explain the importance of practicing your script so you're ready to record your demo.

Authoring Your Own Script

Writing your own original copy guarantees that you don't have to go through any copyright hoops or fret over whether or not the copyright has indeed expired on a work you want to sample from. If you aren't confident in your inner William Shakespeare or J.R.R. Tolkien, you can always hire someone else to write the custom script for your demo.

If writing your own text is the route you want to take for your demo, these sections can help you overcome any writers' block so you can come up with an inspiring script.

Gathering ideas

When you want to write your own script, you need to have a good understanding about what to write about. When writing your own script, be sure to write about things that you know quite well. Writing about topics you are knowledgeable of and have a genuine interest in will make your spots more believable. Take care to research anything you're unsure of, such as how to pronounce certain words or names.

One way to gather ideas for demos quickly is to listen to the work of others, specifically those voice actors who have already established themselves as professionals and are working regularly. Their voice samples are like low-hanging fruit in terms of what may be popular right now, how long your demo and its respective spots should be, the kinds of spots you could write, and also for how the voice actors present themselves. Chapter 3 discusses different ways you can listen to other voice actors' demos.

Putting pen to paper

When writing a script, you need to know everything, from what the commercial is about, who it targets, and what the message is, to how to best communicate the value being offered to the prospective buyer. You also need to know who the characters are and what roles they play in the process. You may want to start with picking an industry that you're writing about, such as a particular kind of product or service commonly offered, and then decide who the sales message targets. Avoid using clichés unless you can find a way to make them funny. Remember that for a demo, you're using snippets from a script to make one spot. You still may want to write out a 30-second spot and then choose a portion of it to use as a spot in your demo.

We suggest you write your own script by listening to a commercial, say about a fast food restaurant, and then developing your own text. For instance, you can write a spot for a gourmet catering business and how its food is organic, why its food is better than fast food, and what makes it unique.

Does your script still have to do with food? The answer is yes, but it has absolutely nothing else to do with the ad that inspired you. You can create a fictitious company name (double-check on the Internet via keyword searching that the name isn't being used or registered by anyone) and run with it.

Here is a sample script based on this example:

> Looking for a better, cheaper way to eat well at your next event? Most people think organic means expensive and local translates to boring. Not so with Chic Gourmet. Our company caters events, both large and small, serving locally grown produce and free-range meats raised without antibiotics and other harmful stuff. When you want pure taste, you need Chic Gourmet.

As an example, you may take the following out of this script to use as one spot on your demo:

> Most people think organic means expensive and local translates to boring. Not so with Chic Gourmet.

Determining how many spots to write

You want to keep your demo about 60 to 90 seconds in length, and within that time, you want to easily showcase between five and seven spots, give or take. A spot is basically 7 to 10 seconds, so you want to write at least six spots. Chapter 6 explains more about how a basic demo is structured.

A good demo covers a wide range of topics, products, and services. When you're writing, remember that it's best to write about what you know. You may want to start by identifying five or so different companies that you love and jotting down what they do and why you enjoy their products or services. The result can be the basis for spots that highlight the company's strengths and value proposition.

Consider writing spots for household goods, such as food and beverage, personal hygiene products, cleaning supplies, electronics, automotive, and banking spots. Just be sure not to include a mention of a year or particular model that may date your demo and make it sound older than necessary before you've enjoyed the full extent of its use. You can then change the company's name or decide to leave the company's name out altogether.

Using Preexisting Material

If you want to use preexisting material for your script, such as from books, advertising, or the like in your demo, you need to pay special attention to what you use. Some of the material may be copyrighted, which means you need permission to use it. Other material may be in the public domain, which means its copyright has expired, been forfeited, or is inapplicable, which means you don't need any permission to use it for your demo script. These sections help you locate appropriate preexisting material for your demo and help you figure out whether the preexisting material you want to use needs permission or not.

Identifying a good piece of material

Recognizing a good piece of material is easy if you're aware of what to look for. Not every work is a masterpiece or worth recording. Ultimately, whether or not a piece of copy is any good boils down to the following:

✔ The text's quality and nature

✔ How it comes across as a spoken word recording

✔ Whether it lends itself to your particular voice type and voicing style

A good piece of material, unless you're making a demo specific to works by writers such as Shakespeare, Donne, or Dickens, should sound like it's in the present era and should use words that sound normal to the 21st-century ear, as opposed to language that is outdated. The copy should be interesting, have substance, and be relevant in some form or another to a modern audience or target market. Remember that your voice is in the service of the words. Even the most painfully dull copy can be read in a manner that engages the listener and communicates a desired message.

You may look at the material in terms of its popularity or subject matter, but make sure you only record material that you believe in and know to be true. The potential exists for you to be held responsible for what you're saying, even though you aren't the party being portrayed in the advertisement or voice-over recording.

Considering copyrighted work

When you're looking at potential text to record, you also want to keep in mind whether the work is copyrighted. Each country (and even each state or province) has its own policies for copyright, so you want to be prudent and aware of copyright laws concerning the material. Using copyrighted material means you must acquire permission to use it and often pay for the rights. Obviously doing so can be a time-consuming and expensive process, so that's why we suggest you stay away from copyrighted work.

A *copyrighted* work means that someone owns the rights to the work and that person is the only one in a position to legally grant its usage to others. The copyright holder would likely desire financial compensation through a fee or royalties for the work's use. Copyright protects someone's intellectual property. *Intellectual property* is the creation of the mind, expressed in many forms, including inventions, literary or artistic works, art, names, designs, and so on.

The Berne copyright convention, having been approved and supported by the majority of leading nations, deems that every creative work is copyrighted the moment it is established in a tangible format. Although the owner of a copyright doesn't need to give notice of the work being copyrighted, it does help to take this step should a legal dispute occur. Registration of a copyright is only necessary for those who wish to be able to sue someone for using their material. A copyright lasts until 70 years after the author or creator of the work dies. Note that facts and ideas cannot themselves be copyrighted. Only expressions of a creative effort can be copyrighted.

Although some individuals in the industry use copyrighted material and brand names in demos (refer to later section, "Avoiding Brand Names in Scripts" for more information), if you want to be on good terms with others, we suggest you observe all copyright laws and rules. Just because everyone else may be using copyrighted materials without getting permission or paying for the rights doesn't mean it's right.

Nearly all the text you uncover, whether it's a print ad or commercial, is probably copyrighted. Using the ad or the brand name or slogan could be a trademark violation. As a result, you may want to just write your own spots. (Refer to the earlier section, "Authoring Your Own Script" for ideas.) Copyrighted material can inspire you, but make sure you take only the core or the spirit of those ads and then translate them into something new.

Keeping updated on copyright legislation

When you're considering using copyrighted material, you want to take note of the potential of copyright extension and how it may affect works you were hoping to use in a demo or otherwise.

The US Congress passed The Copyright Term Extension Act (CTEA) in 1998, which extended copyright terms by 20 years. Copyrights used to last 50 years after an author's death or 75 years after the publication date (whichever came first) before the work belonged to the public domain. However, based upon the CTEA, an author's work is made available in the public domain either 70 years after his or her death or 95 years after the publication date (whichever comes first).

The law also extended corporate authorship. Disney's Mickey Mouse, for instance, actually enjoys 120 years' copyright protection after creation or 95 years after its publication, whichever date comes first.

Locating public domain material

If you don't want to write your own script and you want to use preexisting material that isn't copyrighted, you can look for work in the public domain. *Public domain* works are available to use free of charge. You aren't required to get permission to use them or pay any royalties.

When it comes to playing it safe as a voice actor making demos, you need to know the work's copyright and be able to determine whether something is in the public domain.

Public domain works generally include anything published before 1923. These works may include music, poetry, literature, and so on. Another qualification of public domain includes the number of years that have passed since an author's death. To be sure, double-check on a per-case basis because some copyrights expire based upon how long it has been since publication or the number of years it has been since the author's death.

One great resource for finding works that are in the public domain is Project Gutenberg.org. Project Gutenberg does a great job in presenting public domain material and posts the texts verbatim on its site. You can search through 33,000+ public domain ebooks in a number of ways, including by authors, titles, and subjects. In addition to being able to download free ebooks, you can volunteer in Project Gutenberg's community as a proofreader.

Avoiding Brand Names in Scripts

Using an unauthorized brand name in a demo can spell some trouble for you with a capital T. Unless you're the voice of an official campaign, stick to fictitious company names or leave the product and/or company name out altogether. If you have permission from the copyright holder to use the brand name, that's a different ballgame, but overall you should stay clear of using brand names in scripts. Some of the most effective demos don't use brand names. In fact, they're engineered not to.

Rather than misrepresenting yourself and companies named in the demo, we recommend that you craft your own copy or work with someone, usually a copywriter or demo producer, who can help. Although a brand may not seek legal action against you for including its name in your demo, it certainly has the rights to sue.

A good writer can weave snippets of a commercial together without even dipping his or her toes into copyrighted territory. Instead of relying on the name to carry the commercial or spot, you can create a feeling of brand. These kinds of spots on demos not only avoid brand names, but they also set out to highlight the benefits of a product or service and draw more closely upon emotional responses from their listeners. Through copywriting, you can generate the feeling of selling an emotion or experience that a brand may give without actually including the brand name. (Refer to the earlier section, "Putting pen to paper" for help.)

Recording public domain audiobooks is a great opportunity for you

Voice acting has hit the mainstream with the recording of audiobooks. If you're interested in becoming a narrator of audiobooks, you can get involved with a wonderful resource and community to foster your growth in that area called LibriVox (www.librivox.org). People who use LibriVox often record from public domain works. You may want to check librivox.org for additional resources and to see how this community is making an impact on aspiring narrators and seasoned voice actors alike. Sites like this also give you an opportunity to practice, both as a voice actor and recording engineer.

Figuring out who an audition audio belongs to

A couple of years ago, we interviewed a lawyer, David Canton, for our blog VOX Daily and asked him a number of questions about whom audition audio belongs to. Here we provide a portion of that interview.

Please note that laws vary by country, and even by state/province within countries. Legal answers always depend on the specific facts at hand, and small changes in fact can lead to different results. So David Canton's answers here are for general guidance and information only, and aren't to be considered or relied upon as legal advice.

Another thing to consider is that rights owners vary greatly in their inclination and desire to enforce their intellectual property (IP) rights. Some may not care, or may let violations slide on the basis that it is good publicity. Others may be overly aggressive and try to stop things that one is legally able to do.

VOX: Voice actors do auditions every day at Voices.com and through other services. Usually a script is provided by the client that a voice actor can partially record for demonstration purposes. This allows the client to review the samples and get a better idea of how that person would sound representing their company.

Should that ad copy or script be considered off limits to voice actors if they don't get the job? In other words, is it okay for a voice actor to use the audition spot they recorded as a sample of

what they could do and post it publicly on the web or include it in demo materials that they send out to prospective clients or agencies?

David Canton: If the script is provided by the client, the best approach is to ask permission to use it as a sample and get that permission in writing. Indeed, that should be standard practice for the voice actor. In addition to removing all doubt, it shows a very professional approach that the client may like to see. One factor here is that if the sample script is close to the final ad, the client may not want versions other than by its final voice choice to be floating around.

VOX: There have been a couple of instances where we have received complaints from clients who noticed that auditions submitted featuring their scripts had been used as promotional materials by voice actors who weren't hired for the job. Those voice samples were removed from the profiles of the voice actors in question and the client was pleased with those actions. This may seem obvious, but would you advise that voice actors simply archive their auditions and not use the audio for other purposes, particularly promotional purposes that may endanger or misrepresent the company's brand?

David Canton: Yes, that's a wise approach. Again, the best approach is to always ask if one can use the audition for samples.

The bottom line: You should obtain written permission before using ad copy or a brand name.

Furthermore, another reason to avoid using brand names is to eliminate any chance that you confuse yourself with being associated with the brand. A voice actor who is actually hired to voice a particular spot may have the right to ask a voice actor who didn't book it to remove a fake piece from his demo. In addition, if a client wants to hire the real voice associated with a brand name but then backs out because the client can't find the real voice actor or the client thinks the voice actor who recorded that material (illegally) is the actual voice, the true voice actor loses work over it. Although that may sound rare or severe, imitating the real spot may cause confusion for those listening who don't know any better.

Practicing the Different Types of Scripts You May Encounter

No matter the type of script you use (whether you wrote your own or you used preexisting material), you need to feel comfortable with the script. The best way to get comfortable with the different scripts you may use for your demo is to practice reading a range of scripts. Doing so can help expand your vocabulary and expand your voice-acting skills.

Focus on reading as many books, news clippings, pieces of ad copy, and audition scripts that you can. Diversify the type of material that you read. As you read, focus on the content, application, and style to improve your reading skills. Basically, as a voice actor, you want to become a voracious reader.

Reading is such an important part of doing effective voice acting, and the best way to improve your reading is to practice. The following sections give you some pointers about how you can practice (or rehearse, as people in the biz refer to it) so you're more comfortable with your scripts.

Rehearsing by yourself

What good to a team is a pitcher who spends his time idling in the bullpen and twiddling his thumbs? When called upon, he is rusty, and his performance is lackluster. On the other hand, a pitcher who spends his time wisely when off the field will be prepared, sure of himself, and is able to step in at a moment's notice.

Edison's wisdom applies to your success in voice acting

The great American inventor Thomas A. Edison was famously quoted as saying "Genius is 1 percent inspiration and 99 percent perspiration," followed by a lesser known quote, "Accordingly, a 'genius' is often merely a talented person who has done all of his or her homework."

We feel that this very same quote is so relevant to voice acting. Voice acting is 1 percent inspiration and 99 percent perspiration. You can make the most practical strides rehearsing scripts and practicing behind a microphone. Be a genius and spend the time doing your homework and mastering the skills you need to be successful in voice acting.

Differentiating characters: Taking a more cerebral approach

You were hired to record a job that has multiple characters. How do you differentiate them? Many voice actors enjoy taking time to create a system for how they do their character and voicing work. Your system can be as simple as a note here and there or as complex as an entire spreadsheet dedicated to each and every character and each character's voice, and how to make the transition between characters. Here are some ideas that voice actors we know do to differentiate characters.

✔ **Maggie Mustico** has mastered the art of organizing characters, sharing "I did an audiobook that had 34 different voices, including the narrator. I would go through each chapter and write down who was in the chapter that had lines, then I would go and distinguish each character by highlighting main characters, and then went to a large box of different color markers and underlined where I couldn't highlight or I put a dash next to the line. I also had my cheat sheet of colors to characters. I was lucky that each chapter would at the most have between four to ten voices at a time. Before I sat down to record the book, I would figure out each voice, record a few lines for that character and save it as sample file so when I needed to do that

voice I could go and listen to my sample file and recreate it."

✔ **John McLain** uses a couple of different methods to differentiate characters, but finds that his usage of these techniques depends on the complexity of a passage, noting, "If a passage has a lot of non-attributed dialogue, I will highlight and/or annotate. But for short, well-attributed passages with just a couple of characters, I typically don't need to. It just depends on the writing."

✔ **Bob Derro** takes a slightly different approach. "I use a variety of 'hooks' which work well for my brain. Everybody's brain works differently at recognizing text variation. Try it . . . you'll see. No one easily understands my printing or writing; however, my brain gets it. When I hit a challenging spot in a script I write it out, then the coordination between my eyes, brain, and mouth is automatic. If I have a text problem in reading flow or a stressed word is needed, I will add a stroke line before and after the word. Automatically it stands out, and after reading it aloud a few times, the brain accepts it as a normal sentence without hesitation on that word. Some people 'stroke' entire sentences. Whatever works for *you* is all that matters."

In the same way, a voice actor who exercises her instrument and improves her skills on a daily basis is ready to step up to the microphone with confidence at the time of need. Rehearsing should be a part of your regiment as a serious voice actor. As a voice actor, you want to make time to practice and rehearse. Even though you work from home and may wear a number of hats, including actor, recording engineer, producer, and so on, you want to rehearse by going over scripts as part of your homework.

When rehearsing, you need to have a feel for the text, study it, know its internal rhythm, and make note of appropriate places to breathe. You also need to know how to change the mood of your voice (tone) (see Chapter 5 for the how-to), and how to consistently carry a theme or interpretation for the vocal marathon ahead. Doing so is particularly true with regard to narration and documentary voice-overs.

When you're rehearsing and figuring out what homework means from a voice acting perspective, consider the following:

- ✔ **Understand your instrument.** You need to know your voice, respect it, and take proper care of your instrument, which means drinking lots of water and warming up your voice before you use it. Keep track of what irritates your voice and what makes it flourish. Chapter 3 has a lot of information that is helpful in this regard.

  You may want to write in a daily journal so that you can refer back to specific instances or observations. Explore your vocal range and play with different aspects of your voice. As you gain more experience, you'll want to be able to exercise your voice with the same understanding and skill as a concert pianist tickles the ivories.

- ✔ **Keep your cold reading skills sharp.** You should be able to read well out loud with confidence. Even the most enthusiastic bookworms have trouble articulating a well-phrased passage when asked to do so out loud. Taking time to read out loud can do you a world of good when it comes to reading copy.

  Most voice actors get this exercise when auditioning and apply the ideas and skills we offer in Chapter 11. If you aren't auditioning yet, read anything and everything from cereal boxes to news articles online. Encountering fresh copy regularly throughout your day can make reading for auditions and jobs easier.

- ✔ **Listen to your voice.** You are your own worst critic, but you're also the person who knows your own instrument best. Be sure to record your exercises and read-throughs. After you have recorded, sit down and listen to your voice being played back through the speakers. What do you hear? Compare your most recent work with what you have done in the past to see how far you've come.

  When listening to your voice, be aware of what it sounds like when you're tired versus well-rested, when you're anxious versus calm, and so on. Know how your voice reacts to things, such as caffeine, dairy products, and spicy foods.

- ✔ **Be aware of what's going on in the industry.** Keep your eyes open and your ears tuned to what's happening around you, especially in areas of interest and to voice-over work that you typically book. You may need to listen to commercials, watch cartoons, or purposefully hit up kiosks and websites to hear how the voice actors who got hired delivered their lines. The sky is the limit for finding free goodies on voice-over related topics (Chapter 3 discusses your many options in greater detail.)

✔ **Train on your own, with peers, or with a coach.** You can train in so many different ways — alone, with peers, or with a voice coach. Many voice actors train by themselves each day and take the initiative to attend gatherings of local voice actors to work on reading skills, character development, and improvisation skills. Some train weekly with a coach.

Whatever you choose to do, be consistent and do your best to have fun with it! Encounters with other voice actors often help you to challenge yourself. Working with a coach can help you to set attainable goals. Chapter 3 talks about more about training.

Rehearsing and researching your script

Doing your research and rehearsing upfront can save you a lot of valuable time going back and forth with the client for questions and potential revisions to the script. You want to gain a proper understanding of the script so you can then interpret it and give a polished reading. Chapter 5 explains some tips you can use to research and interpret a script.

When rehearsing your scripts, we find it helpful to have a number of photographs on hand to inspire you. You can produce a more authentic read by looking at an image of a loved one and speaking to this image as though he or she is your audience.

Keeping characters straight

When you're reading for a project that involves multiple voices and drastically different characterizations, keeping all those voices distinct while maintaining a steady read is important. Refer to Chapter 5 for ways you can take more in-depth notes in a script.

To differentiate the characters, you can rely on many different techniques. The primary methods are as follows:

✔ **Highlighting:** Use a number of different colors to identify where certain characters speak. Assign a special color to each character so that each time you see that color coming up in the script, you know who is about to speak and can prepare to change voices.

✔ **Annotation:** Add comments on your script to remind yourself of what you're supposed to do. Explain with a "note to self" what you need to do to either create that character or shift your voice to another character.

✔ **Hooks:** You know yourself better than anyone. That being said, you likely have shorthand or a way of notating that works best for you. If you need to include little pictures, symbols, or markings on the script (think like the markings on a musical score), use these types of *hooks.*

✔ **Cerebral:** If you like color coding, highlighting, or other visual indicators that you can connect thought or expression with, you can find this method particularly useful. See the nearby sidebar, "Differentiating characters: Taking a more cerebral approach" for some examples from voice actors.

✔ **Physicality:** Sometimes you need to get your whole body into a read or a character. Changing your posture, facial expression, or moving in a certain way can help you to get into character. See the nearby sidebar, "Combining vocal touchstones with physicality," for some examples from voice actors.

Combining vocal touchstones with physicality

Although you perform voice acting behind a microphone, you don't have to be limited to just movement and fluctuation regarding your voice. Here are what some voice actors we know have to say about this topic:

✔ **Melba Sibrel** has some great tips for how she goes about developing each one of her characters' sounds. Melba says, "When developing the sound for various characters, I use the old acting trick of picking a phrase from each character's lines and using it as a touchstone, to create a sound memory of how that character talks. Letting a physical attribute accompany it also helps me — a hand motion, head lean, facial tic, even sometimes holding an object — developing the characters physically will lead to their unique sounds. For reference I record each character voice in a separate file and listen to them just before reading the chapters in which they appear. I don't mark the manuscript to delineate unattributed characters' lines. I think doing so would throw me off."

✔ **Diane Havens** internalizes the characters she voices combining both physicality and their back stories, sharing "I try to completely visualize and physicalize the characters, become them when I reach their parts, and use a stance, expression, or gesture unique to them to cue myself into them. Creating complete back stories on even minor characters helps — and then even similar type characters end up sounding different — at least to me."

Chapter 8

Recording Your Demo

. . . .

In This Chapter

▶ Figuring out whether you're ready

▶ Knowing whether you'll record yourself or use a professional producer

▶ Contemplating music in your demo

▶ Reviewing your demos

. . . .

*R*ecording your voice-over demo is one of the biggest steps you can take professionally to move ahead in voice acting. Most people feel comfortable making a demo after they've gone through some training and often work with a producer to help shape the best sample of their voice as possible.

Making a voice-over demo is a very personal, artistic, and technical process. You can go about doing this on your own, but we advise that you consider the possibilities of having a professionally produced demo. Your voice-over demo can be your ticket to success and often serves as the first impression of your voice to a prospective client.

In this chapter, you discover the ins and outs of recording and how to make sure you're ready to record. You take a look at the approaches of recording — recording at home versus recording in a professional studio — and whether to incorporate music. We explain how you can evaluate demos, decide when to update your demo, and get some tips for taking your demo to the next level.

Are You Ready to Record?

You can combine many elements of interpretation and performance to create the presence you're aiming to achieve in order to make a killer demo. In this section, we give you several tips to prepare yourself for recording.

Asking yourself the right questions

Before you start to record a demo, you need to be prepared and understand what to expect during the process. Ask yourself these questions to help you gain a better appreciation about the process:

- ✔ **Have you invested in regular vocal training with a professional voice coach?** No amount of producing or background music will cover a voice actor's inability to effectively deliver a variety of scripts. Get proper training and coaching before you cut your demo. Chapter 3 discusses the benefits of voice training and the options available to you in great detail.

- ✔ **How much have you practiced?** Your personal comfort level using your voice as an instrument and performing reads determines whether or not you're ready technically to record a voice-over demo. Wait until it feels just right. Flip to Chapter 7 for how to practice your scripts.

- ✔ **Do you feel confident in your abilities?** A major part of this battle has to do with how you perceive your abilities and whether you think you're ready to move ahead with a demo. Remember that recording a demo is an investment. Whatever you have recorded will be the crown jewel in your marketing efforts. Make sure you feel confident in your abilities before stepping into this process. Chapter 5 has information that you may find useful for building your confidence in areas of script interpretation and performance.

- ✔ **Have you set achievable goals?** Terry Daniel, professional voice actor and voice coach, says that every spot on your demo should be unique with the goal of highlighting your range and vocal abilities. Additionally, each spot should sound real as if it were a paid gig. Pay attention to detail in your takes because the client most certainly will. You want to make them want you.

- ✔ **Do you have realistic expectations of yourself?** When you receive training, you have the opportunity to explore not only your voice but also whether your expectations are realistic. Your voice coach can help you to set achievable goals to help build your skills and confidence in preparation to record a demo. You may find Chapter 6 to be of interest for determining which demos are essential when creating your audio resume.

- ✔ **Have you listened to demos of established voice actors?** You can find many demos online. Try www.elance.com, www.voices.com, or www.youtube.com.

- ✔ **Are you taking advantage of free resources?** With so many wonderful helps on the web today, there are no shortages of ways you can find out more about voice acting and specifically what goes into a great voice-over demo. Do everything you can to take advantage of credible resources online to help you develop your voice acting abilities as a career voice actor. Chapter 1 details some great resources and ideas for studying on your own.

Getting ready before you make a demo

You need to take baby steps before you can make sure you're ready to record your demo. You're in control here, so consider our suggestions here about what to do to be prepared:

- ✔ **Invest in vocal training with a professional voice coach.** Guidance when you're preparing to record a demo is of absolute importance. Some coaches specialize in creating demos. Even if it's just for a short while, working with a coach can make a big difference. You can flip to Chapter 3 for more information on training with a coach.

- ✔ **Practice.** Knowing your stuff pays off and keeps your voice fit. Read each day and also try different ways of saying the same thing. Always practice by reading the script as it's written. Chapter 11 talks more about going over scripts and interpreting them.

- ✔ **Have confidence.** Believing that you can do something will come through in your performance. Recording a demo is preparation for sharing your voice with the world and those individuals who can hire you. Chapter 4 talks about understanding your role as a voice actor, which is critical to giving a confident performance.

- ✔ **Set achievable goals.** If you want to do your best, you need to set goals you can reach. A voice coach can help you with this. Setting realistic goals is very important so that you can achieve them.

- ✔ **Have realistic expectations of yourself.** What stage are you at as a voice actor? Have you done a voice-over before? Being realistic with where you are experience-wise is a healthy way to approach making a demo.

- ✔ **Listen to demos of established voice actors.** Go online, like to `www. voices.com` and other voice acting marketplace websites, and listen to how a good demo sounds.

- ✔ **Take advantage of every free resource you can.** So many ways exist that can give you more information about demos, the do's and don'ts, and samples of other voice actors' demos for inspiration. It's amazing what a simple search query about a voice-over demo can turn up. See Chapter 1 for more resources that can help you.

Choosing Your Approach

Your voice-over demo is vitally important, so proceed carefully and thoughtfully when planning how your demo will be produced. This section gives you some guidance on producing your own demo or choosing a professional to work with.

Taking the DIY path

Your demo takes a lot of careful planning and ultimately should cater to your strengths as a voice actor and producer. When recording your own demo, first take into account the number of *spots* (or segments on your demo) you want to voice and script and their arrangement, the pace of your reads, self-direction, and the production of certain elements, such as music and sound effects.

If you're going to take production seriously, set your sights on creating solid production value that takes your audience on a journey through varying sounds. Refer to the chapters in Part V for help with the specific aspects of production.

Despite what some people may think, there is still value associated with having a CD with your voice-over demos to send to clients or agents. As a result, make sure to have a number of promotional CDs available for those who request them.

Figuring out what to record

Make sure to map out what parts of your demo you're best equipped to handle on your own. If you're a technical mind, focus on the length of each spot, ways that you can quickly indicate where you may need to edit the session, and prepare for additional tracks, such as music or sound effects. You also want to pay attention to the ordering of each spot to ensure that it flows well from one spot to the next.

If you're more artistic, creating the demo can be a lot of fun for you. Focus on the roles you're interested in playing, and how you wish to differentiate those segments from each other through characterization, vocal range, mood, and so on. You may also want to think about what kind of music you'll have under your voice-overs and customize the music for each spot or part of the demo. (Refer to the later section, "Using Music in Your Demo: Yes or No?" for help.) Set the mood for your performance and use visual aids, such as photographs or physicality, if it helps you with your reads.

Producing specific elements

A voice-over demo has more to it than just your voice-over recording. Additional tracks for music, sound effects, and additional voices can come in handy during post-production. If you're good at the technical side, you can enjoy producing the demo and have fun with the bells and whistles. On the other hand, you may want to partner with a studio or a friend who's a proficient audio engineer to help you with the technical recording aspects.

You may even want to try creating your own sounds instead of relying on premade sound effects. As with all things, use good judgment when deciding whether you should purchase professional sound effects, music beds, and so on versus creating them yourself.

Checking your work

Regardless of your producing skill and abilities, make sure you run your demo by a few seasoned sets of ears before sharing it with the world. Getting feedback to check your work in these ways is helpful:

- ✔ **Ask your peers for their opinion.** This option may be good if your peers have experience in the field. This option is free.

- ✔ **Receive a demo review from a voice coach.** This option is probably better, especially if the voice coach has a strong casting or agency background. These people have their fingers on the pulse of the industry and know what sounds good and what doesn't, and how you can make your demo offering even better. You don't want to send out demos that fail to meet contemporary standards or present a diluted version of you and your abilities.

- ✔ **Join a voice-over forum or networking group.** This option is free, and you may find a thread set aside specifically for demo reviews. In such cases, members are invited to share their demos to gain feedback through peer reviews. One caveat is that not everyone sharing his or her opinion is listening with the ears of a casting director or someone who genuinely wants to help you.

Don't take the feedback personally. Whichever route you choose to take, be sure to keep in mind that any feedback, good or bad, is simply someone's opinion. Don't be discouraged if someone rips your demo to shreds. View the feedback as a way to improve your voice-over and your voice acting business.

Budgeting your production money

If you're recording your own demo, you need to have a proper studio set-up and the right software and editing tools to get the job done. You also need to find music that you can use, which has an associated cost unless you're able to compose and or perform your own music. Refer to Chapter 17 about setting up your own in-home studio.

Think also about your time as a factor in cost. How long do you anticipate spending on the process? Remember that it takes twice as long to edit a recording as it did to record it. Your time is valuable so you also need to budget for it. The average cost of recording your own demo, when you factor in your time spent on copywriting, music, voice-over recording, editing, mixing, and mastering can be up to $1,000.

Although the DIY method may appear to save you money, don't forget the extra time, resources, and energy necessary to get the job done right. It may cost you more in the long run.

Working with a professional producer

Many producers help you to create a demo that is uniquely you. They want to use fresh scripts, music, and ideas that highlight your brand. Working with professional demo producers can be an exhilarating experience. They can make you sound your absolute best and help shape your brand as a voice actor. If you work with someone professionally on your demo, realize that it will cost more than doing it yourself, but your demo is well worth the investment. Your demo, after all, is what helps you to get work.

If you're working with someone in Los Angeles on a demo, you can expect to pay in the neighborhood of $1,000 or more, which may include a couple hours of rehearsal and coaching, a couple hours in the studio, and the producer's private editing and production time. If someone is charging less than $600 to do your demo, take caution. Most demo producers advise you to look elsewhere because anyone charging less than $1,000 probably isn't devoting enough time to give you a real professional demo that you can market.

Using Music in Your Demo: Yes or No?

Is music necessary to include in a voice-over demo? The answer varies. Music can either be a good thing or completely inappropriate depending on the type of work that's being represented in the demo. One example of a demo that needs music is a commercial demo. On the flip side, a demo that shouldn't have music is an audiobook narration demo.

You can often deduce which demos should or should not have music by considering whether work in this category has music or not. For instance, do you hear a voice-over in the elevator that tells you which floor you are on? No, that doesn't usually happen. However, because you generally do hear music on radio commercials, the expectation would be that a radio demo has music and is fully produced.

Music can set the tone and immediately distinguish your voice-over demo from other demos. A musical underscore performs three basic functions:

✔ Sets the theme of the audio/video presentation

✔ Prepares the listener for individual segments or features within the demo

✔ Entertains the listener by introducing and promoting new music

Music, just like any other element in a production, enhances the copy and adds to the overall presentation in a relevant and aesthetically pleasing way. In this section, you get a feel for the role music plays in a demo and how to best include it and know when not to use it.

Including music in your demo

Although music seems to be everywhere, there's a time and place for it in terms of how you present yourself as a professional voice actor. Many producers find that music is a wonderful addition to a demo.

Demos that typically have some kind of music in them include commercials, animations, promos, telephony, trailers, imaging, and jingles. Music can relax people, get them excited, carry them to far off places, and stick in their heads. Music is just as much a voice in the production as anything else.

Next time you're listening to a voice-over, take note of what music accompanies it and how it affects you positively or negatively, and apply that research to your own demo. For specific information on selecting the right music, see the later section "Selecting Music for Your Recording."

If you include music, use musical backgrounds (known as *jingles* or *music beds*) or other non-music interludes (referred to as *bumpers, stagers, sweeps, and IDs*) to transition between topics. These topic breaks are typically described as bumpers or sweepers to help listeners digest the content you just presented.

Steering clear of music in your demo

Music generally isn't used in demos for audiobooks and narration. Exceptions to this rule, outside of audiobooks for children and preschool audiences, are few and far between. Other markets of voice-over work that don't necessarily include music are interactive and talking toys. Typically it's just the voice that's required so as not to hinder someone's ability to hear the message being delivered.

Selecting Music for Your Recording

How do you pick the right kind of music, or maybe even sound effects, for your demo? What should you consider and why does it matter? Music and sound effects help to brand a demo, making it easy to recognize and differentiating it from the recordings of other voice actors. Your voice-over is the key element that your listeners will identify with, which is why it's important to provide your audience with the best performance possible, including complementary music.

When selecting music, keep the theme of the demo and your target audience in mind. Each voice actor is different and has a unique instrument, so the music used should reflect both, in a complementary fashion.

In this section, you consider different styles and sound effects and how to acquire music that you can use that doesn't require permission. You can also get a good idea for when it is and isn't appropriate to use it.

Considering different styles of music

Many different genres of music exist that you can consider when selecting music for your audio recording. You can contemplate adding a multitude of different styles of music, depending on what your spots are about. Most importantly, use music as a tool to enhance your voice-over recording and not to compete with it. If the audio recording is about agriculture, for example, the music and sound effects can mimic the farming industry, or include country western sound effects, such as the sounds of a horse, rooster, pig, and so on. Your voice can also be more laid back and down to earth.

If the demo serves the financial industry, specifically the stock market, the music may be more energetic and riveting. Sound effects may include the opening bell of the stock exchange, heartbeats, clocks ticking, background noise, people talking, and other related sounds. The host may be authoritative and exciting, keeping the audience on the edge of its seat.

If you have the monetary resources, you may consider hiring a composer to provide you with customized theme music. This idea is great for branding.

Finding royalty-free music

Royalty-free music is music that is sold relatively inexpensively, which freelance voice actors and producers can license for use for their productions. You can use this type of music in your productions without having to pay *recurring fees* (paying money each time the music is played). Music beds are great for using underneath your voice-over to accompany the read. You can purchase them either as a single track or as a package with variations on a theme. You can also purchase royalty-free sound effects to use in your demo.

As with anything, purchase the music from a trusted source with licensing agreements, which you can refer to and save for your records after purchase. Visit sites such as www.audiojungle.net and www.istockaudio.com.

Adding sound effects in your demo

You can intersperse sound effects throughout the demo while you're speaking, or you can nestle them into the musical theme and variations. When selecting sound effects, make sure that they're appropriate to your voice-over and are used sporadically to complement your voice.

Sound effects function as another voice in the recording, and you need to be careful about how the sound effect is used in conjunction with your vocal. You don't want the sound effect to overpower your voice or distract from what you're saying. Make sure that you position sound effects in places where they don't interfere with your voice and what is being said.

Living Up to Your Demos

Your voice-over demo is truly your calling card. The demo, while not necessarily representative of work you have actually done, is representative of what you're *capable* of doing.

Although many voice acting talents have professionally produced demos, not nearly as many are able to replicate every subtlety or element on their samples when called on to do so. What happens when the voice-over demo promises more than what a voice actor can actually do on his own, unassisted by producers, directors, or coaches?

So you can replicate what you produce, keep the following tips in mind when recording your demo:

✔ When recording a voice-over demo with a coach or studio, keep the production elements minimal depending on the demo type, especially if you aren't particularly skilled in this area.

✔ Present your abilities with *dry voice samples* (no production elements, only the voice). Dry voice is typical of narration and audiobook demos as well as GPS, telephone, and other types of voice-over work. Another benefit of dry voice is that people can immediately hear the quality of the recording and also focus on your voice as the sole instrument in the mix.

✔ Invest time in the art of direction. Study, watch others, and make choices, not guesses.

✔ Be consistent with your vocal regime. This includes warming up, maintaining dental hygiene (the last thing you want is food stuck in your teeth, which can produce excess saliva and impact the way you speak), being well-hydrated, and allowing your voice to act as a vehicle for the written word. (Maintaining good dental hygiene is also important to avoid the extreme where you may lose some teeth and need dentures or implants, which can affect your voice's sound.)

Evaluating Demos for Updating

Your demo, especially if someone produced it in a professional recording studio, is a thing of beauty and deserves to be shined up every now and then. But when is that time? If your demo represents what you can do and only needs a bit of tweaking here and there, just remove spots that aren't working anymore and replace them with some new spots or a sample from a more recent job you've done.

In this section, we explore the telltale signs that your voice-over demo, or a given spot on a voice-over demo, has reached its expiration date.

Avoiding dates and times

Dates and times, particularly as they concern cars, concert tours, and political campaigns drastically limit the potential for your demo to endure. Marking a date will almost always give your demo a shorter shelf life unless the date is referring to an historical event, such as the reenactment of the Battle of 1812.

 Generally, if a product is mentioned to be older than two years, try to edit out the date or leave the dates out altogether when recording initially. For instance, if you have a commercial read in your demo about a model of a car that was new in 2005, take some time to update that demo.

Being careful about music selections

Music often sets the tone for a voice-over demo and helps to establish your personal branding style. But don't let styles of music that have been shelved for too long give clients the wrong impression of your production or music selection skills.

Ask yourself the following questions:

- ✔ Does the music sound retro in a bad way? Is the music from the 1970s, 1980s, 1990s, or early 2000s?
- ✔ Are the sound effects in line with what you would expect to hear today?
- ✔ Are there cheesy synthesizers in the background?
- ✔ Does the music selection support the essence of the spot?
- ✔ Is the spot supposed to sound retro as in a parody spot or throwback?

There may be exceptions to the rule where certain spots need to have an aged or vintage sound. You may find these sounds to apply to game show spots, old time radio drama, or the stereotypical announcer read from decades ago. In those instances, you can get away with using those elements because they support the spot in general and contribute to its authenticity and overall effectiveness.

Recognizing your voice age

If you recorded your commercial demo in the 1980s or even the early- to mid-1990s, the demo itself may not only sound aged, but your voice may have matured since that recording, too. Voices age, just like bodies do.

Men's and women's voices age differently as well. Although the vocal aging process isn't as noticeable in men after they pass puberty, the voices of women continue to mature until they're 40 years old. That's a lot of changing and readjusting for a voice and vocal technique in the span of a voice-over career.

Maybe you're in your twenties and have done some growing up. You may find that your voice doesn't have that youthful ring to it anymore. Unless your voice is pliable and can reach into those spaces where your performance is still within the realm of believability, your days of voicing roles for children and or teenagers may be over.

If you know that your voice has changed and you're no longer able to do certain reads believably, consider passing on the audition or removing voice ages that you can no longer do from your demo.

Making references to pop culture

If you have a mention of something in the ad copy on your demo, make sure that it's still relevant or at least accurate. For example, if you have a spot that mentions a Beatles reunion with Paul, George, and Ringo, it may be time to cut that bit.

Perhaps it isn't something in the popular realm but a political campaign advertisement. If the candidate mentioned in the spot isn't currently running for office or didn't succeed in her attempt, strongly consider removing that spot. It may confuse people who are listening to your demo, and of course, reveal the age of the demo.

Don't forget that when you make references to pop culture, you may also be including popular or trendy music from that time. That's a double no-no!

Adding new work

One alternative to re-creating a demo from scratch is to add new work to refresh your demo and give it some zing. Subbing in a current sample may be one of the easiest ways to keep your demo on the up and up. If you decide that this is something you're interested in, keep good records of the work you do and assess it for demo potential.

If you have more than one demo, document the spots that are on each demo at any given time and include details about them to help you keep track of their content and how long you have before certain spots may become tired. Some demos are more evergreen than others but all have an expiration date.

After you've created a list of your demos and what they consist of production and copy-wise, you can more easily earmark new work or samples you've recorded that can serve as material to update a demo or possibly even serve as material for an entirely new demo.

Getting permission to use work

If you find that something you've recorded fits the bill for any of your demos, make a note of it and be sure to ask the client for permission to use part of that project as a segment in your demo for promotional purposes. The holder of the copyright is ultimately the person you want to consult. If it's not the client you worked with, he or she can look into finding out whether you can use it by going to the client with your request.

Most clients will be fine with this, but you do need to ask. Voice actors we've worked with have asked us if they could feature voice-overs they recorded for us on their website or in their demos, and we've always said yes. Some of our commercials are hosted online, and voice actors who've worked as narrators on our videos are also able to promote the video as a sample for their prospective clients to consider.

Whatever you do, don't use auditions as spots on your demo or as stand-alone demos to promote your voice. Not only is this misrepresentative of work you've done, but also doing so without permission could spell trouble for you in the long run. If you ever want to use an audition on a demo, which at times may be appropriate, you need to ask the client and obtain permission.

Replacing spots

Something else you can do at this point is to create an entirely new spot that fits with the current spots on your demo. Whether it's a spot you've repurposed from a job you did or a new spot altogether, you're still replacing a spot on your demo.

If you're given permission, decide which segment of that work you want to use as a spot in your demo. Listen to your demo a number of times to see where your new spot can fit. You may need to rearrange spots to accommodate your addition, especially if you're replacing more than one spot and if music is involved. If you don't feel you can do it well, employ a mixing engineer who can help you.

After you have replaced some spots on your demo, consider archiving them so that you can remember how far you have come. Demo by demo, spot by spot, you'll be able to track your growth as a voice actor and also provide you and your family with an interesting way to monitor your voice and observe changes in how it sounds and ages over time.

Older demos of your voice can also serve as good learning tools. Listen to your demos and take notes on what you did. Documenting your progress can be fun! Perhaps listening to the demos will even trigger memories of your training, of investment in your career, and of the creative process. You may even get a few giggles out of them! A lot of hard work goes into making them in the first place, and you don't want to see them fade into oblivion.

A demo is like a time capsule in some ways and each voice-over demo you've recorded or work that you have done in general tells a story of what you've accomplished and what was important to you as voice actor. Just because a spot or demo has been replaced doesn't mean that it needs to be forgotten.

Part III
Auditioning and Finding Work

The 5th Wave   By Rich Tennant

"Okay, but this is the last cat food commercial
I'm doing."

In this part . . .

Here we detail the bulk of a voice actor's day-to-day activities concerning auditioning and finding work. As many voice actors probably agree, doing the auditions is the work. Booking a job is gravy! You can find out all you need to know about how to audition both online and in the real world.

If you're new to voice acting or you've been away from voice acting for a while, make sure you review the increasingly dominant role that the virtual casting environment plays in the industry for searching, auditioning, and hiring voice actors. If you have auditions in traditional settings on location, we also include tips for how to conduct yourself at in-person casting calls.

Half the battle is showing up! This part shows you what is expected of you when you're auditioning for work and how to promote yourself in a professional manner.

Chapter 9

Marketing Yourself and Promoting Your Work

. . . .

In This Chapter

▶ Getting noticed online with a website

▶ Using a profile on a voice acting marketplace site

▶ Enhancing your visual brand

▶ Seeing what professional associations can do for you

▶ Reaching out to your connections: Drumming up business

. . . .

*W*hat do you need to do to get noticed? As you may have heard, half the battle is just showing up. In order for your brand to show up, you need to know how to market yourself. Particularly online, marketing yourself includes investing some time and effort into building your web presence.

You may also consider the possibility of paying to get your name out there to attract potential customers to your website. After a visitor arrives at your website, your earlier diligent work along with a clear visual expression of your brand can help persuade people to do business with you.

You can also market yourself in other ways, including sharing your story and explaining to others how you can potentially work together. Networking is a way to expand your territory while making new friends. So many different businesses need voice-overs recorded, and they may not even realize how voice acting can help them. When you network with other people, you may be the first person they've ever met that does voice acting. As a result, getting your story down pat before you head out into the world of business networking is a must.

In this chapter, we explain how to create a web presence to help people find you and how to advertise your website using pay-per-click options. We share a glimpse of how you can shape the way people visually perceive your brand and how you can network to help you drum up business for keeping your microphone warm, and hopefully, cash flowing steadily into your studio.

Creating an Impressive Web Presence

An effective Internet marketing strategy is one of the keys to a successful voice acting business. Your business needs a multi-pronged approach to ensure positive results. One of the first things any voice actor needs to do before jumping in full force to self-market is to build a website. This website can be a traditional one or it may be having a profile on a voice-over marketplace. Most people have both. In the following sections, we focus on how you can build your web presence with a personal website that you can be proud of, how you can utilize social media, how you can maximize how people can locate your presence, and how you can advertise online. (We discuss a marketplace site in the "Utilizing a Voice Acting Marketplace Website" section in this chapter.)

Building a personal website

When you modestly invest in securing a domain name and hosting a website for your business, you're able to use this virtual real estate to maintain an aesthetically pleasing and up-to-date website that promotes your voice. In other words, you have a place to hang your hat and show people who you are and what you're about.

Many voice actors prefer to brand their websites using their name, while some take a more creative approach with how they are branding themselves. When picking your domain, you need to factor in availability, how easy it is to spell/type, and also how well the domain name reflects your brand. Even if you aren't a computer genius, you can find innovative ways that beautifully reflect your business while giving you the ability to update your content easily using a content management system such as WordPress. Look on websites like NetworkSolutions, Yahoo!, and GoDaddy to see if the domain name you want to buy is available.

After you know that your desired domain name is available, secure the name by purchasing it and perhaps even extending your ownership by more than just the one-year option. You also need a web-hosting package. In the event that the company you bought your domain name from doesn't provide a web-hosting package, you can find several good web-hosting companies out there, including www.hostgator.com, www.rackspace.com, and www.1and1.com.

After you have a web host, one of your first orders of business should be to install a content management system (CMS) such as WordPress. A CMS gives you the flexibility to update your content as often as you want. You don't need to know about computer programming to have a beautiful and functional website. These platforms allow you to change the graphics and text of each page using a WYSIWIG editor ("What you see is what you get") that also helps you to rank higher in the search engines.

Wondering what you should write

On your website, highlight and promote your abilities so clients know what you can do. You're the only one who knows exactly what you are great at, so make sure you prominently and honestly feature those skills.

Along the same lines, your spelling, grammar, and choice of words definitely impact your audience. If you write in the third person (he, she) rather than the first person (I), you can use your name in the body of your profile and increase your visibility in the search engine. Whichever you choose, use it consistently.

Telling customers what you can do for them

Clients require your services because you can do something for them that they can't do for themselves. As a result, you want to write text for your website that addresses their needs while respecting the fact that they need something specific and have limited time to find what they're looking for. Some needs that someone requiring your services may have include artistic and technical needs.

The customer expects that most voice actors can also serve as audio engineers to a degree, meaning that you can record your own voice, make edits, and also present the best audio quality possible. Some may even expect that you can include music or sound effects, or you can draw upon the talent of other voice actors when producing their project.

Refer to the later section, "Filling out your profile" for more help. That section focuses on using a voice acting marketplace website, but the same premises apply about how you can write compelling text about yourself and your abilities for your website.

Marketing on social networks

These days it's not just about who you know, it's about how many people you know that matters. Social media now plays such an important role in getting more friends — and thus more business prospects.

With social media, virtual friendships have increased the number of friends and potential networks you are connected to. You can have similar interests and business goals with those friends, which in turn allows you to share opportunities and successes in your voice acting career.

The three main social media sites that we suggest you use to market your voice acting include Facebook, Twitter, and LinkedIn, which we discuss in the following sections.

Facebook

Facebook (www.facebook.com) allows you to join groups, add friends, and incorporate applications into your profile to share content and help direct people to your website. You can include links from your profile to your own website and blog. The ability to post notes and update your status on the fly also gives you an opportunity to communicate to all your friends at once. Your profile can promote your voice and invite your clients to join. You can send out emails to your members easily to announce and share a new demo, talk about work you've recently completed, share your studio news, and more.

We suggest that if you want to keep business and personal matters separate, you should create separate profiles — one for your personal self and one for your business. You can opt to create a Facebook page for your business that people can "like" and follow you on a professional basis. That isn't to say that you can't share personal things through your professional profile, but you can be more selective with what elements of your personal life you choose to share, given the audience viewing the updates.

Twitter

Twitter (www.twitter.com) is a channel that many techie social networking types have embraced as an alternative way to keep people up on what they're doing. Twitter gives you the ability to sign up and provide a flow of personal updates while also allowing you to follow or subscribe to the Twitter update feeds of your family, friends, colleagues, or your favorite movers and shakers. For example, you can be on the lookout for people in the industry who share interesting things on their Twitter feeds. If you follow them, they may follow you back! Similarly, you may be followed by those who are interested in what you have to say. When you use Twitter, you can share recent work you've done or general things like how to take care of your voice.

One of the more popular ways to classify a tweet is by using a hashtag (#) before a word. Doing so makes it easier for others with similar interests to find what you're talking about. For example, a popular hashtag being used in the voice-over industry is #voiceover.

Twitter updates can be searchable on the Internet and also published in the public timeline. If you want to limit access to your updates, you need to check the box to "protect your updates" Twitter feed.

Avoiding social media burnout

If you're feeling overwhelmed by social media and social networking, you may find that maintaining too many profiles on social networks may become one more thing on your to-do list or the straw that breaks the camel's back. Having several profiles on social media can also become addicting if you're constantly updating, tweeting, or reading what others are doing instead of actually doing anything yourself. Social media has a lot of noise, so be careful and spend your time social networking wisely.

LinkedIn

LinkedIn (www.linkedin.com) is one of the oldest social networking sites specific to professional networking. It focuses on facilitating the connection of service providers in a traditional manner. Why is LinkedIn great for voice actors? LinkedIn classifies nearly every aspect of what people do in their professional lives and makes it simple to connect with others in the industry of your choice or related industries. You can add friends and develop a network of other voice actors, producers, casting directors, and so forth. You can also observe a "six degrees of separation" type family tree of who knows who, how they know each other, and how you may also become acquainted with someone who is a friend of a friend by means of an introduction from a mutual friend.

Optimizing for search engines

Search engine optimization, also referred to as SEO, is one of the most powerful Internet marketing tactics. *Search engine optimization* basically is the process in which the careful and strategic placement, analysis, and use of keywords on a particular website can enable optimum search engine rankings. Being found in the major search engines is vital to anyone who conducts business on the Internet.

SEO has two unique areas — on-page optimization and off-page optimization, which we discuss in the next two sections, that you can use to quickly increase your site's visibility in search engines.

On-page optimization: What you can control

When you think of *on-page optimization,* focus on all the elements and factors in good search engine ranking that you can control. Examples of on-page optimization include the following:

- Domain name or website address, also known as the *URL*

- Website content, such as the articles you write about and the pages that describe your product and services

- *Page formatting,* which is the specific layout of the page, and keyword selection (*keywords* are words searched for by those individuals interested in what you offer. For example, you can use keywords, such as "voice-overs," "announcer," or "narrator"), use of images, and any element you can edit, modify, or delete at a moment's notice

- How your web pages are linked to each other

Having good, well-written content on your website is your first priority. Why do we say your first priority? Because all search engines display search results by ranking the content of a specific page within a website. Google doesn't always just list the home page of a website as being the most relevant. Google also provides the searcher with the page within a website that contains the text that is the most relevant to the search phrase.

To take your text to the next level, jot down pictures that come to mind when thinking about your keywords. You may find doing this activity offline with a pencil and paper is helpful when you're sketching out your vision and setting your mental juices in motion.

To help you come up with important information about yourself to include on your personal website, check out our suggestions in the "Utilizing a Voice Acting Marketplace Website" later in this chapter, which also apply here.

In addition, you want to pick keywords that improve the chances of your website appearing in a search engine. To do so, think about what you're great at and also about what people searching for your skill set may be looking for. If you're trying to attract work in broadcast, for example, you can include keywords such as "radio imaging," "liners," "sweepers," or "station IDs." If you work primarily as a character voice artist, you may wish to consider words such as "cartoon voice," "animation voice actor," "video game voice," or "character voice." You can also try *keyword analysis* to see which words are better than others in terms of how often people search for them on a monthly basis through search engines, such as Google or Yahoo! For more information about picking keywords for optimizing your website, we encourage you to read *Search Engine Optimization For Dummies* by Peter Kent (John Wiley & Sons, Inc.).

Off-page optimization: What is out of your control

Off-page optimization includes all the activities and aspects that are out of your control, and, more to the point, are controlled by what other people think of your website. Off-page optimization includes some of these factors:

✔ **Link popularity:** *Links* are the currency of the web. Links that are placed on a particular website and point to another website are seen as a vote of confidence. Link popularity is all about quantity, meaning the number of links you have pointing to your website.

✔ **Link relevancy:** Links pointing to a website within the same industry are seen as a vote of confidence from a relevant source. Industry-related links are sometimes considered a higher quality because the support demonstrated through those links is indicative of your website's perceived authority and standing, based upon the support of others in your field.

✔ **Anchor text:** *Anchor text,* which is the visible and active text used to enable the link (often making the text blue with an underline), provides additional information about the source of the link and what the linked-to site will be about.

Many search engine marketers consider that links are the most important factor in getting those all important natural (non-paid) search engine results. Many inconclusive debates discuss whether the quality of the links or the sheer quantity of the links is more important in the eyes of Google, Yahoo!, and Bing. Regardless of the answer, links clearly play a significant role in obtaining great search engine results. (For example, Google has a patented method for determining the number of links of a website known as PageRank. Websites with a higher PageRank have a greater number of links from other websites.)

Considering paid advertising

Build your website to be useful and relevant to those individuals seeking your services. Doing so helps to not only better position you in the search engines but also makes your website a better fit for when you try to attract visitors to your site using directories or pay-per-click (PPC) advertising programs. These sections show you the difference between getting listings in a directory, which requires an annual fee, versus paying on a per click basis to attract visitors to your website.

Launching a Google AdWords campaign

To complement your organic search engine optimization efforts, you should consider advertising your services using Google AdWords (`www.google.com/adwords`), which is the pay-per-click advertising model. When you create an account, you're able to craft your own text ads and determine the landing page for each ad.

Some keywords cost more than others because of how competitive they are. If you do some basic keyword research, you can discern which keywords you want to target and also decide how much you're prepared to budget for your Google AdWords campaigns on a daily basis. Other factors include which devices you want your ads to run on (desktop computers or mobile devices) and also which countries you want to have your ads displayed in.

You can get started with Google AdWords for as little as $5, but realistically, you can expect to pay around $100 per month for a few hundred visitors to your website. Try running a small test campaign for a month and then evaluate the results. If it's working for you, then continue advertising. If you feel your money is better invested elsewhere, this chapter has plenty of ideas for you.

Getting listed in the Yahoo! Directory

Yahoo has two kinds of listings that you can use to purchase paid advertising and increase your web presence. The two are

- Yahoo! Directory, which is organized by topic
- Yahoo! Search, a search engine based on keywords

  Being listed in Yahoo! Directory costs $299, which places your website alongside your competitors and colleagues within the industry. More importantly, a listing in the Yahoo! Directory greatly increases the odds that your website will be noticed by other search engines, such as Yahoo! Search and even Google, Bing, and Ask.

You can submit your website to Yahoo! Search (http://yahoo.com/dir/submit/intro/), although like Google, there is no guarantee your website will be listed in the natural search engine results.

Utilizing a Voice Acting Marketplace Website

If you don't have your own website, a voice-over marketplace is the ideal place to begin developing your presence online. These sites are referred to as *online marketplaces,* where clients and voice actors can connect to complete a project. The following sections explain the benefits to these sites, what some sites are, and how you can use these sites.

Seeing how these sites can help you

When considering membership at an online marketplace, be sure to consider the following:

- ✔ Easy to navigate
- ✔ A professional site where you will feel proud to be featured
- ✔ Free from overt advertising by third-parties (no ugly banner ads)
- ✔ The ability to manage and edit your profile on your own without a fee
- ✔ A consistent track record of clients posting voice-over jobs
- ✔ A good number of projects that you can audition for every week
- ✔ Easy-to-use auditioning process
- ✔ Efficient system that provides you with a record of auditions submitted
- ✔ Opportunities for voice actors to be found in multiple ways
- ✔ Active marketing campaigns on your behalf
- ✔ Acknowledgment in the press
- ✔ Recognition by industry groups resulting in awards or other achievements
- ✔ A good variety of testimonials from both voice actors who use the service and clients who have experienced the service first-hand
- ✔ Good customer service and support, both online and offline
- ✔ Access to resources and templates that can save you time
- ✔ Responsive to voice actors' suggestions
- ✔ Looking out for your best interest
- ✔ Considerate to your needs
- ✔ A trustworthy and transparent site with open business practices
- ✔ Accountability
- ✔ Integrity
- ✔ Reasonably priced annual membership fees, ranging from $299 to $1,995

Having a web presence and a subscription to an online voice-over marketplace are appropriate steps that can be taken to draw more opportunities to yourself.

Naming some of the available sites

Some marketplace websites are obviously better than others. The following three are the best in our humble opinions:

- ✔ **Voices.com:** `Voices.com` is an online marketplace that connects business clients with professional voice actors. Voices.com is home to more than 200,000 customers and serves companies from Fortune 500s to small businesses. In addition to its role as a marketplace, it provides helpful resources and business developmental tools to nurture its customers, including blogs, podcasts, a digital trade publication, and award-winning customer service unparalleled in the industry.

- ✔ **Elance:** Elance (`www.elance.com`) helps businesses virtually hire and manage. The site helps clients find qualified professionals who work online, includes tools to hire, keeps track of the progress, and pays for results. Elance also offers you access to qualified clients, a virtual workplace, and guaranteed pay for your work.

- ✔ **Guru:** Guru (`www.guru.com`) is another site that gives you a chance to market your skills to prospective clients at a low cost. It includes features such as profiles to showcase your skills and experiences.

Filling out your profile

Your profile (this section may called a bio on some sites) gives you the opportunity to customize and brand your website and display resume information, feature voice-over work, and monitor the types of feedback you receive.

Having a profile on a voice acting marketplace website provides you with a means to effortlessly build a web presence and feature your abilities, describe your voice, upload demos, and more. A great profile not only tells clients what you've done but also about what you can do. It should capture their interest and motivate them to contact you for their project.

Your profile is

- ✔ **An advertisement:** It allows you to highlight your voice quality and feature your skills and experience as a voice actor.

- ✔ **An online storefront:** It allows you to conduct business with clients from around the world.

✔ **A business card:** It informs prospective clients of your capabilities, and it provides contact information.

✔ **A forum:** It allows your clients to leave feedback so you know what you're doing well and what you can work on.

Your profile presents you in the best light and convinces clients that you have what it takes to complete this project to their satisfaction. When you create your profile with the goal of attracting the client rather than a personal statement of what your goals are, your opportunities increase. We explain how you can take advantage of these benefits in the following sections.

Completing your profile simplifies the process of marketing your business. You can write about yourself and often distribute multimedia files that show samples of your work. Whether your prospective clients contact you is based on first impression. Clients will quickly glance through your profile, trying to find the one thing that they need. As a result, your profile descriptions can either make or break you.

Maintaining a complete and engaging profile can represent your body of work and attract prospective clients. Some sites are linked to online search engines, so the more detail you have, the more you will be indexed in the results for search engines.

The following are parts that you may need to complete on the voice acting marketplace website. These sections may vary, depending on the site. No matter if you use your own website or a voice acting marketplace website, including the following information is a smart idea to give prospects a better idea of who you are and your skills.

Describe your voice

Writing your vocal description is a necessary step in the branding process. Your *voice description* is basically a quick summation of what you can sound like that makes people want to click play and hear your demo. When you're drafting your voice's description, make sure that it features your strengths, specialties, and unique characteristics. Your vocal description is the first impression for the majority of clients that encounter your profile page. For example, you may describe your voice in terms of your range, acting abilities, and the kind of work you specialize in. Chapters 2 and 3 have foundational information that you may find useful when describing your voice.

When describing your voice, make sure you specify your age ranges so prospective clients can get a better appreciation for it when visiting your page. As you specify, select only voice ages you can confidently and believably perform. Featuring demos that showcase each voice age you selected is also helpful to those visiting your profile. For example, if you can perform a variety of voice ages, provide examples of your reads for each age you can do. You may have a teen demo, a child demo, and a young adult demo, for instance.

Identify the languages you speak and accents you know

Voice actors who are able to fluently speak multiple languages have a distinct advantage over their peers and can charge a premium for translation and performance services.

Specify the languages that you speak fluently in the order of fluency from most fluent (for example, your mother tongue and dialect) to least fluent. If you state that you're fluent in a certain language, we suggest that you include demos on your profile that reflect your ability to speak that language in case prospective clients want to hire you in that language. Refer to the "Uploading your demos" section later in this chapter about uploading demos to your profile.

In addition to the languages you speak, list all accents or character archetypes that you can perform as well as your regional accent. If you have a neutral accent relevant to your country of residence, state so. For instance, if you live in the United States and speak with a neutral accent, list that you have a "standard nonregional American" accent.

List your skills and areas of expertise

You want to make sure you list your special skills that directly relate to the categories of voice-overs you can record. Some categories include cartoons, movie trailers, audiobooks, and so on. Refer to Chapter 6 that talks about demos for the different types of categories you can list. Chapter 4 refers to the different roles you can do. Be sure to create individual demos that reflect these special skills.

Include your experience and education levels

Include a list of the major companies and organizations that you have completed voice-over work for. Update this list from time to time so people who seek your services see what you can do and that you're still active in the industry.

Make sure you note your experience in the voice acting field. We've seen several people say that they have substantial experience, but then fail to list what it is they've been doing. When stating your years of experience, be sure that you have painted a clear picture of the type of work you have done to better promote yourself.

Experience can be anything you have done up to this date that lets people know where your expertise and talents lie. If you have a degree in a field related to voice acting, such as broadcast or theater, make sure you provide all the relevant information. All forms of education are welcome in this field. Consider adding details about voice-over or acting workshops you have participated in, teachers you have studied with, and post-secondary programs you have completed.

Even if you have a degree in an unrelated field to voice acting, you can benefit from mentioning it. For example, a potential client who needs a medical narration may be more interested in you if you have an educational background in medical transcription.

If you have done any studying with coaches, have graduated from a degree program, or have trained in a specific area, tell people your background. Remember, you never know who may be visiting your page. In addition to your experience and education, you also want to mention any associations you are a member of, including unions or guilds.

Address what recording studio and special equipment you use

Clients want to hear that you can get the job done, but they also want to know how you can do it. Although most clients never ask for technical information, having it handy and including on your profile a description of your high-quality studio equipment, which can be a costly investment, may help justify your fee structure.

Here are the main studio details that you should include

- Microphone
- Recording software
- Mixing board
- Other special equipment (compressors, reverbs, delays, and so on)
- Methods of delivery (MP3, CD, FTP access, phone patch, ISDN, and so forth)
- Royalty-free music and sound effects library

Refer to the chapters in Part V for more in-depth information about this equipment.

State delivery methods and turnaround time

You need to know ahead of time what methods of delivery you can provide and communicate with your prospective clients on the website. Your options include FedEx and UPS overnight shipping of a CD, MP3 via email, or uploading a WAV or AIFF file via FTP. Refer to Chapter 21 for more about file formats and the best practices for sending files over the Internet.

You also want to be able to give an estimate of the total time it will take you to complete an average job. We suggest you estimate 24 to 48 hours with the caveat that how quickly you can finish a job depends on the job's specifications. Be sure that you have the ability to stick to your word because many clients have rush jobs and hire based upon voice actors who can meet their tight deadlines.

Describe your detailed service and list testimonials

You want to elaborate in your profile about the details of your service and share information about how you deliver on your brand promise. Basically answer the question: What do you offer that makes your services unique from other voice acting talent?

Make sure you include in your profile a section on references and testimonials from past clients. If someone you have worked with in the past has glowing praise for you, include a quote so prospective clients can see.

Uploading your demos

While your profile serves as an advertisement for your services, your demo provides the actual evidence of your claims. Some voice acting marketplace websites are all demos and others are all words. Balance is required to keep the client interested, so search for one that is balanced.

Having several demos isn't a bad thing. In fact, the more skills you can feature, the better. A *montage* is a great sampler of what you can do, but you also want to focus on your stronger skills in individual demos.

Including demos on either your voice acting marketplace website or your personal website is so important to show prospective clients the different types of work you can do. Upload files to showcase your abilities. After you upload your demos, view your profile as a visitor would see it and test that the samples are downloading or playing properly.

When you upload demos, you need to describe them so prospective clients can prepare themselves for what they're about to hear when they click the play button. When you upload a demo, make sure you address the following information with each file:

✔ **Demo name:** Make sure the titles of each demo clearly describe what the demo is about. When naming a demo, include keywords that quickly tell the listener what the demo is about (commercial, telephony, and so on) and include your name in the demo name.

- ✔ **Demo age:** Oftentimes, clients seek a specific age of voice talent to connect with their audience. You may be capable of performing voice ages younger or older than your actual age, all of which you should document and record as samples for clients to review. (Refer to the earlier section "Describe your voice" about noting what ages you can voice.)

- ✔ **Demo language:** Clients often search by accents, for example, the British accent or Southern Belle, United States. Including the timber of your voice (your vocal range), for example, bass, baritone, alto, or soprano, is also helpful for clients looking for specific voice types. (Consult the earlier section, "Identify the languages you speak and accents you know" for making sure your profile matches your demos.)

- ✔ **Demo category:** The demo category refers to the type of demo it is, for example, radio, business, telephone, movie trailer, narration, and so on. Ideally, you will have a separate demo for each category you're interested in obtaining work in. If you have a montage demo, try to select the most appropriate category for it.

- ✔ **Demo description:** Some sites have a search engine that not only searches your profile's content, but also your demo descriptions. The more demos and diverse descriptions you have, the greater your opportunities of being found for a variety of queries. In one or two short sentences, describe what types of characters are portrayed, the voice styles used, and, if applicable, who the demo was voiced for.

- ✔ **Demo tag:** A *tag* is a single word description of the contents on your demo. Usually tags are adjectives like "funny" or "serious" and serve to provide insight into the material on your demo. Tags can also be a character type, such as "soccer mom" or "guy-next-door" and prove helpful to clients who are looking for someone who can fill that role.

Considering Visual Branding

Your personal branding is very important, and if successfully mastered, it can set you and your offerings apart. Your *brand* is representative of who you are and what you're offering as a voice actor, which also includes your voice.

The following sections discuss how to choose a name for your brand, select visual images to identify your brand with, create verbiage around how you want to share your brand, such as a slogan or tagline, and create your brand colors. They're all critical pieces in defining, developing, and communicating your brand. You can then share your brand in a variety of ways, including online via your own website.

Selecting your brand's name

When you brand yourself, you need to consider what name you want to use. Many professionals choose to keep their real names, but you can also choose to use a stage name. For many voice actors, a stage name gives them the freedom to create a unique persona and helps separate their work from their home life.

You can select a memorable name, a unique name, basically any name that you feel suits you and is in line with the services you provide. Be sure to select a name that is easy to remember, easy to say and spell, and is non-offensive to others. Check to see if the name you want to use is available by contacting your local government office when registering your business. You may also want to cross-reference your desired stage name with guilds or unions to see if someone is already using it in the acting field. You also may want to do an Internet search to verify no one else has trademarked it. After you have a name, go online to Network Solutions or a similar domain name broker to discover whether or not your preferred domain name is available.

If no one else uses the name, opt for your name to serve as your domain name. If the domain name you desire is available, you have an opportunity to purchase it and secure your brand name on the Internet. Having a memorable URL or website domain name is important because you want people to remember how to get to you easily. The closer the domain name ties in with your brand and what you do, the better.

When devising a name for your brand, you want to differentiate yourself. Brainstorm names and use alternative imagery that evokes emotion. Try something new like a plant, animal, household appliance, something conceptual, a play on words, or something completely off the wall. The point is, be different.

Before going too far down this road, we recommend that you consult with a lawyer to learn more about how to properly apply for and/or register a stage name for your business.

Adding a photo or image

When establishing your brand, you want to include an image to show prospective clients who you are. Many voice actors add a traditional headshot as a graphical representation. Others commonly use a microphone, which is simple and to the point. Whatever you choose, make sure you're original.

You can upload a picture of yourself or a graphic that represents who you are as a voice artist and businessperson. Many voice actors opt not to reveal their visual identity, although voice actors with an acting background or on-camera experience are more comfortable with marketing their personal image as a representation of their corporate voice-over image.

You may not want to include a photo of yourself, which is fine. Voice actors expect to be cast based upon their voice, not how they look. Given that the medium is audio, this makes a great deal of sense and enables the customer to focus on your voice when listening to a performance.

No matter what type of image or picture you use, if you want your brand to stand out, we suggest you use something else besides just a headshot of yourself. A couple suggestions include the following:

- ✔ **Use online services:** These services, such as www.istockphoto.com or www.gettyimages.com, offer royalty-free photographs, royalty-free illustrations, and digital artwork. For a few dollars (most images are only a couple dollars), you can license an image to promote your business that's likely not being used by anyone else. Using these types of sites can be very helpful in branding your business visually and cost effectively.

- ✔ **Hire a graphic designer:** You can hire an artist to create an image (or logo; see the later section on having a logo). Make sure you own the image and its rights. A graphic designer is a professional who has the expertise and can come up with something unique.

For best results, upload a square image with equal dimensions because the website may resize your photo during the uploading process, and you want the image to be able to scale properly and be displayed well.

Designing and creating a logo

A *logo* is the most readily available representative of your voice. Your logo can accompany press releases, be used as a link to your website and for advertising purposes, and give potential audiences a glimpse at what you and your voice are all about even before listening to your demo.

Logos are very important in the world of branding because your logo is often the first impression of you and your voice. As a result, your logo should be friendly to all age groups and sized appropriately, making sure that it doesn't take up more than the normal allotted dimensions for logos. The dimensions should be no less than 500 pixels wide and 500 pixels high. Ideally, you should display a square, so your image is 500 pixels by 500 pixels. An image that is cropped correctly loads much faster, uses less bandwidth, and creates the positive first impression that you're aiming for. Stick with .gif or .jpg files because they display better on the Internet.

To create a logo, you have a couple options:

- ✔ **Hire a professional graphic designer.** A freelance professional just like you with an expertise in graphic design can create your logo. This individual can send you a web-ready image in the appropriate dimensions and format. Check with friends for referrals or go online and search for individuals who can help you create your logo. If you use a professional, make sure you own the rights to the image so you can do with it what you want.

- ✔ **Design it yourself.** If you have some experience, you may want to design your own logo. If so, you can use tools such as Adobe Fireworks and Adobe PhotoShop to achieve your branding goals. Designing your own logo may be the best route if you don't want to deal with licenses or other arrangements.

If you already have a logo, you can further brand your image by incorporating your business logo or designing a variation of your corporate logo to strengthen and reinforce your brand.

Coming up with a tagline

A *tagline* is a brief statement that qualifies what you do and how it relates to others. Having a tagline as a voice actor is important because people will quickly see how you are different from other voice actors and figure out the benefits of working with you. You can use a tagline to instill, validate, and affirm your brand. You may want to use it on your website, business cards, and in your demos.

To come up with your own tagline, take a good half hour or so to brainstorm slogans and taglines for your voice-over services. Consider what you think you do and how others see what you do. Perception is important, and you can help to shape how your brand is perceived. Think about what you want to say about your voice to someone who doesn't know you or your brand. Ask other people who know you and your business about what they think your tagline should be. A tagline helps to extend your brand and identify what you do at the outset.

A smart one-liner can do wonders for staying front-of-mind. For example, voice actors on Voices.com include "Cowboy Dave, The Voice of the West" and "Melanie Haynes, The Tasty Voice," which do a great job of giving prospective clients a snapshot into who the voice actor is. No matter what tagline you come up with, make sure you have fun with it.

Picking colors

When choosing color themes to represent your voice-over services, make sure you select complementary colors, that is, colors that go well together. After you pick the colors that will brand your services, be consistent and use only those colors, including on your website, in your logo, on your business card, and any other product you distribute. You want your brand to be consistent, and an easy way to do so is use the same colors all the time.

Colors often have certain emotions or connotations associated with them. For instance, the color yellow is often associated with the sun, cheerfulness, and innovation, whereas blue may be associated with the sea, tranquility, and freedom.

To select colors that suit you and your voice-over abilities, consider

- ✔ Using colors that you like (it's your brand, after all)
- ✔ Staying away from colors your competition is using
- ✔ Pairing colors that are complementary to each other
- ✔ Considering what those colors mean to you and how you can weave them into your brand

At the time of this writing, Voices.com uses green, blue, and a little bit of orange in our branding. We want to project a fresh, vibrant, and natural look that reflects our brand and corporate culture.

If your business already has an official color(s), you may wish to incorporate those same colors into your branding scheme for your website, logo, and business cards.

Drumming Up Your Own Business: Network Your Way to Success

Although the web offers an abundance of opportunity to network and get the word out about your business, you can also rely on developing personal relationships with people through different types of networking. These flesh-and-blood connections can introduce you to prospective clients.

Having a firm handshake, making eye contact, being friendly and open, and exuding confidence and an attitude of service were and still are key in developing meaningful business relationships. The challenge faced today is making those skills translate to networking in a virtual environment. Even though a large part of your voice acting work is online, you can still apply these similar techniques and person-to-person communication skills to online efforts.

The following sections identify some places where you can utilize your networking skills with people who can potentially get you jobs and help you improve your craft.

When you network in the following places, you want to be prepared. The best way is with what is called an *elevator speech* in the industry. You sum up who you are, what you do, and how you can be of service to someone in less than 60 seconds. It basically lasts the time it would take you to travel on an elevator with a person of influence from the first floor lobby to their executive office, ten floors or higher. You have a limited window of opportunity to make an impact, so you want to practice and master it, so it sounds natural but polished. If the person you're talking to has follow-up questions, then you know he or she is interested and your elevator speech worked.

Visiting recording studios

A recording studio is a unique place to gain perspective on the technical side of voice-over acting and to connect with people in the industry. Those people can potentially assist you in improving your skills and getting work.

At a studio you may be able to watch actual recording sessions and listen to professionals at work. Becoming familiar with the technology is a definite plus that can help you to become more independent. You can also discover more about the process as a whole and develop a greater respect for how hard audio and sound engineers work to make you sound good.

If you're interested in watching live sessions take place, call a local recording studio to see if it's open to observers. You may also ask a peer if you can accompany her to a recording studio and observe her work as a guest.

Connecting with casting directors

Nowhere else can you get the inside scoop on casting trends better than in a casting house. These companies are responsible for organizing casting calls and auditioning voice actors with a casting director.

You may be able to observe the auditioning process and see first-hand what directors look for in a read and also gain invaluable insight into how the business works from the inside out. Take the information you acquire and be sure to incorporate it into your own business for better audition to booking ratios.

Reaching out to talent agencies

Employing the help of a voice acting talent agent can deliver real benefits and results. Agents don't charge you any fees upfront; they get paid in commissions after you get hired. Unless the agent is successful in getting his voice actors work, he doesn't make any money. As a result, he's motivated to find appropriate work for you.

Agencies are always looking for new talent, which is the only way that they can remain fresh, competitive, and viable. In order to be considered for agency representation, you need to provide the agency with a demo CD or MP3, portfolio, and professional headshot or portrait. You can send these items via mail, and they become the property of the agency once they arrive. If you're thinking of hiring an agent, check out Chapter 16 for more details about what an agent can offer you.

Partnering with other voice actors

You may be the type of person who really wants to learn from other more experienced voice actors. By working with a voice actor who is already established, you can see the business, technical, and artistic side of her work. Your mentor may take you under her wing and ask you do certain tasks, such as take phone calls while she is recording, submitting auditions on her behalf, editing audio files, sending out marketing materials to customers, or managing ad campaigns. All these tasks can help you gain a better appreciation for what goes into being a voice actor.

Similarly, voice coaches are great people to work for because they already value education, and they'll see that you get everything you need while you're with them to succeed. A coach may ask you to do a wide array of tasks, including organizing his class schedule, booking clients, promoting workshops, or even sending out email newsletters to students about upcoming opportunities to train. You may even be able to work out a deal where you take classes with the coach and pay off what you owe by serving as his assistant for a set time. The coach's generous nature can do you good and introduce you to numerous possibilities in his area of expertise. (Refer to Chapter 3 for more about using a voice coach.)

Attending local meet-and-greet events

Although a lot of business is done online as a voice actor, most relationships either start or are strengthened by meeting in person at conferences or networking events. As a voice actor, especially if you're just starting in the business, you want to connect with local people and establish new relationships. You can take advantage of many opportunities for networking and becoming known locally, especially if you seek out membership in an advertising club, a chamber of commerce, or any other organization of businesspeople looking to connect on a regular basis to socialize.

Joining (or even starting one if one isn't in your area) a monthly meet-up group is a great way to network with peers and get referral business. You can introduce yourself and make a connection with all different sorts of people. You can let them know what you do and how you could potentially help them. Whenever you can, make sure you make an effort to do some face-to-face networking and make some real, in-person contacts.

If you're working for yourself and selling your voice-over services, you have every right to be involved in the corporate fabric of your city or town. Don't be afraid to show up. Many voice actors often forget that they're running a business. You have so much to offer other people and businesses near you, so make sure they know about you.

When you're at these meetings, work the crowd to meet as many people as possible. The last thing you want is to talk to the same person for an hour and not get the chance to meet other people. Make sure you have business cards and CDs with your demo ready to give to people who are interested in talking to you more.

Offering your voice to complementary service providers

The voice-over industry isn't just about creativity and audio production; it can also be about marketing and public relations. If you prefer working with a creative business that involves creative yet business-focused people, you may want to consider a position working with companies that provide services or products complementary to your own. Some examples you can look into are advertising agencies, video production houses, language translation companies, and retailers for recording studio equipment.

If you have the personality for it, try cold calling local creative businesses and introduce yourself. Find out if they're interested in using your voice in their next radio commercial or offer to be the voice of their telephone auto-attendant.

People everywhere admire and are moved by the personal touch. Receiving something that you know has been touched, written by hand, or sent especially to you in the mail means so much more.

Using your demo

Being able to hand someone a physical representation of your work is very important. Some people who may want to hire you aren't comfortable with receiving attachments via email, especially when it's the first encounter. The best way to do so is by having CD copies of your demo ready to hand out.

Include a business letter that accompanies your demo that shares that you're looking for work and have the talent and ability to help meet your prospective customer's needs. Remember to follow up with the people to whom you give your demo. Many people lose business because they don't follow up and ask for the business. If you really want to work with someone, follow up to see where they are and how you can serve them.

Make sure you keep a copy of your demo with you because you may never know when opportunity knocks. Handing someone a demo CD, even though it may seem to be low-tech when compared to emailing an MP3 file to someone, is still a viable and potentially preferred way to present someone with your offering and show them what you can do.

If you prefer a more high-tech way of getting people to hear your demos, you may consider printing QR Codes on your marketing materials and business cards. (A *QR Code* is basically a graphical link; see Figure 9-1 for an example.) The recipient can scan the code using a QR Code reader on his or her mobile device to easily access your demo and other material online. Check out *QR Codes For Dummies* by Joe Waters (John Wiley & Sons, Inc.) for how you can easily create a code for your marketing material.

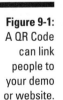

Figure 9-1: A QR Code can link people to your demo or website.

Illustration courtesy of Voices.com

Generating local publicity

If you have a compelling story, journalists are more likely to write about you. As a result, you want to figure out what makes you unique. Did you just open for business? Did you land a national project? Are you sponsoring a local event? These are good reasons to reach out to trade magazines, blogs, and local media, and pitch your story idea.

Publicity has an incredible tendency to beget more publicity. After you get covered in one article or you land one speaking engagement, you'll be amazed at how that piece of publicity snowballs into more opportunities.

Before you make your pitch, read these different publications to get an idea what they cover. Familiarize yourself with the writers who cover arts, entertainments, voice-overs, and small business. Reporters are interested in human interest angles because they're the most popular articles with the public. Think about what you like to read and pitch a story accordingly to the appropriate reporter.

Reporters are busy people. They have tight deadlines and are almost always short on time. They may not respond to every pitch. Keep these suggestions in mind when contacting reporters:

- ✔ **Reach out a couple times per month, depending on the circumstances of your story.** Don't hound them.

- ✔ **Find different angles to your story.** Don't send the same pitch over and over.

- ✔ **Respect the reporters' deadlines.** Avoid contacting reporters during their crunch time when their stories are due. This time varies on the news source.

Being written about in the local newspaper or covered in some other news source helps you reach people that normally wouldn't otherwise be thinking about the wonderful world of voice acting.

If you want to more formally pitch your story, you can draft a news or press release. A press release is an unbiased and objective third-person report of your newsworthy story. Press releases should be about a product launch, website launch, company report, event, or announcement that the public would find interesting.

If you live in a larger metropolitan center, start a media list, which can be as simple as a Word document or Excel spreadsheet, with the names, phone numbers, and email addresses of journalists at each of the local radio and television stations, and magazines and newspapers. Then, when you have news to share, pull up your media list and spend the day pitching your story. Doing so is worth it, even if a single media outlet publishes your story.

If you've been in the business a while and are interested in enlisting help to promote your business to the media, consider hiring a publicist. A *publicist* makes it her business to pitch your story to the press and may also line up speaking engagements for you. To find a publicist in your area, consult your local ad club or chamber of commerce. You can also search online to find a publicist who specializes in working with actors and creative types.

Sponsoring an event

You can also sponsor an event, such as a conference, seminar, workshop, or other gathering, to get out your business name. When an event takes place, sponsors are acknowledged publicly for their contribution to the event and are able to promote themselves to a degree throughout the program.

Sponsorship doesn't have to be expensive. Event organizers often have a community sponsor level typically starting around $250. If the event has a good turnout, of say at least 250 people, you're basically paying a dollar for each person to see your name.

You can also consider an *in-kind* sponsorship, which means that you provide services free of charge in exchange for recognition at the event. Approach the conference organizers and ask if they need any voice-overs or audio production done. Perhaps they need an announcer at the event. Having your name seen in printed materials and having event organizers hear your voice make announcements throughout the event can be a great opportunity. You can also demonstrate your abilities to event attendees.

However you choose to approach event sponsorship, be sure to ask to have your name and logo in a few key spots. You want visibility on the event website, in the event program, and on any other printed materials. Ask for at least one verbal mention during the event. You can also inquire about setting up a small booth where you can provide more information about your services.

Joining Professional Associations

You can promote your business and skills even more by joining one of the many professional associations available for voice actors, radio announcers, actors, recording engineers, and other industry professionals. You can join different types of professional organizations, including unions.

The following organizations appeal to voice actors. Some are more accessible than others, but we include them all to give you a broad spectrum of your choices to consider when finding an association you can be part of to benefit you and your business.

- ✔ **Unions and guilds:** *Unions* are organizations of employees that bargain with employers, while *guilds* are groups of people with similar interests or pursuits, especially merchants or craftsmen. A few unions and guilds that you should be aware of as a voice actor are SAG-AFTRA (United States), ACTRA (Canada), and Equity (United Kingdom). Though joining a union isn't mandatory, a union may be appealing to voice actors who live in big centers such as New York or Los Angeles because more union jobs are available in those cities. That being said, a significant amount of voice-over work is non-union. Remember, if you join a union, you will not be able to do any non-union work. Refer to Chapter 16 for more discussion on unions.

- ✔ **Nonprofit trade organizations:** These organizations help people learn more about their craft and provide resources. You can join these organizations and network with others who do what you do or people who work in closely related fields. The following are some nonprofit organizations you can join:

  - **Audio Publishers Association:** The Audio Publishers Association (APA) (www.audiopub.org) is a nonprofit trade association of audio publishers related to audiobooks.

  - **PromaxBDA:** PromaxBDA (www.promaxbda.org) provides education, community, creative inspiration, and career development for marketing, promotion, and design professionals within the entertainment and information industry.

  - **Voice and Speech Trainers Association:** The Voice and Speech Trainers Association (VASTA) (www.vasta.org) is a nonprofit organization run by volunteers in the profession that provides service to voice and speech professionals.

  - **Southern California Broadcasters Association:** The Southern California Broadcasters Association (www.scba.com) is a trade organization for advertising agencies, clients, and the community on behalf of radio broadcasters throughout Southern California.

- ✔ **Chambers of Commerce:** A chamber of commerce is a local organization that helps nurture businesses in its area. Any kind of business can join. Members are encouraged to network at chamber events and take advantage of resources to further their businesses.

  - **US Chamber of Commerce:** Check out www.uschamber.com for more information.

  - **Canadian Chamber of Commerce:** Refer to www.chamber.ca for more information.

Following Up with Your Past and Prospective Clients

If you've been in business for any amount of time, more than likely you know that getting repeat business is easier than selling your services to a new customer. As a result, following up with your current client base is an important step to promoting your voice acting talent and growing your business.

No matter whether you're brand new or have some experience in voice acting, you want to focus on getting a new (or your first client). The following sections identify how you can call on prospective clients to get new customers. After you get your client, you can ask for referrals that can help you garner new clients.

Calling on prospects

Whether you're calling on prospects to land your first job or you're simply prospecting to generate some new business, the process is the same. You can stick to these simple steps to help:

1. **Identify and understand who your prospects are.**

   Match the kind of work you're looking to do with the people who will need to hire you. For example, if you're most interested in doing voice acting for animation, then you need to identify animation producers at video production companies. If you're interested in recording commercials, then you can focus your time on radio and television stations and advertising agencies.

2. **Create a detailed prospect list.**

   This list should keep contact information for all prospective clients, including full name, phone number, email addresses, mailing address, description, last contact date, and any call notes. Refer to Chapter 16 for how to manage this information.

3. **Develop a telephone script so you're ready to start calling.**

   The *script* is an outline of the conversation you want to have. Your script can have an opening, such as

   > "Hi. My name is Peter from Got The Pipes Studio. How are you?"

4. **Respect the prospect's time by qualifying her.**

   You can say something like,

   > "You're busy, so I'll make this quick. How often do you work with voice actors?"

Notice the open-ended question. You didn't ask whether the prospect hires voice actors, but rather how often, which can start a conversation.

5. **Write the script so you ask important questions.**

For example, you can write something like this that directs the prospective client in answering key questions that will let you know how you can best meet her needs.

"Can I send you an email with a link to my demo? Great!"

6. **Develop a consistent close.**

Your close is important because it sets the tone for how your prospect may respond and also provides options for how she can move ahead. A good example close is

"Thank you for your time. If you have any questions, you can contact me at (phone number) or email (email address). I look forward to hearing from you and would be grateful for the opportunity to serve you."

Follow those steps on your phone calls, and you can turn your prospects into customers in no time!

Asking for referrals and testimonials

If your clients are happy, then they're sure to refer you to others. Sometimes all you have to do is ask. A *referral* is someone recommending to others that they should work with you, while a *testimonial* is a brief account detailing a customer's positive experience working with you.

You may have heard in life that you shouldn't care too much about what other people think, and to a great degree, that's true — just not when it comes to promoting your business or helping others to define their perception of what you offer as a business.

Repeat business and word of mouth are both amazing ways to acquire new customers and get your voice in front of others who may need what you have to offer.

So when is the best time to ask for a testimonial? We recommend asking a client for a testimonial right after you have delivered the completed audio. Usually when your client replies to confirm receipt of the files, she has something nice to say about your work or the experience. At this time, you want to get those sentiments in writing to use as a testimonial, with the client's permission, for promotional purposes, whether it be on your website, as a reference, or in your marketing materials.

Given that you're a voice actor and the medium you work in is audio, having some of your testimonials in audio format is a nice feature. Ask your client whether you can record her saying something about you or whether your client can send you a brief clip detailing the experience. Some people are better speakers than writers, so this option may be popular depending on whom you offer it to.

After you get the testimonial from your client, you can send a standard template like the one in Figure 9-2 to show your client what you'll use.

If the client replies in the affirmative, you can then use that testimonial as a reference on your website or in other marketing material.

Dear   ,

Thank you for your kind words! I really enjoyed working with you, too.

What you've said means a lot to me. Can I publish what you've shared as a testimonial on my website? Here's how it would appear:

"Quote what you want to use as a testimonial here."

If you're agreeable, please let me know. I look forward to hearing from you.

Thank you again for your business.

Sincerely,

Your signature

Figure 9-2:
Send a letter like this to your clients and ask for a testimonial.

Illustration by Wiley, Composition Services Graphics

Gaining public acknowledgement in other ways

In addition to testimonials and referrals, you can build credibility and recognition for your work in three other ways:

- ✔ **Getting a public feedback rating and review:** Most online marketplaces that facilitate transactions give you the opportunity to rate and review your experience working with someone at their site. Ratings and reviews are opportunities for publicity and acknowledgment that you receive if a client hires you online. These ratings and reviews are public, and you don't have to ask permission to share them because they're available for all to see on the website you worked through.

✔ **Being featured in a case study:** Some companies do case studies, so ask whether those sorts of opportunities are available to you to gain a higher profile on their website. A *case study* typically consists of identifying the initial challenges you faced before using the service and then detailing how you went about achieving your goals. Case studies document a process but also give insight into your personal experience from start to finish. Although case studies may only be used for internal company purposes, sometimes they're published and even used in university and post-secondary settings.

✔ **Writing a success story:** Did you know that companies love hearing from people they've worked with, especially if they were successful? Contacting the editor of a company blog or connecting with a customer service or public relations representative can be your foot in the door to publicity via a larger platform. A success story can be about a great experience, a job you booked, and the like.

Chapter 10

Uncovering Voice Acting Jobs

. . . .

. . . .

*N*o matter whether you've been in the voice acting business for a while or are just starting out, if you don't know where to find the work, then you're going to be unemployed for quite a while. Even if you know where to find the work, but don't know what kind of work you want to do, then you'll also be in trouble. Voice acting has so many different criteria that factor into it, including the vocal requirements, creative direction, and more that if you aren't sure, you may have a difficult time growing your business as a voice actor. Becoming knowledgeable and being selective can serve you well as you navigate through the thousands of opportunities that may come your way.

One of the best ways to uncover voice-over work is to have an online presence and have a website or create a profile on an online marketplace. That way, opportunities that match your profile are sent to you for consideration. Chapter 9 discusses creating a website or joining an online marketplace. This chapter can help you find auditions, how to read job postings, and how to determine which jobs are a good fit for your abilities and interests.

Finding and Reviewing Job Postings

The good news: With the Internet, voice-over job postings are just a click away. You can find voice-over jobs in quite a few places online, including the following:

- ✔ www.craigslist.com
- ✔ www.elance.com
- ✔ www.guru.com
- ✔ www.odesk.com
- ✔ www.voices.com

When reviewing a job posting for voice acting, some bits of information are more important than others. As you gain more and more experience in the voice acting field and look at more and more jobs, you'll become more experienced at spotting great opportunities that you have a really good shot at landing.

Later in this chapter in the "Researching and Evaluating Job Opportunities before Auditioning" section, we discuss how you can make objective decisions regarding whether you should audition or not. In Chapter 16, we explain how thinking like an agent can help you answer the decision whether to audition or not. These sections run through what you should keep an eye on, starting with the most important pieces of information. You can then use this information as you peruse the postings.

Knowing what to look for in a job posting

When you first see a job posting that interests you, you want to double-check a few key specifications about the job, including the following:

- ✔ **The language or accent required:** Verify you can speak the language that the job is calling for. Sometimes a job wants you to speak a language such as Spanish or French. Other times, the client wants a particular accent, such as a British or Australian accent. Pay attention because even though the language states English, you want to double-check the accent requirement.

- ✔ **The gender:** On a similar level of importance, clients state in their job postings the gender of voice they want. On the one hand, if the job calls for a deep male announcer and you sound like a teenage girl, you can save yourself the embarrassment and skip the audition. However, if it's an animation job, you may be able to perform a voice for the opposite gender.

- ✔ **The work type:** Identify the type of work the job listing is for. Different types of work include radio and television commercials, animation for film and cartoons, audiobooks, and so on. Check out Chapter 6 where we discuss in depth the many types of work you can do with voice acting.

- ✔ **The deadline to receive auditions:** Consider when the client has set the deadline to receive auditions. If you aren't able to audition in time or are booked solid when the client needs the voice-over recorded, you need to pass on the opportunity. You don't want to give the impression that you're available when you aren't and then potentially disappoint and come across as being unreliable.

✔ **How the client needs the work delivered:** Most of the time the client wants it uploaded to a website, but the possibility remains that some clients may require that you have access to ISDN, phone patch, or Source-Connect. Refer to Chapter 21 for how these technologies differ.

✔ **Pay rate:** This may be the deal maker or deal breaker for some people. Does the pay line up with the amount of work required? Look for a budget range, for instance between $100 and $250 for shorter recordings and a range of $500 to $1,000 for longer projects. (Refer to the later section, "Paying attention to the pay," to help you know whether to audition or not based on the pay.)

After you review a few job postings, you can get better at scanning them for these details.

Making VoiceMatch work for you

Voices.com has a feature called VoiceMatch, an indicator for how qualified voice actors are for a particular job, saving time when auditioning online. The VoiceMatch score is out of 100 and puts a numerical value on their direct match and helps to take the guesswork out of their chances for being considered for a job.

Knowing how well matched a voice actor is helps to prioritize which auditions to respond to first. The higher a VoiceMatch score is, the more relevant a voice actor's audition submissions are when submitted to clients for review.

To maximize your VoiceMatch score, you want to

✔ **Complete your profile:** A voice actor's VoiceMatch score is based upon how well his or her profile matches a client's job posting. The more complete a profile is, the more job invitations and opportunities a voice actor receives. A complete profile also dramatically increases the potential of being a closer match for a given job posting and by virtue of that fact, the actor may be the recipient of a higher VoiceMatch score.

✔ **Have unique demos in each category:** If you have three or fewer voice samples, you may want to consider recording more demos and uploading them to your account. If you have a number of demos, but they all fall under the same category, see if one or more may fit in multiple categories, and edit your demos to spread the wealth. For instance, categories such as documentary and Internet may be considered interchangeable depending on the contents of the demo. The search engine searches your demos. Being listed in more categories can help you to show up in additional searches as well as provide you with a boost to your VoiceMatch.

✔ **Tag your demos:** We encourage voice actors to use ten tags per demo to help increase their VoiceMatch scores and search visibility. A *tag* is a descriptive word that can be used to reflect the demo's contents. These words can be adjectives that describe how the voice sounds, vocal range, moods, qualities embodied in a read, the kind of character being portrayed, and more. You also want to diversify your tags. Make sure that your tags vary from demo to demo and try to incorporate as many diverse tags as possible that relate to your voice samples.

Spotting vital project information before an audition

Job postings provide important information about the client and project. By thoroughly reviewing this information, you can fully grasp what is required before submitting your audition. Figuring out whether or not you can meet these needs is a very important decision to make.

In this section, we examine four important areas of client requirements that can give you a better idea of what the job posting is about.

Artistic requirements

When you view job listings, consider *artistic direction,* which gives you instruction on how the client wants your read to come across. This may include how old your voice sounds, the register of voice you speak in, or vocal characteristics, such as mood. Artistic direction also can relate to a manner of speaking or characterization.

You need to be honest with yourself and objective about your voice and abilities and discern whether you fit the specifications for artistic requirements. Not everyone has the skills that the job listing asks for so when reviewing job listings, look at what artistic direction the job requires and do those auditions you have the confidence you can deliver.

Artistic requirements include the following areas:

- Vocal range
- Ability to produce a certain voice age
- The tone quality of a voice
- Characterization

For example, a role is being cast for a boy's voice aged 7 to14. A grown man probably shouldn't audition for this role because his voice is too deep for the range needed. Women whose voices sound younger or can be made to sound younger may want to audition, because a woman's voice falls within a treble range similar to that of a child, and a woman can more easily stretch her voice to sound like a younger boy (although the perfect fit would be a boy in that age range).

In addition to knowing if you're a good fit, you also need to be able to interpret scripts well and direct yourself. Most voice actors working independently from home spend time developing their skills in the area of self-direction. As we discuss in Chapter 5, you can inspire yourself in many ways to create a more effective and believable performance.

Kids are sometimes best for the job

When a job listing asks for a child's voice, sometimes the best actor for that job, surprise, is a child. Many children have been cast to give a more authentic read in their normal speaking range. The cast of the *Backyardigans,* a show for preschoolers, is a good example because all the characters were voiced by children, lending greater authenticity to the characters and more connectivity with the audience.

Another great example is the cast of *Dora The Explorer.* The original voice of Dora, Kathleen Herles, didn't do anything out of the ordinary to change the way she spoke when voicing Dora, a role she booked as a child. She simply delivered her lines with feeling as Dora in her own voice. As she got older, she needed to adapt her read slightly to keep with the younger Dora voice she started with.

Technical requirements

In your perusal of job postings, you also want to be aware of the technical requirements for the different jobs. Technical requirements include the following:

✔ **Special equipment:** Some jobs specify that you have equipment to do a job. Some of that special equipment includes

- **ISDN line:** Technical requirements may include how the voice-over is recorded. Some means of recording, such as using an Integrated Services Digital Network (ISDN) line, literally bridge multiple studios so that they're all involved in the same session. (AT&T and Bell Canada offer ISDNs.)

  Other technical requirements include a *phone patch,* which means that the client wants to call in and listen to you as you do the recording and provide feedback and direction in real time. Source-Connect is another popular option. Similar to ISDN, Source-Connect leverages the power of the Internet. Refer to Chapter 21 for how this equipment works.

- **Uncommon audio file format:** Some clients specify in job listings that they need an uncommon audio file format for their telephone system recording. Be sure you can export in that format or at least search online to find software that allows you to convert for recordings into the required format.

✔ **Special skills with editing, producing, mixing, and mastering:** Whenever you see those skills listed in a job posting, what the client expects is someone who can not only serve as a voice actor, but can also provide audio engineering services. Audio engineering is an art and a science, so only step up to the plate to audition if you're competently skilled in this area. If you aren't, find someone who is to help you with the production of a piece and be sure to include what it will cost for him or her to provide those services in your quote.

Location requirements

Another area to consider when reviewing job postings is the location requirement. Location requirement basically means the client requires that the work be completed in a particular location, such as New York or Los Angeles, where the industry is more concentrated and established. In fact, we know of a global industrial company that flies a gentleman from Montreal to Chicago because the company wants him in person when he records its French voice-overs.

Animation is one area of voice acting that requires actors to be in a particular city. Most producers and voice directors want to have their voice cast recording on-site at their preferred recording studio. That explains why a lot of people who do voice acting for animation tend to live where the work is. In Canada, Vancouver is a hotspot for animation voice acting and dubbing, with Toronto offering some work as well. In the United States, Los Angeles is the hub for animation voice acting.

The good news is that with a huge amount of voice acting nowadays being done online, your physical location may not be relevant. However, some clients still prefer a collaborative process that requires you to visit their recording studio. That's right; you may actually have to drive or catch a cab to the recording session. Although location requirements are becoming rarer, keep your eyes open for them when reviewing job postings.

Location may also have to do with how someone communicates or pronounces his words, coming across as naturally as possible to the specific audience he is recording for. Such a job requires understanding of the culture and the ability to fluently speak the language. This requirement may come into play if the casting director needs a native speaker who not only sounds like he comes from a particular place, but also is familiar with the colloquialisms of that group of people and whose delivery of the script comes across well to the audience.

Legal requirements

As you review job postings, you also want to keep in mind the legal requirements. Consider these legal questions as you read through the postings:

- ✔ **Is the job union or non-union?** Most voice-over jobs posted online are non-union, which means you don't need to be a member of SAG-AFTRA (see Chapter 16 for more on this union). Having said that, more union work is being conducted online. Look to see if you meet the union requirements.

- ✔ **Do you have to sign a nondisclosure agreement?** The company may require you to sign a *nondisclosure agreement*. This type of agreement typically limits you from being able to reveal information about the job, the company, and that you've done the work. The nondisclosure agreement may even state that you're not allowed to include the company on your client list.

✔ **Do you have to acquire or license music and sound effects?** If the client needs only the voice-over from you without production, that's great! Sometimes the client will also supply you with preselected music. Other times, a client may let you find music from which the client can choose. Make sure you're versed in what royalty-free means and also understand licensing music for use. (Refer to Chapter 8 for what you need to know about choosing music.)

Researching and Evaluating Job Opportunities before Auditioning

When you're looking for work and different job opportunities, we can't state enough the importance of taking the time to research and evaluate the postings to find a good match for your skills and abilities. Some due diligence on your part can help inform you beforehand when making the decision to audition or not. Understanding how a voice-over can impact you personally should factor into this process. What we mean is that you need to weigh the opportunity with your own values and beliefs before pursuing it. Your integrity is far more important than making a quick buck.

In this section, we discuss the significance of the work you choose to do and provide you with tools to discern opportunities that may prove invaluable to your career. We also provide you a healthy dose of everything you need to know to properly understand what is being asked of you in an audition situation.

Selecting your auditions

Although auditioning is part of what voice actors need to do to get work, most voice actors want to do work that satisfies both their personal interests and business needs. That means being more selective with the jobs that they apply for.

As a result, when you're researching and reviewing job listings, you more than likely want to have a positive experience with a job opportunity. The way you feel toward the project in general may be enough to help you determine whether auditioning is the way to go. Voice acting is living truthfully under imaginary circumstances. That being said, you can act out imaginary circumstances with integrity by using discernment. Whenever you do something you feel comfortable with or know to be right, your read will sound better and more genuine, and your conscience will be clear, saving you from compromising yourself both personally and professionally.

Disregarding your own convictions simply because you can make a dollar in the short term has long-term implications. If you're not in favor of a job opportunity or the company associated with that job, and you decide to take it despite your reservations, remember that you're the one who is making the compromise, not the company in question. Ultimately, it's your decision to participate in the process and live with the consequences. (To help you identify potential red flags with a script or project, check out the next section.)

When you're selecting an audition and trying to find the right fit for you, consider your own perception or opinion of what is being presented and by whom. Carefully read the copy and identify anything that might be misleading or incredible.

Some people think that if you can fake sincerity in this business, you've made it, but you may not be able to mask your underlying feelings or apprehension regarding a script or project. Can good acting camouflage how you really feel about a script or your depth of knowledge?

In a time when very few people are fooled by advertising and marketing, many voice actors who don't agree with a script's content or don't understand its meaning think they can still convince an audience to believe otherwise. Your voice conveys more than you think it might! As Marice Tobias, also known as The Voice Whisperer, said, you can liken the voice to the mirror of the mind.

Making sure the project is in line with your personal beliefs and convictions

When you're researching different job listings, it's time to pull out your Sherlock Holmes gear and thoroughly examine the script for any potential traps or red flags. What do we mean by traps? *Traps* or red flags basically consist of anything that goes against your personal morals, beliefs, principles, and/or politics. If you identify any potential problems and don't feel comfortable reading a script, don't even think about auditioning for it!

Just because you make a living as a voice actor doesn't mean you have to audition for every job you see. Be selective and remember that although the listening audience probably won't know who you are, you do and so will other people who follow your career or employ you. In other words, if you wouldn't publicly affix your name to it or you wouldn't want anyone to know that you recorded it, don't stress over the content and don't bother auditioning for it.

Say what you mean and mean what you say

Words play an enormous role in voice acting. That being the case, every word that comes out of your mouth comes from you regardless of how you came to voice it. When you don't fully invest yourself into a project because of personal reservations, that incongruity can come across in your read, which in turn can negatively impact the performance and how the listening audience receives it. People can spot a hypocrite a mile away.

How often do you publicly support something that you strongly disagree with in private, or do you say things to your family and friends that you don't really mean? Not at all, we hope. Being authentic also applies to your work. Words that come from a voice actor's mouth are still words with meaning. Voice acting doesn't separate actors from their tongues, minds, or hearts.

That isn't to say that there aren't instances where voice actors record for projects with content that they don't personally agree with. On one occasion, we contacted a voice actor to congratulate her on work she booked with an offer to share the YouTube video she had narrated with our Voices.com community to celebrate. After presenting her with the opportunity, she turned it down and asked that her name not be associated with that project.

On the flip side, one voice actor shared that he has never regretted a decision to turn down work that wasn't aligned with his morals, values, and beliefs. You can't put a price on integrity, he said.

Never be afraid to turn down an audition or work that compromises who you are and what you believe. What you gain is the knowledge that you emerged with your dignity intact and were counted among those who possess both honor and conviction as a business professional and as an individual.

Some examples of red flags or traps may be scripts for products or services that you've never used, for products or services that you have tried and don't want to recommend, for testimonials or political ads where you disagree with the parties, or anything else that you don't endorse or support. These examples are where you can fall away from your moral convictions, just for the sake of making money.

Ask yourself different questions, such as

- ✔ Does the copy promise the moon?
- ✔ Is it targeted at a demographic or segment of the population that the advertiser may be trying to take advantage of rather than serve?
- ✔ Does anything stand out in the script as potentially misleading or that otherwise makes you feel uncomfortable?

As a voice actor, you have many freedoms. True freedom means that you don't need to compromise on your morals, beliefs, or otherwise to get a paycheck. That being said, freedom doesn't come without sacrifice. If you stick to your game plan, it may mean standing alone, turning down work, losing friendships, and having others who disagree with you scrutinize you. If you're working with an agent, we suggest you discuss your hesitations with her.

If you find yourself sitting on a fence about whether to audition or not for a project, reconsider what it would mean for you to take the job. Although voice acting often goes without public acknowledgment, if you record something you aren't in agreement with, remember that you must live with that decision for years to come. Refer to the nearby sidebar for more on this philosophical discussion.

Investigating unfamiliar brands

Whether the voice-over is promoting a hotel, computer software, a loaf of bread, or an automobile, you need to know what the word on the street is about that company and product so to speak before auditioning.

In your research to determine whether the job is a right fit for you, you should research the company offering the job, especially when it's an unknown company. Even though research can be time-consuming, you can find lots of information about a company through its website as it relates to the brand, mission, vision, and values. Type the company's name in your favorite search engine to read about the company's services and products.

When evaluating information from the company, keep a lookout for social media pages and customer support forums. Peer reviews, as well as customer reviews, play a large role in helping people decide nowadays whether or not they purchase a product or enlist a service to meet their needs. They can tell you a lot about a company. If you come across a job promoting a new product or service, see what others have said about their experiences to better gauge how the public is receiving the product.

In a recent Nielsen survey featuring degrees of consumer trust in a number of forms of advertising, about 90 percent of survey respondents trusted recommendations from people they know while 70 percent trusted consumer opinions posted online. That's significant, isn't it? A company's website turned up third on the list at 70 percent, so if you have limited time to put your ear to the ground, at least consider visiting the company's website.

Paying attention to the pay

Another important aspect to eye when you're considering whether to audition for a job is the compensation. After all, voice acting is a business and career for you, and you want to be paid accordingly for your services. You can certainly use the client's budget to help decide if it's worth your time auditioning. In fact, you may find that being proud of your work and association with that client takes precedence over the compensation.

Sometimes, though, you may encounter gray areas where you're not sure about auditioning when pay is a question. You may have to make some decisions, based on these circumstances:

✔ The job doesn't pay as much as you think it should yet you're comfortable with everything else about the project. If so, you may choose to move forward with the audition. Make sure you factor in how long the audition and the job will take (if you get it) and what the possible long-term gains are if you choose to submit an audition. (For example, you may be able to network and meet other people who can lead to more work.)

✔ The job pays a handsome sum, but the project doesn't align with your views. If money was the only factor you considered (and not what you thought of the company or the message, like we discuss in the previous section, "Making sure the project is in line with your beliefs and convictions"), then you may decide to go ahead with it. However, your opinion of the client, product, or the script may make you uncomfortable, and no amount of money can ease your feelings.

To quote the lovable Walt Disney character, Jiminy Cricket, "Always let your conscience be your guide." As Jiminy sings in this song, taking the straight and narrow path isn't easy, but it does yield the best results.

Understanding the script

Fully understanding the contents of a script can help you decide whether you want to audition for a job. When you can appreciate and comprehend a script's meaning, you have a better idea what the project is about. You can then determine whether that message matches your values (refer to the earlier section, "Making sure the project is in-line with beliefs and convictions.").

Do a little research to help. Although you may think researching aspects of a story or script are beyond your responsibility, doing so can give you a better idea of the nuances and themes of the project. Research can serve as a tool for greater discernment in addition to simple fact gathering that buttresses a read.

Something else you'll want to look for in a script to determine whether or not to audition is the character role. Knowing your skills and abilities is important. Some roles will appeal to you more than others. For instance, if you're great with accents and character voices, be on the lookout for those sorts of requirements. If your voice and talent are better reflected in a corporate read requesting solid narration, be mindful of those opportunities and audition for them as they come your way. If you see something you want to try but haven't quite honed, such as an accent, wait to audition for those sorts of jobs after you've mastered the related skill.

Chapter 11

Auditioning 101: Just the Basics

Al aspiring voice actors need to cut their teeth on something . . . what better than a steady, daily diet of auditions? The need to read can't be over-exaggerated. Many wonderful opportunities exist to audition in the world of voice-over just waiting to be had.

In this chapter, you look at how auditioning can be likened to the lifeblood of your voice acting career and the different kinds of auditions. Both online and in-person jobs are waiting to be filled with actors whose voices hit the mark and match a casting director's vision.

You also gain an appreciation of what it means to interpret, mark up, and rehearse a script. A little preparation goes a long way when creating a read that not only sounds good, but also is memorable and stands out!

Identifying What You Need to Know from the Get-Go

When you're a voice actor, auditioning is your work. Think about how you spend your day. As a voice actor, it's the pursuit of work and auditioning — getting your name out there — that occupies most of your time. When you're not auditioning, you're either working on projects for established clients or you're extending your brand through marketing and networking with others. Although auditioning may appear to be tiresome and may not financially yield immediate fruit, many voice actors use these special opportunities to exercise their minds, test their creativity, and stretch the limitations of their voices while presenting their talents in front of clients directly, one audition at a time.

For some, auditioning is the day-in, day-out drudgery that they'd rather, but can't, do without. But consider this: How can you reap if you don't sow? Having many targeted, purposeful irons in the fire can only help increase your opportunities to succeed.

Part of auditioning is being purposeful and selective with the opportunities that you invest in. One shift in your perspective can make the difference between struggling and succeeding.

Having a constant stream of auditions flow your way is critical to the success of a working voice actor. Each audition has the potential to help you grow, become more experienced, develop new business relationships, and lead to a booking. All things considered, auditioning is what keeps voice actors going and through perseverance refines their skill and dedication to the craft.

Recognizing the Differences between In-Person and Online Auditions

In recent years, more and more clients are searching the Internet for voice-over professionals. New methods of conducting casting calls have emerged, simplifying the process of searching for, auditioning, and hiring a voice actor. As a result, auditioning has broken many barriers including time, geography, and agency representation.

The traditional method of auditioning meant that you had to physically show up at an agent's office or studio location to give a read. Aside from having to show up, you drove around a lot and spent incalculable time, commuting from place to place simply to audition. Although actors did get some time to socialize with other voice actors and staff at the casting as well as opportunities to be directed on site, most of this activity could only happen in big centers like New York City, Los Angeles, Chicago, Toronto, and Vancouver.

Today, you can do voice acting from literally anywhere there's a connection to the Internet, a computer, audio recording technology, and a voice actor for hire. For specifics on auditioning online, check out Chapter 12. If you're interested in auditioning in person, flip to Chapter 13.

Downloading the Script

Some clients will deliver scripts in newer file formats or require their audio sent to them in various bitrates and file formats. To meet the needs of today's client, you have to be quick on your technological toes and have the most recent versions of the most popular software packages used in the industry — or know a really good workaround.

Many software updates are free and those that aren't are comparatively small investments that you can and should make if you want to service people who have already adopted newer technologies.

Do you really want to send the client a note saying "Hi Client, I can't open your script as a .docx file (or Excel, PDF, or text file) and hope that you will send it to me in another format so I can send you my audition"? Not only is that a wasted opportunity (you can only reply once to a given audition), it's an outright declaration that you can't meet the client's needs!

Doing Your Research: The Script and the Client

When you first receive a script, one of the most important things is to read the script in its entirety before committing to a read or submitting an audition. You may have a gut reaction as to how you ought to read it. Having an idea of where you want to take the script when auditioning is a great feeling, and when there's direction to interpret and guide your read, all the better!

When you read through a script, you're told information about who you are as a voice actor, what you're communicating, the value proposition, and also a call for action. The script may even include details about the audience or help you to determine other important clues, such as how you should sound when delivering your lines.

In a good script, the author's intent should be crystal clear. When auditioning, you may not always be given creative direction, but what you'll nearly always have is the script to aid you in how you plan your read. When you audition, receiving some kind of artistic direction about what type of voice and delivery style the client wants, but what happens when that information isn't as specific as it could be?

Although having that kind of information can be useful, it isn't always provided, so you need to use the script as your primary guide and look for clues. When you gain more experience, you may find that just like established voice actors, you'll be able to rely on your instincts, experience, and ability to self-direct, given the script provided and the demographic it's reaching. Chapter 5 explains some specific ways you can interpret and mark a script so you can understand your character.

The following sections explain more about what you need to do when reading a script for an audition.

In addition to having a good backdrop for your script, knowing a thing or two about the client you're auditioning for can also give you a unique perspective and understanding of the client's expectations and how the read can reflect those expectations. Doing research in general helps you understand upfront who the client is and what other types of projects the client has done in the past.

To have a better feel for the company and the script, research the following pieces of information;

- ✔ **Text analysis:** When you're reading through the script, take note of the kind of language the company uses when communicating to its target audience. Words go a long way and are chosen very carefully. The words communicated in the script embody the essence of the brand and may even be speaking in the brand's voice. If you look closely enough, you may be able to tell what the brand's values are, its culture, and how it wants to be perceived by those hearing its message simply by reading the script.

- ✔ **Corporate culture:** Take a look at the logo(s) of the client you're auditioning for and any images that the client may feature on its website that are related to how it presents its brand. Logos can sometimes embody more than just graphical insight. They can also display a slogan that may be helpful to you. Visiting the client's website can provide more information about the client than what the script may tell you.

- ✔ **Historical context:** Consider reviewing previous ad campaigns around products in that line to see how the client has tried to reach its audiences in the past. Is the script in line with how the client campaigned before or is the client trying a different approach?

Rehearsing the Script

After you've done a very quick analysis of what you see in the script, you're ready to start practicing. Yes, you should rehearse your script several times to make sure you're comfortable with how it reads and the notes that you've made before you audition. Rehearsing a script means that you take the time to practice how you plan to deliver the voice-over when auditioning.

 The best times to rehearse are when you're most awake and have the most energy. Many voice actors also rehearse a script just prior to recording their voice. Make sure that you're well-hydrated and your voice is warmed up. Be sure to observe any markings you have made on your script and keep rehearsal to a minimum before getting in front of the microphone. You don't want to tire your voice before you've even begun the audition!

Before you audition, remind yourself about the following:

✔ Who's meant to hear this message?

✔ What does it mean?

✔ Why is it relevant to the people hearing the message?

✔ Who would the person on the receiving end want to hear from?

✔ How can I best communicate the message?

Keep in mind that clients don't always know exactly what they're looking for and are usually open to hearing all kinds of voices and interpretations. If the clients have a preference or know what kind of voice and attributes they want to cast for ahead of time, they will indicate that in the job description and details.

The following sections focus on some basic script analysis aspects that we suggest you study in the script before you audition to give you the edge over your competition.

Phrasing

Phrasing refers to how you choose to use your breath and shape how you communicate a sentence, question, and so on. Planning how you will phrase ahead of time allows you to be confident in where you intend to breathe, pause, or pace your read. The way you phrase in one area of a script may differ from how you choose to do so in another part of the script. Generally, a phrase contains an idea, a statement, or an expression. You need to budget your breathing to accommodate the phrase. Observing punctuation can also help you to determine how to best phrase a line you're reading.

Shaping the arc of a phrase is important regardless of what you're voicing. When planning how you'll read a passage, take into special consideration the flow of a sentence, its peaks and valleys, and also the terrain. How do you want to paint the picture? Everything you put into a script marking-wise helps you make your vision a reality! Check out Chapter 3 for extended information on phrasing. You can read more about voice production, proper breathing, and support, too, in that chapter.

Timing

Have you ever heard that timing is everything? Voice-over is an art that requires the utmost attention to *timing*, whether it be sticking within the confines of a commercial, dubbing for animation and film, or simply pacing out a read so it sounds natural. Timing is also important when recording with other voice actors in a cartoon, commercial, video game, or film where your pacing needs to match the other actors' speed.

Characterization

Getting into character is one of the most exciting and delightful aspects of the auditioning process. You get to step into the shoes of someone else, read a variety of copy, and play with your voice. Know your character and the audience that you're speaking to, and be aware of how your voice is coming across.

Being conscious of your voice is very important. Practice recording and listening to yourself perform to hear your artistic choices. Did they sound informed, deliberate, and committed? Were you able to identify any areas, whether technical or artistic, that you'd like to further develop or explore?

Using the "series of three" audition trick

Using the series of three, based on a method taught by voice coach Pat Fraley, is an excellent way to provide direction for yourself when auditioning for voice-over work. Essentially, what you do is prepare three different takes in your audition for a client to consider. This can be done either in person or through an online audition. You can also use this method when working on a project in your recording studio or practicing at home. If it's a long script that you're recording, simply do a portion of it.

The series of three is as follows:

✔ **A:** Your primary interpretation

✔ **B:** An interpretation different from A

✔ **C:** A mix between takes A and B

You can easily make your C role how you interpret the copy for any voice-over job, not just character voice work. You'll certainly notice a difference in how you perform and your clients will too. Most directors end up casting your C role. Think of this as the Goldilocks method — too hot, too cold, just right:

✔ **Too hot:** In voice-over terms, the read is over the top, perhaps aggressive or overly confident. The feeling or interpretation motivating your read may be the first thing that comes to mind and needs to be clear and effective so you have something to build on for your other reads.

✔ **Too cold:** The read contrasts significantly from the first read. Maybe this read is happy, perhaps cheerful even! Whatever it is, it needs to be different from the first read and express a different feeling or sentiment using the same words.

✔ **Just right:** This read is somewhere in the middle of hot and cold. It's described as a warm read or combination of the two.

You can play with pitch, inflection, timing, and more when compiling a series of three sets of reads. Something helpful in this case would be to let clients know that you've prepared a number of contrasting reads for their consideration.

Your first two choices don't have to be complete opposites to be effective. If you want, you can experiment with using a sliding scale, hovering around the same feeling with ever so slight changes in interpretation. Employing a lighter variation strategy can result in complementary rather than polarizing interpretations and produce a more targeted series of reads, if the client has been quite clear with his requirements and creative direction.

Achieving Success during Your Audition

If you're auditioning for voice-over jobs on your own, we hope you've adopted an agent's mindset for qualifying your opportunities. Thinking like an agent saves you time (which can also equate to money) and energy, and doing so also gives you a better shot at booking the projects you're auditioning for.

See each audition as a means to keep in shape. When you audition, know that with each piece of copy you read, you're getting better and better. Whenever you invest time and effort into something, it begins to yield fruit.

Being consistent is important in terms of achieving success with regularity. Having a membership on a marketplace site allows you to "speak to the world" from the privacy of your own home and provides opportunities for you to work with repeat clients.

Some things you can do include

- ✔ Auditioning multiple times a day
- ✔ Inviting clients to add you to their Favorites
- ✔ Teaching clients how to leave feedback for you after completing a job
- ✔ Responding to a job posting as soon as it arrives

Something you can do to make your auditions sound better is editing out breaths when it makes sense to do so. Editing breaths out of auditions may be a reasonable thing to do, especially if you're having some respiratory issues or have a cold. You can remove the breaths to make the audio sound cleaner, but the end result could be that the voice-over loses an aspect of its humanity and may sound unnatural. Check out Chapter 19 for more specifics about editing.

Slating Your Name

What does it mean to slate your name? Simply put, *slating* means to read your name aloud prior to performing the audition copy so the casting director, or decision maker, knows who he's listening to. A slate can also foreshadow what the listener will hear as well as potentially surprise the listener depending on how the slate is executed.

Slating your name, whether in person or online, is part of the auditioning process and is as industry standard as anything. Given the frequency that you may be using it, something you may wish to do is record your slate as a separate file and store it in your session template/settings in your digital audio recording program.

These sections explain the importance of slating, what you can gain from good slating, and how you can slate for auditions.

Giving a good first impression with a slate

The basic slate is simply stating your name at the beginning of the file. A slate doesn't serve the same purpose as a watermark. A slate doesn't compromise the trust between actors and their prospective clients.

Slating serves many these purposes:

- ✔ Readily identifies you, the speaker
- ✔ Sets the tone for the audition
- ✔ Gets your name in the client's head
- ✔ Sets an industry-standard auditioning technique
- ✔ Serves as another way to document whose voice is on the file, should it get downloaded

Identifying the main benefit to slating

One benefit of slating your name is that people in the press or podcasters can instantly know how to say your name. Having a slate can help to prevent mistakes and embarrassing moments for people trying to contact you, promote you, hire you over the phone, or reference you on a program.

People, whether in the media or otherwise, mean well, and they want to say your name right the first time. Give them the opportunity to ace it by having a slate accompany your demo.

Knowing the different ways to slate

Slating can come in two different ways:

- ✔ You can slate your own name.
- ✔ You can enlist a colleague to slate your name.

Many voice actors who incorporate slating into their promotional and auditioning techniques choose the second option and have one of their voice-over pals, usually of the opposite gender, record their name in an MP3 file that they then use to introduce their demos and auditions.

In the majority of instances, having someone slate your name works in your favor, but sometimes the actor who slates your name can end up getting the job. Rest assured that this isn't the norm, but it's still another good reason for having a voice actor of the opposite sex slate for you. Try working with a voice actor who has a different accent altogether from your own and is the opposite gender. Above all, the slate is supposed to prepare the audience and enhance your performance, not take away from it.

Getting a Callback

When you get a callback, you're over the moon! You're that much closer to booking the job. Only a select number of voice actors receive invitations to read again, so this feedback is wonderful for actors who wonder if their read was what the client was looking for.

Feedback of this kind is rare as are callbacks for most voice-over jobs. If you do receive a callback, you are on the right track and are one of the select few who caught the client's ear with your interpretation of the client's script with the help of your voice.

For the callback, here are a few things to consider:

✔ **Respond to your client.** One of the best ways to communicate with clients where documentation is concerned is by using the internal messaging system with your online account or sending an email if you're working with someone who hired you through other means.

If you book a job at Voices.com and communicate using the internal messaging system, all communications, from the audition through feedback reviews, are stored safely within your account for you to reference if need be.

✔ **Ask what the client liked.** Given the opportunity, you may wish to ask a client what it was about your audition that he liked. This isn't always an option, but if you find that you do have access to a direct communication line, you can dig a little to discover more about what it was that singled you out.

✔ **Improve from your original audition.** If you made it this far, whatever you did in your original audition can serve as your benchmark for success. If you made any technical or artistic mishaps in your original audition, you can now fix them.

✔ **Understand the client's requirements.** Make sure you know what the client expects of you. Doing so is a surefire way to best prepare yourself in a callback situation. You may find that the callback contains more detailed information and requirements that the client only wanted to disclose to contenders for the job.

Thinking beyond the Audition

Although curiosity can be a healthy thing, you can take it too far, and it may prove to be a point of frustration. This can be especially true when pondering the potential outcome of a job application, auditioning for a role, or submitting yourself for consideration — all of which put the ball in someone else's court.

Auditioning requires a boldness to step out and the willingness to become vulnerable in the presence of someone else. When you give of yourself, you'll experience a certain level of vulnerability. The decision ultimately resides with the person you're trying to please and convince on the other end.

After putting so much of yourself into an audition, it's no wonder you feel curious and want to know what came of your efforts, but that's part of your job as an actor. If you were to spend all your time worrying about past auditions, you'd have time for little else.

How can you get past the audition and move on, even though you don't have a definitive answer? Try these suggestions:

✔ Don't use the word *rejection.* Just tell yourself that you weren't the right voice for the gig.

✔ Remind yourself that not getting the job or not hearing about the job has left you time and energy for the right gig to come your way.

✔ Think "I'm perfect for the next project!"

✔ Use the fire and forget method. Do the audition as best you can and then forget you did it. Then if you get the call, it's a pleasant surprise. If you don't, you haven't lost anything.

✔ Think of supplying the best audition you can as your job. After that, it's in the client's hands.

Modeling What Other People Who Book Regularly Do in Your Auditions

What sets successful voice actors apart from those individuals who don't get jobs? When you get right down to it, people who book as their own agent have mastered the arts of communication and marketing and are able to meet the artistic and technical needs of their clients.

Voice actors who are their own agent have less time to complain or second-guess themselves. Many voice actors in the business like to not only receive demo feedback from prospective clients offline, but they also want to receive feedback from clients online. For instance, they want to know details, such as whether the client has listened to a demo, what the client thought of the performance, and also why they weren't chosen for the part.

Based on what we've experienced, these actors

- Were the right voice for the job
- Quoted an amount that the client was prepared to pay
- Customized auditions (both demos and proposals)
- Made clients feel at ease and reassured them of their professionalism
- Added value to the customer and had a unique selling proposition
- Were able to identify and relieve their customers' "pain"

For most actors, the proof is in the pudding. A paycheck is equivalent to a client's feedback and pat on the back for a job done well. Those actors are busier working and have no time (and certainly waste less time) to contemplate why they did not book a particular job. They adopt and live out a send it and forget it mindset. In their opinion, it's not about rejection. It's about selection.

Reflecting on Why You May Not Win an Audition

Take a moment to pause and think about what it is that may have contributed to your not landing a gig. For some actors, they can point their fingers directly at the fact that they didn't record a custom demo, provide the client with a sample read from their script, and so one. But for the most part, focus on the Big 3: the right equipment, desire, and ego.

The right equipment

Do you have the time to just stop everything and record a custom demo? For those of you who work at home, equipped with industry standard studio gear, recording on demand can be as easy as creating a new session, positioning yourself in front of your trusty microphone, and getting down to business, script in hand (or in browser window, whichever works for you).

That's wonderful for actors with pro studios, but what about actors who don't professionally record from home? This is where the custom demo may go out the window.

"But, what about recording it through an online system or on a portable, hand-held MP3 recorder?" you may ask? We don't want to be the bearer of bad news, but online recording software that allows you to simply use your computer's internal microphone often comes across as tinny, poor quality, and incredibly difficult to enjoy from a client's point of view. Recording in this manner jeopardizes your chances of landing a job.

Right away, you face

✔ Distortion

✔ Reduced quality

✔ Low fidelity

✔ Limited amount of time to record

✔ Not being able to edit the recording

✔ Having no record of the recording on your personal computer

✔ Relying on a particular service to submit lower quality audio

✔ Clients not being able to or not wanting to share your demo with colleagues

✔ A poor first impression of what you can do for the client

If you have the choice to record a really solid custom demo with proper equipment, don't settle for providing a potential customer with inadequate audio and a poor first impression of your work. In most cases, if you aren't prepared to record a sample of the script (and have the time and resources to do so), perhaps you really aren't as interested in the job as you may have thought.

Desire

When it all boils down to it, do you really want this job? Client feedback has revealed that submissions without custom demos aren't worth reviewing. They interpret a stock demo as obvious disinterest in the project.

If you truly want the job, prove it to the client and give the client a taste of what you can do for them.

Ego

Do *not* let your ego get in the way. Don't think "I've been the voice of superstar blue-chip clients, and I don't need to prove myself to you." This position is a dangerous place to be for a voice actor who's trying to find himself work.

You may have numerous credits that indicate your extraordinary voice acting roles, clients, and so forth, but odds are that the majority of clients will have no concept of the breadth of your voice acting history. In most instances, clients won't make the decision to hire simply because of past credits and one's clout as a voice-over phenomenon. It all comes down to how you can serve clients and how you can serve the people in their charge — not about the latest voice acting project you've starred in or the most recent national commercial you've recorded.

Chapter 12

Auditioning in the Virtual World

· ·

In This Chapter

▶ Knowing the ins and outs to auditioning online

▶ Recording your audition and naming your demo file

▶ Safeguarding your auditions

▶ Quoting pay rates for clients

▶ Giving your audition portions a second look

· ·

*A*uditioning leads to work. When you audition for a voice-over job, you need to concentrate on what's being asked of you, and how to best convey the purpose and sentiment of a script, and you need to persuade clients to work with you on their projects.

In this chapter, you discover how to submit an audition online at a voice-over marketplace, including receiving job posting notifications, reviewing job details, interpreting a script, recording a custom demo, deciding whether to include music in your audition submission, and filing naming conventions. You also gain insight into the quoting process, find out how to write a great proposal to accompany your custom demo, and move on after you've sent in your audition.

Following the Steps for Auditioning Online

When you're listed on an online marketplace, some membership levels give you the opportunity to not only showcase your voice but also apply for work. This application process is commonly referred to as *auditioning.* The process is simple and designed to help you put your best foot (or voice) forward. Here are some sample steps you can follow when auditioning online, on a marketplace website.

Step 1: Creating an online account

Clients are constantly in need of people who can do voice-overs. They create a job and post jobs for you to see on a marketplace site. The job postings outline requirements and what types of voices are needed. After the job postings have been submitted and approved, you can peruse the listings. But you can only do this if you have an online account.

To create an account, find the audition sites you're interested in and register. Some online sites where you can find voice-over auditions include Voices.com, elance.com, and guru.com.

Step 2: Locating jobs

You can locate jobs through sites that you are registered for in two ways:

- ✔ Peruse job listings. Check out Chapter 10 for where to locate job listings.
- ✔ Email links from clients.

Only voice actors who are logged in to their accounts can audition for jobs.

After job postings are submitted and approved to registered sites by clients, email notifications are sent out to the voice actor profiles that match the project requirements. Some of these requirements include language, gender, voice age, and the kind of work needing to be recorded. This is the reason why you should have an account and upload your profile.

Job notification emails include a direct link to where you can see the postings or glean more information regarding what's required of you. If you're clicking through a link in an email, finding jobs is much easier than having to browse listings on your own (see the preceding section).

Step 3: Reviewing job postings

When looking at job postings, take every detail into account, particularly where it pertains to areas that the clients have typed in, such as the job description and sample script. Check out Chapter 10 for what to look for when reviewing job postings.

Step 4: Downloading the script

Most jobs have a script attached to them that you can download and review. The script is more often than not the final copy and may contain additional information such as storyboards and sides. Some voice actors directly read the scripts off their computer screens or iPads, and others prefer to print them off and put them on a music stand.

If you're reading the script on a screen, use the word processing tools to high-light, italicize, or bold anything you need to be aware of. Don't be afraid to add your own direction and analysis of the script if none has been provided. If you're working from a printout, grab your pencil and get marking, highlighting the same things you would on screen. Check out Chapter 5 for more help on marking up your script.

Step 5: Replying to a job

Replying to a job is an exciting prospect, don't you think? Every opportunity you take advantage of can lead to something bigger and greater than you ever imagined. Taking time to reply is important. Showing up is important! In the online world, showing up is easier than it is in the physical sense, but you still have to be ready and present yourself professionally.

Being selective with the jobs you reply to can also be of great benefit both to you and to the person who's posted the job. If you feel that you're a wonderful fit and can confidently deliver on all that's being required, go for it! If you find a job posting that interests you, you can reply to the job by submitting an online audition that consists of a brief message, your voice-over demo, and a quote for the job.

Step 6: Getting a response

After the client posts a job, the client logs in to his account and listens to the audition responses. Clients can contact you directly through the marketplace using the site's internal messaging system to further discuss their projects. After a final selection has been made, the client awards the project to the best voice actor for the job (hopefully, that's you!), and if a payment service is offered, the client makes a deposit to your account to secure your services.

You'll receive a notification via email stating that you're the winning candidate! Don't you just love to hear things like that? You have the job! This email includes instructions on what you have to do next and links to where those actions can be taken when logged into your account.

At this point, you may have direct contact with the client and discuss details pertaining to the job. The marketplace may disclose your contact details to the client and vice versa to facilitate easier communication between the two of you. After you complete the work in a recording studio, you upload the file(s) to the job and await the client's approval of the work, which triggers authorization of payment.

Recording Your Custom Demo

Custom demos are more attractive to clients. In an audition situation, voice actors who submit custom demos, meaning a sample read of the client's script, are usually rewarded with extra attention from the client receiving the auditions.

For you as a voice actor, the goal is to present the client with something that best reflects the project requirements while demonstrating your vocal abilities in a practical manner. Recording the custom demo also gives you the option to include that significant tidbit of information in your written proposal, catching the eye of the client and raising interest levels in your submission. (See the section "Preparing the Proposal to Accompany Your Audition" later in this chapter for more information.)

That being said, when clients receive custom demos, they usually give them more weight than a stock demo submission, especially if they're presenting the demos to their own clientele. From the client's point of view, a voice actor who submits a custom demo is more keen to work for the company in question. Considering the interest level and the time invested to record a custom demo, clients may also perceive you as more qualified to work for them.

Think about this recording like a job interview. Do you show up to an interview knowing nothing about the company? Would you send in a general cover letter instead of personalizing it for your prospective employers? Not likely (at least we hope not). Record a custom demo and address the client by name in your proposal to get the best results.

Custom demos take time, but if recorded with the right motivations and precautions, they more than serve their purpose. You're giving clients something greater than just a sample of your voice reading copy — you're giving them a taste of precisely what their voice-overs will be like. (For detailed information about recording your own demo, check out Chapter 8.)

Submitting a Dry Audition

You should submit auditions as *dry voice* samples, which means that they don't have any other production elements involved, such as music, sound effects, processing of the voice, and so on. In other words, the recording should consist of just you reading the copy.

A dry voice recording reveals the qualities of your voice and captures the recording environment. Very rarely are voice actors asked to include music in an audition, but make sure you follow the client's instructions. For more information on including music in your demo, check out Chapter 8.

Protecting Your Auditions

Because today's auditions are typically digital audio files, your demo is more accessible and in some instances can be downloaded and potentially used without permission or without paying you. In this section, we identify methods and techniques for how you can protect your custom demos in the online voice-over marketplace.

Watermarking

Think of *watermarking* as how a photographer provides sample proofs with a logo on them or words across the image that render the image less polished and therefore less desirable for professional use.

In the custom demo scenario, the higher quality version isn't made available to the customer prior to purchasing. Although this option seems good in theory, clients aren't keen on watermarked demos because they distract them greatly and ultimately detract from the read. As a result, clients are less likely to consider voice actors whose initial audio submission is less than desirable.

Fading in your audio

How about an alternative to watermarking (see the preceding section)? Consider fading your audio out. The easiest way to protect your audio is to fade out the last sentence, preferably before the end of that last sentence. Bleeps and bloops are distracting and can put a bad taste in a client's ear.

A *fade* is a gentle way of saying that you really want to work with a client, but you're protecting your work from fraud. Clients should respect this method. You can also try leaving the name of the client, service, or product out when recording the audition.

Naming Your Audition File

How can you find a file that you need if every demo you have is called "mydemo.mp3" or has a meaningless file name? Consider naming your demo appropriately so it catches the eye of the client you're pursuing.

You can also name the file to reflect the company's name that you're recording for. This naming convention helps you readily identify files related to that account or group them together by using the same naming convention (if a number of files are associated with a particular job).

For some proper ways to label your demos, check out the following list:

- ✔ yourname_company.mp3
- ✔ yourname_company_chapter_1.mp3
- ✔ yourname_jobIDnumber.mp3
- ✔ yourname_character.mp3
- ✔ yourname_company_product.mp3

When working with clients, you may find that they have their own preferred file naming conventions and ask that you save the files according to their requirements.

Pay special attention to file naming conventions. This is important because some systems may not receive your file properly or kick your audition into a spam folder if not labeled correctly.

At Voices.com, all audition demos must be in MP3 format using a bit rate of 128 kbps and a sample rate of 44.1 kHz in order for the client to successfully play back your demo in the Flash players. Also, the file name can't include special characters such as !,@,#,$,%,^,&,*,(,) or spaces. When in doubt, ask clients how they want your file named.

Preparing the Proposal to Accompany Your Audition

A *proposal* is only the beginning of a contract negotiation. Having a proposal that is well-matched with the job you're auditioning for can go a long way in getting the client's attention. Don't be afraid to come right out and ask for the job! Figure 12-1 gives you three samples to look at to help you draft your own proposal.

The most rewarded auditions that clients consider when they look for a voice include custom written proposals for their project. A persuasive and relevant note will catch more eyes quickly than even the most creative demo.

Dear Client,

I am pleased to provide you with a custom read of your script. My rate is negotiable, and I can provide you with a finished product within 24 hours of your request. For a different style of read, you may visit my website at www.mygreatvoice.com to hear more of my work.

I look forward to working for you and giving your business a voice.

Regards,

Your Name

Figure 12-1: Sample proposal letters.

Dear Client,

Your script and project present a very exciting challenge that I look forward to working with you on. My demo showcases the work I've done in a similar genre. Because this project is such a unique one, my quote is for dry voice only. The additional editing, background music and production costs will depend on the length of the final project.

I look forward to working for you and giving your business a voice.

Regards,

Your Name

Dear Client,

I would like to thank you for considering me for your corporate training video project. I have recorded a custom audition using a portion of the script you provided.

After reading your project details, I can confidently say that I am the best candidate to record your project. I have recorded several educational and commercial narrations, many of which include training video narrations for corporate and government clients.

For a two-hour corporate training video, my proposed quote for your project is $1,500, full buy-out, fully edited and delivered within seven business days.

I look forward to working for you and giving your business a voice.

Regards,

Your Name

Illustration by Wiley, Composition Services Graphics

Researching the client

Showing knowledge of the company and familiarity with its brand is a huge help. You can research companies by visiting their websites and social media channels. If you're on the company's website, be sure to go to their "About Us" or "Contact" page for key information.

A brand typically comes across best through a company's social media channels. Facebook is an excellent social network for seeing brands at their very best. No doubt you can already think of a number of brands you follow on Facebook and just how well you know them and their culture based upon the updates, photos, videos, and discussions on their pages.

Using these sources helps you better understand companies and highlights how you would best represent their corporate image from the insight you have gathered. This information can be embodied into your read — for instance with the essence of the brand presented in the style in which you read. You could also use that information to further customize your proposal to mention a recent success that company has experienced and congratulate them.

Looking at the pieces of the proposal

For best results, your proposal should include the following parts:

✔ An introduction and brief recap of their project

✔ Explanation of your skills related to their project

✔ Your project action plan

✔ Quote and turnaround time

✔ Closing statements and contact information

If your proposal is long, the client may not take the time to read it. You should aim for ten lines or less so the client can review your full proposal quickly.

Personalizing the proposal

You'd never guess how far some simple personalization can take your audition. Addressing the client by name in the greeting is one of the easiest and most critical steps you can take to personalize a proposal. Also, be sure that if you're using audition templates for your proposal, that you personalize other areas and clearly state such things that may, in theory, appear obvious, such as "I recorded a sample from your script."

One of the drawbacks of the audio medium is that you can't really "preview" it before you listen, and unless you spell it out for clients, they may assume you have sent a stock demo, especially if the proposal included with your audition appears to be generic and unrelated to their specific project and needs.

Becoming relevant to the client

Say something specific to clients about why you want to work for them and record their voice-over (remember, this project is their baby so they may want to feel an emotional connection with your reasons for wanting to record). Mentioning something of particular note that relates to them is a great way to connect and become memorable; however, if clients aren't addressed by their names, this strategy becomes less effective than it could be. You don't have to write them a sonnet, just a sentence or so that sets you apart while connecting with the heart of the project. People make decisions with more than just their pocketbooks and their ears.

Reassuring the client

You need to affirm that you're able to meet the clients' needs as outlined in their job postings. If they say something like, "I need this done by phone patch," include the fact that you can do so in your proposal. It may seem redundant, but it affirms for the client that you are on the same page.

Similarly, if clients want a particular sound, let them know that your audio sample embodies the sound they asked for. Clients have revealed their most pressing needs in the posting. Be sure to identify and acknowledge those needs by briefly reassuring them of your ability to meet their requirements, both technical and creative.

Handling parting words

When you wrap up your proposal, be sure to thank clients again for the opportunity and express that if there's any way you can be of assistance to them, that you can be contacted through the site you have auditioned on. Make sure that you have

- ✔ Thanked them again for the opportunity
- ✔ Expressed a desire to work with them
- ✔ Provided them with instructions on how to move ahead (hire you on the site) or contact you for more information using the tools provided for messaging between clients and voice actors

Quoting for the Job

Voice-over is a competitive industry, and you need to decide how you will be quoting for your services. Will it be by word, per spot, per hour, per package, per project, per market, or per page or usage? These are all items that you should consider before you quote a project. You may even consider a combination of these if the situation requires it.

It seems like all voice actors have their own preferences when it comes to quoting, but one thing they all have in common where non-union work is concerned, is that all jobs are quoted as full buy-outs. A *full buy-out* means that there will be no residual payments made to the voice actor from the client in the future for use of the audio. A full buy-out also means that clients can use the audio for whatever they want, for however they want in perpetuity. Chapter 15 discusses important issues related to quoting, to ensure you get paid appropriately for your work.

Taking Care with Each Submission

When you're auditioning and have the convenience of using a template such as what is available to you via Voices.com, it can be easy to go on autopilot and let technology get in the way of important choices requiring thought and social interactions.

This section gives you the opportunity to review key pieces of your audition submissions before they fall into the possession of clients who hold the power to hire you in their hands.

Proofreading your proposal

When your proposal is finalized, double-check everything with the following checklist:

- ❑ Make sure your proposal is well-worded and contains no spelling mistakes. Maybe have someone else read it.
- ❑ Personalize the proposal to the specific client.
- ❑ Make sure the proposal is short and concise.
- ❑ Contrast and compare past proposals to see which ones may have worked best when communicating with clients. This is easy if you have stored a number of templates and can reference them within your account.

Be careful to customize templates or edit parts out of a template on the fly that don't directly relate to the client you're auditioning for at the moment. For instance, say you were auditioning for a movie trailer voice-over, but the template you chose to use was recording telephone voice prompts. If you're not careful and don't edit the template, the client may get the impression that your reply is a stock response, and you may not even know what you auditioned for in the first place.

Uploading the correct audio file

Wouldn't it be awful to have taken all that time and care crafting a custom demo only to send the wrong audio file? You'd be surprised to discover that this can happen, even to the best voice actors!

When you go to upload an MP3 file during the audition process, check these steps:

❑ Browse your desktop to find the correct file to upload. This is when naming files properly really comes in handy (see the section "Naming Your Audition File").

❑ Listen to the file to make sure it is the right one.

❑ Upload the file after you've confirmed that it's the right file to send.

Some marketplace sites have a preview feature that allows voice actors to listen to their voice samples before sending them to the clients with their auditions. The file may also be stored in a voice actor's audition history in case the actor wants to replicate that voice-over style for the client if the actor books the job.

Verifying your quote is accurate

Of all the factors that will be most glaringly important, your quote takes the cake. When using a marketplace, your quote is often one of the first things that clients see when evaluating responses to their job postings. Make sure that

❑ You've quoted an amount that compensates you fairly and falls within a reasonable range.

❑ Your quote isn't lower than the budget that's stated.

Quoting less than what's been budgeted for is not only silly but also may give the impression that you're desperate to get the job and perhaps may not actually be as qualified to do the work. Many voice actors have a poor impression of what they should be able to command for their services.

These voice actors typically fall into three groups:

✔ People who are new to the industry who decide to undercut industry standard rates due to lack of experience or belief that they're undeserving

✔ People who come from broadcast radio who work on volume, making their money by working numerous jobs for less

✔ People supplementing their income with voice-over who are either moonlighting or retired

Because the money is over and above what they're already bringing in, some feel charging less for something they consider to be a hobby is justified.

Above all, submitting a quote that you are comfortable with is paramount, particularly if you're relying on the money you make from doing voice-overs to feed your family, keep a roof over your head, and send the kids to school.

Agreeing to work for less than you believe you should be paid will only make you resentful, leave you with not enough money, affect your working relationship, and may even come across in your read.

Submitting it and forgetting it

Do ghosts of auditions past linger in the back of your mind? Have precious time and emotions been wasted contemplating the outcome of a casting call? Although it's human nature to wonder, fixating on things that are out of your control can be exhausting and make it harder for you to keep moving forward. How can you liberate yourself from questions such as "what if?", "who got it?", and "why not me?"

Even harder than letting go of a submitted audition can be getting an audition to the point that you're comfortable submitting it period! When you're in the director's chair, the decision rests with you as to how many takes you produce or how you approach a read.

How many takes are enough? You ask yourself. Some voice actors beat themselves up to get what they perceive to be the "perfect" take. After they get that perfect take out, they need to release it through the auditioning process and let it go as a whole. We cover this topic extensively in Chapter 11.

Chapter 13

Auditioning in the Real World

· ·

· ·

*W*hat's it like to go into a real-world, bricks-and-mortar audition? Most of these kinds of auditions only happen in the major city hubs for voice acting, but you may find yourself in a situation where you're called on to show up and give a few reads for a casting director to consider.

This may happen if you're represented by an agent or the producer's client wants to hold auditions at a studio. Being professional and looking the part, that is to say, not showing up in your pajamas, will provide all involved in the decision with a good first impression of who you are and how you work. That being said, if you're working from home, pajamas or casual around-the-house clothing (even slippers) works just fine.

This chapter emphasizes the importance of making a great first impression, following studio etiquette, and correctly interacting with a casting director, studio engineer, and anyone else who may be present at an audition or recording session.

Don't forget that while being professional is important, so is having fun! Building relationships and participating in the social world of in-person auditioning is an experience you want to be prepared for as well as enjoy many times over the course of your career.

Making a Great First Impression

In voice-overs, the first impression clients get of you is often determined by your résumé and the voice-over demos on your web page or voice demos submitted in an audition situation. When it comes to auditioning in the real world, there's so much more that goes into putting your best foot and voice forward. In this section, we cover professionalism, touching on areas such as dress, punctuality, presentation, and relationships.

Dressing for success

A variety of things certainly exist that you should and should *not* wear when in a live audio recording session. In this section, we take a closer look at the kind of clothing real working voice actors wear when doing auditions in person.

 Your clothing choices can impact your performance, both in terms of how you can use your instrument and parts of your ensemble the microphone picks up that you may not have considered. You must look the part and sound the part. So, what are winning combinations when stepping into the booth at a live audition?

- ✔ Cottons and blends such as blouses, khakis, rugby shirts, and so on
- ✔ Knits such as sweaters, cardigans, and shawls
- ✔ Well-worn denim that fits well and isn't tight
- ✔ Soft sole shoes, sneakers, or slip-ons (anything that doesn't make noises or squeaks)

Now that you have a good idea of what kind of clothing is acceptable, perhaps it's time for some enterprising fashion designer to start her own line of fashionably quiet outfits and accessories for voice and on-camera actors.

The microphone hears all

You'd be surprised by just how much the microphone hears. When you're auditioning and your necklaces are clanging together or your phone is beeping or vibrating, the microphone will pick up those noises and your audition may be affected. For your convenience, we include a list of distracting noises:

- ✔ Audible body movements
- ✔ Breathing
- ✔ Clothing ruffling
- ✔ Coins in your pocket
- ✔ Coughing
- ✔ Jangling jewelry
- ✔ Mobile phones
- ✔ Mouth noises
- ✔ Pagers
- ✔ Pages being turned
- ✔ Rolling pencils
- ✔ Room tone
- ✔ Touching the music or mic stand
- ✔ Vibrations of any kind
- ✔ Wind-up watches (tick, tick, tick)

Something even as obscure as a coffee cup can change the quality of a recording. Be aware of every single thing that can cause noise and do whatever you can to eliminate it.

Choosing quiet clothing

Picking the right clothes to wear in a session or at an audition makes a difference in terms of what the microphone picks up and also your personal comfort level. You may want to have a few outfits set aside that are only used when recording or auditioning in person. They could be your recording clothes, maybe even your uniform so to speak. When you feel comfortable in your clothing, you can definitely give a better performance.

That being said, your choice of footwear is also going to either help or hinder your performance. Most people prefer to wear shoes that help them feel grounded in their stance. Good actors or public speakers know the importance of standing well and being able to access their air using good posture. A solid pair of well-worn shoes serves as the only boundary between your foot to floor connection. Be sure that the shoes you wear bring out the best in your posture and performance. Don't wear anything that may obstruct your access to the microphone.

What not to wear

When you're in the booth, you want to be both comfortable and only generate audible sound from your mouth. That means no jangly earrings, clothing that makes a ruffling noise such as polyester or nylon, anything with buttons that clank, zippers, or jewels. You may not want to wear a hat because the peak of the hat could interfere with the microphone itself or somehow get in the way of your voice making its way through the signal chain.

Don't give anyone a reason to not pick you. Sometimes castings are very close, and you never know what their final decision may have been swayed by, be it what they ate for lunch, or their impression of how you chose to dress.

Perfume, cologne, or strong smelling moisturizing lotions are also on the list of items you should avoid when going to an audition. You may want to add hair spray, gel, or any other product you may use that carries a punch.

By no means are we telling you not to shower before going to an audition, but we are suggesting that being aware of and considerate of others where fragrances or scents are concerned is just as important when entering the studio environment as anything else. Those are tight quarters! When you leave an audition at a studio, it shouldn't smell any different than when you entered the booth.

Although you would likely not wear a ball cap to a session, it has come to our attention through talking to voice actors that depending on the situation, it's sometimes okay to sport a hat. This seems to be more prevalent in animation voice acting circles. In most situations, though, err on the safe side by removing your hat before arriving at the studio and stepping in the booth. Ultimately, the decision of whether you can or can't wear a hat in the studio belongs to the recording engineer or the person running the session.

Heeding Some Tips for Professionalism

Always be professional. Remember that your brand is on the line. Being courteous and considerate as well as prompt and ready to work are fabulous ways to set the tone for your audition and create a lasting first impression that will be crystallized in the minds of those around you. This section gives you some extra pointers for auditioning in person and being professional.

Mute the mobile phone

Thanks to mobile devices and access to the Internet, games, and so on, people bring their cell phones everywhere and sometimes into places that they wouldn't have normally done so in the past. Although you can ensure your phone doesn't ring by changing the settings or muting the phone, that won't necessarily stop it from becoming a distraction for you in terms of its use.

When people mute the volume on their phones, sometimes they forget that the vibrate option is still on. When a phone vibrates, it can sometimes be even louder given the surface it's placed on than if the ringer is set on a lower volume. If you have a mobile device, be sure to turn it off at an audition so that it doesn't become a point of contention between you, your peers, the casting team, or anyone else.

Showing up on time

When you have a job interview, you want to arrive with plenty of time to spare so you can allow for traffic, find parking, and arrive fifteen minutes early. In the world of in-person auditions, arriving to the venue early for your audition will make a good first impression.

If you're going to be late, which we run into a lot here in Los Angeles, make sure you call the studio and let them know you're going to be late. Studios are all based on an hourly rate. So if you're late, it's costing the client money and in turn, that could cost you money.

Following the list of don'ts

Whenever you walk into an in-person casting call, you need to remember to come prepared mentally, emotionally, and free of any ego (be sure to leave that one at the door). Being prepared means so much more than just showing up and giving a read for consideration.

Voice actor and voice-over coach Debbie Munro created the following tips for what *not* to do in an audition:

- Don't direct, rewrite the copy, or point out any mistakes unless you've worked with this client in the past and know it's safe to do so.

  Each of these traits are taking away someone else's job and putting you in charge. You're in charge of the choices you make, but ultimately it's the clients/directors who are in charge, so know your place in the room.

- Don't come in with only one choice prepared; always have a backup plan.

- Don't ask to redo something if they are saying they are fine with what you did.

- Don't apologize.

  This is a big pet peeve among directors — in fact they often bet on how many times an actor apologizes in an audition.

- Don't come into the audition with a closed mind and not willing to make different adjustments or choices.

- Don't ask what the client wants with this character.

  This part is your job, and you're supposed to know. After all, you're the expert, right?

- Don't draw attention to or point out your mistakes.

  Just make mistakes in character, have fun with them, laugh them off, and keep on going. If you need to pick it up again and redo it if it was a very obvious mistake, do so.

- Don't worry about all you have to do when the engineer is trying to adjust your microphone.

- Don't be too chatty or a distraction; make sure you are there and focused and paying close attention.

Abiding by studio etiquette

When it comes to studio sessions and voice actors, recording engineers and studio owners have seen it all. How should voice actors behave themselves in a studio session?

If you've ever wondered how to behave at a recording studio, especially if it's your first studio session, follow these tips:

- ✔ Before you book for your first session, be sure to rehearse your scripts in advance. Being prepared will save you time in the studio and money while affirming your professionalism.

- ✔ When you arrive at the studio for the first time, be sure to properly introduce yourself. Building a good business relationship starts as soon as you make your first contact. Building a relationship with a local studio is a must if you don't have your own home studio.

- ✔ Don't bring food into the studio. A water bottle is the exception and even then, it's advisable to ask the recording engineer if he minds if you bring your water bottle into the recording booth.

- ✔ Bring a pencil with you to the session for taking notes on the script.

- ✔ Don't touch the microphone; let the recording engineer adjust it for you.

- ✔ Don't tell the client what to do.

Remember that this isn't the time to give a headshot or your demo. Something you can do though is write a quick thank you note after the session and include your demo CD with the receptionist after the session so the director can receive it afterward.

Interacting with the Recording Equipment

When you come to a professional audio recording studio, keep in mind that the equipment you're using costs tens of thousands of dollars if not more. Not terribly long ago, it was the norm for a full out studio to have $1 million invested in equipment. Although recording equipment has come down in price, it's still pricey and as such, engineers are extremely protective of their gear, which for most was a handsome investment.

Microphones

Not touching the microphone is an industry-wide standard that recording engineers expect you to understand. While it isn't necessarily an unwritten code, voice actors who've had any degree of training or professional experience know that touching and/or adjusting the microphone isn't their responsibility. You'll find that because microphones in professional recording studios cost a pretty penny, the only person who should be touching them is the engineer or studio owner if skilled in this area.

When you step up to the microphone to speak, the audio engineer may ask you to give a level. This means that he wants to hear your voice projected into the microphone so that he can appreciate how he will need to work with your voice and how it is being picked up through the signal chain. The signal chain, covered in Chapter 18, is the route that your voice takes once it leaves your mouth, enters the microphone, goes through the microphone cable, and ultimately ends up in the recording software.

The engineer may ask you to stay where you are so that he can adjust the microphone for you. At any rate, when you are asked to give a level, just deliver a line from the script in the voice and volume level that you are going to use when you read. The engineer doesn't want any surprises, which is why he or she will ask. Knowing how loudly or quietly you will voice gives the engineer the opportunity to set his controls accordingly. Whatever you do, don't say "Testing, testing, 1, 2, 3." Doing that will not only sound silly but let the engineer and the client know that you are an inexperienced voice actor and have much to learn about how the business works.

While it may seem to be common sense not to give a level saying "testing, testing . . . ", most recording engineers can appreciate that a significant number of voice actors have not as of yet mastered microphone technique and have more patience for actors in this area. The engineer understands far more than any visiting voice actor would about his equipment, studio environment, and its characteristics, so it is better to trust his judgment when it comes to the equipment and how you're using it.

Once you are properly positioned, your voice will be on-axis, meaning that you are in the best stance possible for your voice to be picked up cleanly and clearly by the microphone, highlighting the timber of your voice. When picked up this way, your voice should sound like it is at its absolute best. Some people call this finding the sweet spot on your microphone. You should know where you voice sounds best on a microphone at your own studio, but doing so on a microphone you've never used before can be tricky.

After you master it, this skill is particularly useful when you go into a studio and are unfamiliar with the studio microphone they have in the booth.

Knowing your microphone technique is critical if you want to enjoy a long, wonderfully sonorous and happy career, especially when working with other professionals in the business. Over time, finding that sweet spot becomes rather instinctive. When you start to work with a variety of microphones and experiment with how your voice sounds behind the microphone, your sessions will progress more smoothly, your comfort level will increase, and the better your microphone technique will become.

The bottom line when figuring out how to use a microphone you're unfamiliar with is to trust the engineer. He will walk you through where to stand, explain how to project, and how you things you can do to make your audition or studio session more successful.

A few other elements equipment-wise may come into play in the booth, such as headphones, music stand, stool, and the pop filter. We cover the pop filter in greater detail, but first address headphones and music stands.

Headphones

When you think of headphones, you may get the iconic mental picture of a voice actor standing in the booth ala Gary Owens cupping his ear with one hand and leaning into the microphone. Cupping one's ear does give you a better appreciation for how your voice is coming across to others, but more often than not, you're going to have a pair of "cans," or headphones as they're more commonly referred to, to help you hear yourself better.

If you aren't used to wearing headphones, this may take some getting used to. If the engineer asks you to wear them or you choose to, you'll also go through a testing exercise to make sure that the sound is coming through on your end and that it's balanced. The engineer controls the volume.

Music stands

The music stand serves as a resting place and platform for the script to sit. The stand should be at eye level and positioned in a spot where you can see it. The objective of any voice actor is to stay on script, so you need to be sure you can easily see the script from where you are in terms of the microphone so that your read isn't compromised.

Pop filters

Do you remember what it sounds like when someone pops their Ps or Bs on a live microphone? Perhaps memories of school assemblies, church services, or public announcements come to mind. Whenever select consonants cause that kind of "pop," which are called *plosives,* you can be almost certain that a pop filter was nowhere to be found! Nearly every photograph I've seen of a voice actor at the microphone during a studio session has been accompanied by a pop filter.

A *pop filter* is the screen that separates you and your voice from the microphone. This little fence as it were helps to let your voice go through to the microphone without popping plosives and instead softens letters like Ps and Bs. A pop filter can also help you to cut down on *sibilance* (the hissing noise that can come from overly apparent S sounds). Using a pop filter cuts out issues on both the high end and the low end, making for easier editing of the recording. In our opinion, the pop filter is a beautiful thing and does have its place. Pop filters are used by voice actors and singers alike to help achieve the best possible performance.

Tricks you can use for avoiding plosives include

- ✔ Smiling through your words
- ✔ Putting a pencil in front of your mouth
- ✔ Cutting the air in half by speaking with your face turned down a bit
- ✔ Speaking across the microphone instead of directly into it

Some things you should never do to a microphone include

- ✔ Blowing into it
- ✔ Tapping it
- ✔ Yelling directly into it
- ✔ Spilling any fluids on it

Interacting with the Casting Director

A casting director, specifically a voice-over casting director, is someone who has an ear for picking the best candidate for a particular job. It's the casting director's responsibility to "cast" the right person in a role for a client who usually has little interest or ability, or lacks the confidence to "pick" the right voice to represent his company, project, or brand. The casting director wants to get the best possible performance out of an auditioning actor.

The following sections take a closer look at what the casting director's roles are, what he asks of voice actors during auditions, and what you can do to decipher a casting director's direction, particularly when he asks you to voice match.

Identifying the casting director's job

The casting director should make a voice actor feel at ease because he needs to evaluate all his options in the best light to pick the most appropriate voice for the client's campaign or project. A casting director charges a fee to the client for his time and expertise.

Casting directors cast for a variety of projects including commercials, movies, animated films, cartoons, and more. Although the casting director may appear intimidating, it's in the best interest of the casting director to solicit the best possible performance from each performer who auditions for a role.

Voice casting is an art. The casting director needs to be familiar with the project he's casting, the audience that will be consuming the production, and also how that audience needs to be communicated to. In essence, the casting director is a voice actor's friend, just as a voice-over coach and recording engineer are.

A casting director has a huge responsibility placed on his shoulders not only to cast the best candidate but also to treat each person who walks in the door with the utmost respect, which helps him keep an open mind when casting for a particular role, voice-over, or shot.

Sometimes, a casting director is responsible for casting an entire voice acting cast for cartoon series, animated films, video games, and audiobooks. These projects are especially interesting and challenging for a casting director because there's so much to consider, including how the voices match each other, how a voice fits a role, whether the voice actors have good chemistry, and whether their voices fit the ideal that their client is looking for.

Giving you direction

The casting or voice director may want to know about how you interpret the script. He may or may not be interested in knowing ahead of time though, so just go ahead and give it your best shot.

A voice director or casting director often helps to oversee the audition; he'll more than likely give you some artistic or creative direction to play around with when giving your read. This experience can be exciting and productive or painful and stressful, depending on how you respond to what's being required.

When the director goes into a casting, he wants the actor to take direction, interpret the script, stay in character, and get the job done. Don't get frustrated; ask for clarifications for anything that may not be clear. Even if bridging the gap means asking the director to give you a "line read," don't be afraid to request more guidance. Your read and perhaps your chances of landing the role depend heavily upon your understanding what is being asked of you as a voice actor.

A *line read* is when a director demonstrates the delivery of a scripted line the way he envisions the actor to read it on stage or in the booth. Line reads, most often used with child voice actors, can also be effective tools for directors to use with grownups. Never be offended if a director gives you a line read, and don't be afraid to ask for one if necessary.

The director may present you with sides. A *side* is a description of a character and tells you about who the character is, what the character is like, how old the character is, and other bits of information that can help you to fortify your read and give a well-thought-out interpretation.

Remember that you are in a creative space, and the people there want to see you succeed.

Asking you to sound like someone else

This information is particularly applicable to an auditioning situation. Typically, voice actors know these things ahead of a recording. You never know, though, when something may be thrown at you from out of left field, so being able to have a number of voices in your back pocket is helpful.

You may receive direction during a recording that the director (or client) wants someone who sounds like a famous person. (Other times you'll already have known this from the information you received from the client after being hired, and you'll have plenty of time to prepare.) No matter when you receive it, rest assured that the director doesn't really want that person or even someone who sounds like the famous person.

What the director is often looking for is a voice actor who, when standing in front of the mic ready to record, can replicate a famous person's speech pattern. In other words, the director is asking you to voice match. *Voice matching* is mimicking the speech pattern and vocal characteristics of someone else in order to sound like him or her. The following sections provide some concrete hands-on information that you can use if you have time to prepare and a director asks you to sound like someone else. (If you don't have the time, do what you can in the moment and ask for some direction if necessary.)

Figuring out how to voice match: The how-to

Even the best sound-a-like voice actors can't consistently replicate someone's voice and way of speaking. Everyone has a unique voiceprint, but you can certainly study the person and figure out how to deliver your lines in the style of someone else.

Your voice, like your fingerprints, is distinct. Although every person has a voice, the human voice is very unique, and that uniqueness sets you apart from everyone else. Consider the following factors when you are trying to voice match:

- ✔ **Voice type:** *Voice type* refers to what we commonly accept as the four main voice classifications — soprano, alto, tenor and bass. Singers recognize different classifications or *fachs* within the four broad categories of voice type; for instance, there is a big difference between a coloratura soprano and a mezzo soprano. If you're going to match the voice of someone, you'll want to make sure that you have a similar vocal range (voicing comfortably) and fall under the same category regarding voice type.

- ✔ **Age:** When voice matching, you need to consider how old the person you're trying to match sounds, not necessarily how old he is in terms of years. The closer your voice is in how old it sounds to how old the person you are mimicking sounds, the closer and more believable your match will be. For instance, if you're a teenager trying to mimic another teenager whose voice age is similar to your own, you'll be a closer match than someone whose voice sounds older trying to sound like a teen.

- ✔ **Register:** *Register* is a series of tones created in a particular range of voice. You have three vocal registers — the chest voice, middle voice, and head voice. Most voice actors speak from the mid-range, bridging chest with head voice. This middle voice is called the *pharyngeal voice.*

- ✔ **Timber:** *Timber* is usually what people mean when they try to describe how a voice sounds. *Tone quality* and *color* are synonyms for timber, often described as bright, dark, light, clear, and so on. Timber refers to the tone quality or resonance that distinguishes your voice from similar instruments.

- ✔ **Accent:** The accent refers to where a person sounds like he is from. If you're trying to sound like someone from New York for instance, you need to study the accent and pay close attention to how he shapes his vowels, where he places emphasis on individual words, and so on.

✔ **Intonation:** You may have noticed that most people's voices in North America rise in pitch when they're asking a question. This is just one way that people intone. *Intonation* in general has to do with raising or lowering your voice in pitch. This falling or rising in pitch communicates meaning and colors how the listener receives what is being said.

✔ **Speaking patterns:** When you speak, there is a bit of a rhythm to how your voice is paced, how and where you choose to use inflection, and just how much of your vocal range you use. When trying to sound like someone else, take note of how he uses his instrument, not just how his instrument sounds. When asked to sound like a particular person, like say, James Earl Jones, you really just need to sound close enough to him in terms of how he speaks.

✔ **Mannerisms:** Depending on who you're trying to sound like, mimicking vocal mannerisms can be something as simple as how someone breathes, how someone clears her throat, and so on. Maybe it's adding in a word or short vocal utterance that she always says, like "huh," "got it," "um hmm," "capiche?," or "eh."

✔ **Placement:** Placement is important because vocal placement determines how the voice sounds. If you speak out of your nose, you sound more nasal. Try speaking "through" different parts of your face to see how your sound changes. When mimicking someone, you need to know where her placement is to match the sound and tone she produces.

✔ **Physicality:** Try to copy the way the person you're mimicking postures himself and incorporate hand gestures or facial expressions that may help you to re-create his sound. The closer you are in terms of physical appearance, voice type, and age to the person you're mimicking, the better your impression of him may be because your instruments are similar.

After considering these factors and the person the director wants you to sound like, you can get an even closer match, based upon more than just the quality and range of a voice. Sometimes you just need to go ahead and experiment to see if you can do the person's voice.

Discerning and developing an historical character with voice matching

Trying to put a voice to someone who lived long ago is difficult, especially if no recordings are available of the person's voice, video footage, or photographs to base an interpretation on. Even so, casting for roles like this happens all the time when epic films are made or documentaries are produced, featuring people who lived in a time before multimedia.

When your director asks you to reconstruct an historical figure and you don't have a voice sample to refer to, you often need to figure out on your own how to make this character. The following tips can help you voice match when you don't have anything to reference. These tips also help you create additional layers and depth to your character's personality.

- ✔ **Study personal accounts and follow patterns in the person's transcribed speech or writing style.** Getting to know the person through his own writings or speeches can give you a greater understanding of how he spoke and provide you with good material to practice with. You can also compare and contrast those writings with what you're being asked to read to see how close the script is to what the person would have actually said.

- ✔ **Go back to the script or historical document for clues regarding his age, demeanor, physicality, and vocal timber.** Some of these details may be self-evident because you know the story of that person so well. Even little tidbits of information can help you form the character and more believably perform his voice.

- ✔ **Observe the person's physical appearance as depicted in photographs or paintings.** Look for details that may tell you something about his speech. For example, focus on things such as missing teeth, a clenched jaw, a broken nose, a foreign object in his mouth such as a cigar, and so on.

- ✔ **Identify where the person came from and consider known speech characteristics or accents from that geographic location.** If you can pinpoint where the person hailed from and are able to amass information about the language he spoke during that time, you may be able to track down voice samples of people speaking in that language in the style of the day to help you with your interpretation.

- ✔ **Read accounts made by people who knew or interacted with the person in question.** Doing so can reveal aspects of that person's personality and his deeper convictions. Even if the source of the writings was a hostile one, the admission of a fact decidedly not in his favor proves the genuineness of that fact and helps you when understanding and better appreciating the person you're re-creating.

- ✔ **Collect adjectives that have been used to describe the person's personality and temperament.** What you find may surprise you! The film *Lincoln,* featuring actor Daniel Day-Lewis as US President Abraham Lincoln, is a great example of how the studious Day-Lewis based his Abraham Lincoln voice on first-hand historical accounts indicating that Lincoln's voice was higher pitched and slightly shrill instead of the deep and rich Lincoln voice that culture often presents us with.

You may be able to find that you can apply these tools when addressing artistic direction for creating voices for character roles in cartoons, audiobooks, and many other types of voice acting jobs.

Maintaining eye contact

You may not realize it, but the casting director or recording engineer can be your greatest ally in the booth. They're responsible for leading you through a session and ensuring that you achieve the best performance possible. When things go well, working together can be a satisfying experience for you both.

Eye contact can convey encouragement and let you know that you're on the right track. Sometimes eye contact is all you have because the casting director or engineer may not want to interrupt you mid-take. Using eye contact helps to build trust between you and whoever is directing you. Maintaining good eye contact is also beneficial to you for gauging how your performance is being received.

Considering alternative roles

How many voices do you have at the ready? In Chapter 11, we talked about how you can prepare a few different styles of read to give prospective clients and casting directors options to choose from when casting. The skills you may develop just right may come in handy for auditions where the casting director wants to see what you've got!

If directors are more of the "I'll know it when I hear it," mindset, the extra effort you put forth to create more interpretations may truly help them "find" the voice that they were looking for. Sometimes it's what we aren't looking for that ends up being exactly what we never knew we needed and/or wanted. The same applies in casting for voice-overs.

Having a few base voices that you work with also helps. If a director calls on you to try out for a character that you didn't anticipate auditioning for, draw on similar characters that you have voiced or developed character sketches for independently.

Even though it may be nerve-racking, you should give it a try. What's the worst thing that can happen? It would be better to try something and allow the director to shape your attempts than to pass on an opportunity because you feel incompetent or unprepared. Some of the greatest roles have been cast to voice actors who didn't come expecting to audition for the roles they were given.

Having Fun While Building Relationships

If there's anything clients like to hear, it's about why you want to work for them and what motivates you to make their project a success. They want to know why you love them, why you love their product, or why you love their service. Essentially, they want to know why you love them so much that you would go to the extreme of publicly representing their company and being their voice.

Does the company evoke memories from childhood? Do you use their products? Have you ever been to one of their events? Are you in love with their brand?

Even though the audition is a time for getting down to business and staying on message, conversations had in the green room or with the casting crew can present opportunities for you to add another layer to the process and make inroads with people in a position of influence.

In this section, you grab hold of how your personality can book you a job, why engaging with the staff at an audition or recording facility matters, and how to leave an audition on a high note.

Letting the real you shine through

Casting directors want you to shine. The more at ease you are, the likelier they are going to receive a bang on audition from you and have something to work with when deliberating with their team. When you think about it, being the real you helps the casting director do her job because she's working with the genuine article. Completing her job successfully depends on getting you to bring the most amazing, spot-on read possible. It's in her best interest to warm up to your personality and help guide you through the audition.

Be sincere, personable, and respectful. If she provides you direction, take it! Show her that you can be directed, that you're able to listen, and also that you can improvise.

Whenever you choose to honor your values, you're being authentic, credible, and have a greater purpose for what you're doing or contributing to. If you truly believe in what you're saying and speak with conviction, the read will come across with indisputable honesty and be beneficial to a prospective client and to your customers.

Each decision you make affects you and those around you. Just as a raindrop lands on the waters and causes a ripple to spread, so do your actions, making an impact on those around you and on others beyond your community.

Engaging the staff

When you go to a recording studio for the first time to work with their crew, you can make a good first impression in a number of ways so that you're asked back again. (See the earlier section "Heeding Some Tips for Professionalism.") But the casting director isn't the only person who holds some kind of influence at a casting. Remember that everyone from the receptionist to the casting director's assistant plays an important role in the success and outcome of the day.

Everyone — from the person making the coffee to the assistant taking notes has a distinct role as each candidate steps up to the microphone. You never know what type of influence each person carries beyond the casting.

Anyone from interns to assistants may one day start his or her own casting house or talent agency. If you're consistently kind to everyone you meet and appreciative of their gifts, you'll make more friends and contacts that may benefit you in ways you never anticipated. Remember, people may forget what you say, but they'll never forget how you made them feel.

Leaving on a high note

Saying thank you never goes out of style. In an industry that is short on gratitude, showing appreciation for opportunities, especially for an audition, doesn't go unnoticed. Make eye contact and thank everyone in sight to express how much you enjoyed the session.

After you go home, write a thank you note to the person who invited you to the casting call to let him know how much you appreciated the opportunity. If it was an agent who sent you, be grateful for his willingness to include you. Mail the card to the person(s) and be sure to include a business card so he remembers who you are.

Part IV
Setting Up Your Voice Acting Business

The 5th Wave   By Rich Tennant

Airwave
Voice Talent Agency

"I can do a caring mother of three or a menacing specter from the gates of Hell. In fact, the menacing specter voice came as a result of being a mother of three."

In this part . . .

*V*oice acting can be a lot of fun, but it's also a business and a way to make money. Understanding how to properly run a business is key to experiencing ongoing, quantifiable success as a professional voice actor. In this part, you discover what you need to know about how to set up your business, what you should consider when building your brand, what to charge for your services, and how to obtain payment after you've been hired to record.

When you treat what you do as a real business, you'll be more eager to develop your craft and invest in your career.

Chapter 14

Working after You've Booked a Voice-Over Job

*Y*ou've booked the job, so now what? When it comes to working on a real voice-over job, you need to be aware of certain things like how to communicate and interact with clients. Understanding simple things like expectations and the like will lay the right foundation for a successful experience and a great relationship that could result in ongoing work.

In this chapter, we walk you step by step through working with clients in both online marketplace settings and jobs you've secured working at a local recording studio. You get a taste of what you should expect, how to communicate professionally, how to handle contracts and non-disclosure agreements, and also what to do for your business if you get sick, are too busy to take on more work, or are on vacation.

Understanding the Hiring Process

Some people like to know what will happen before it does, and don't like to be taken by surprise. Knowing the ropes ahead of time creates more confidence and security when it comes to booking that first job. Say goodbye, anxiety!

This section may be of particular interest to you if you appreciate having as much information as possible when it comes to doing business in the online marketplace for the first time.

Working in an online voice-over marketplace

When you have your own business, you come to realize that you must look after some basic needs and objectives . . . most significantly, marketing your talent and positioning yourself for opportunities to earn money.

Generating leads, prospecting, developing relationships, and earning the business of others isn't easy. This is where an online marketplace provides you with the tools, opportunities, and resources you need to prosper online as a professional voice actor. An online marketplace does the heavy lifting, which includes attracting clientele, attending to their needs, vetting jobs, posting jobs, and then inviting you to audition for opportunities that you're qualified for based on your profile and preferences.

An audition online, as we discuss in Chapter 12, puts you front and center with the client and affords you a means to introduce yourself to him in a safe and welcome environment. Remember, the client wanted to hear from you . . . this isn't a cold call!

One of the most exciting aspects of working with clients via the online marketplace is that everything has the potential to happen quickly. From the audition to being awarded a job, the process could take as little as a matter of hours. Most voice actors perceive auditioning to be the real work, and booking a job is gravy. Many online marketplaces also typically facilitate everything from the audition through getting paid.

Working in an in-studio environment

When you go to a recording studio to voice a job, much of the work you need to take care of yourself is managed by the studio, given it brought you in and you didn't book the job on your own. Working in a professional recording studio harkens back to days when voice actors went from studio to studio to simply perform voice-over jobs they had booked. Voice actors at that point in time were only required to provide the artistic and had next to nothing to do with the actual technical process. In order to work consistently, most voice actors had to commute through the concrete jungle of Los Angeles from job to job.

The late, great Don LaFontaine used to have his own limousine and driver for this purpose. He arrived in his white limo and got to work. This was before it was standard practice to work from a home-based recording studio. It wasn't unusual for Don to take aspiring voice actors to sessions with him on ride-alongs to give them a glimpse into the glamorous world of voice-over that he and those in his small circle of peers enjoyed.

When it comes to studio sessions and voice actors, recording engineers and studio owners have seen it all. How should voice actors behave themselves in a studio session?

When working in-studio, respect the space and most importantly, don't touch the microphone. New voice actors may be tempted to touch the microphone to adjust its positioning, so be forewarned that doing so isn't a good idea. If you need the microphone to be moved, ask the recording engineer to assist you. Taking direction well and keeping to the script are all expectations the crew in the studio will have of you. When you're done, you're done! They will let you know when they are satisfied with your work.

Some things you may want to bring with you to the studio are a water bottle, your pencil, an open mind, and a smile. For more information on studio etiquette, flip to Chapter 13.

Is the customer always right?

The person doing the hiring or directing is your customer, and in many circles, the adage of "The Customer is Always Right" applies.

This could go one of two ways:

1. The client appears to be insatiable and requests more takes.
2. The client likes your work even though you think you could've done better or that someone else was better qualified.

In big league voice acting, it isn't uncommon for a director to request a minimum of 20 takes to get the perfect delivery, so it would make sense that other clients may have the expectation that two or three takes may just be scraping the surface of your talent and ability to take direction.

Although interpreting feedback during a session as criticism may be a natural response, it isn't the healthiest thing, and you have to remember that the director is only trying to communicate his vision through your voice by doing business with you.

Check your ego at the door

If you're able to separate your feelings from the work, any feedback you receive will come as creative direction or a way of trying the same thing a different way, not as a personal insult. Make sense? Remember, if the client likes it, don't offer to do more or question the logic.

If the client needs to take a little while to realize the vision through your voice, enjoy the ride. Make it a game if you have to and use each take as an opportunity to freely explore parts of your voice you may not have known before. While this may be a lot of fun, always remember that you are there to provide a service and remain professional. I think you'll agree that it's more enjoyable (and perhaps less labor-intensive) than most jobs out there!

Communicating with Your Client

Do you know how to communicate well? Depending on how you book a job, you can communicate with your client in different ways. Regardless of tools and options, make sure you present yourself well, are considerate, and affirm your client and the progress of the job whenever possible.

Speak to the best interests of the project and don't say things that could be misinterpreted as disagreeable or ambiguous. Always be clear with what you're saying and quick to resolve misunderstandings.

In this section, you get some tips for conversing with your client, including how to set the tone for a great business relationship, understanding expectations, and keeping lines of communication open.

Setting the tone

People do business with people they like. What happens when we place more significance on ourselves and how we perform than on the message and the people it is intended for? When more emphasis is placed on your gifts and ability to shine instead of on why you're called to be of service in the first place, the doing becomes more about the superiority of your gifts than the purpose which, as you can imagine, often yields detrimental results.

In order to set the right tone, you can do many simple things, such as having a good attitude, smiling, and being grateful. Smiles, like yawns, are contagious. Note also that smiling, even if at first it's a forced act, will eventually morph into an authentic smile and serve as a great pick-me-up for when you're feeling tired or discouraged.

When you smile, your body releases chemicals in your brain called endorphins and serotonin, often referred to as "happy" hormones. In a nutshell, smiling simply makes you feel good.

Last but certainly not least is to have an attitude of gratitude. Any number of voice actors were talented enough to do what you're doing, but for some reason, your audition was chosen. Be grateful.

Understanding expectations

A clear understanding of your goals and how you reach them together should be set. Fewer if any issues arise when everyone knows what's expected of them. Items that may require special attention in this regard are

- Creative direction
- Communicating the script properly
- The cost
- When the client needs the audio

Not knowing what's expected of you can cause an enormous amount of stress and confusion, so if you have any questions or something doesn't seem very clear to you, ask for clarification early on and pick up the phone if you have to.

Keeping lines of communication open

Keeping in contact regularly with the client after your job is over helps open lines of communication. While you don't need to send annual gifts marking your first business deal, you should be considerate of all you've worked to build and let your partners know that you appreciate them. Ways you may communicate with your client include

- Email
- Internal messaging
- Telephone
- Skype

Reviewing the Full and Final Script

Before you take the leap to record, review the final script to make sure that there haven't been any changes or additional text added for you to record. In this section, we cover going over the script, figuring how much work there is, and how long it may take you to record the voice-over and make any edits.

Evaluating the script

Typically, you'll have the full script before agreeing to do a voice-over job, but in the case of some projects, such as an audiobook, for instance, you may receive that script after you've already committed to being its narrator. In rare cases, you may be in for a surprise or two depending on how forthright the client was with the amount of work required or the contents of a script. If those issues exist, you need to discuss them with your client preferably before the recording process starts. You may need to submit a new quote for the work or ask that a word here and there that you take offense to (such as a swear word) be changed in the script.

If everything looks great to you, it's time to dig into the script. Ask yourself the same questions found in Chapter 5 having to do with analyzing a script and developing your character. You also need to gain an understanding of context so far as it relates to your role(s). Marking up your script is another way that you can document your findings.

Determining how much work there is

How long will it take to get through a script? Knowing this is important because time is money. Remember also that it takes twice as long to edit a voice-over as it did to record it in the first place. Our friends at Edge Studio, a voice-over education and production facility with coaches around the United States, provided this resource to our community for helping voice actors better gauge how much work there is in a given script.

This chart is based on: 12 point Arial, double-spaced, margin-to-margin.

- ✔ Speech count
  - Average person reads three words per second (range is two to four)
  - Average person reads 88 words per half-minute (range is 60 to 120)
  - Average person reads 170 words per minute (range is 135 to 215)
  - Average person reads 10,320 words per hour (range is 8,625 to 12,030)
- ✔ Line count
  - Average number of lines per page: 21
  - Average number of lines per 30-second spot: 7.5
  - Average number of lines per 60-second spot: 15

✔ Word count

- Average words per line: 13 (range is 8 to 18)

- Average words per page: 273 (range is 168 to 378)

✔ Reading time

- Average reading time per line: 4 seconds

- Average reading time per page: 85 seconds

The preceding list breaks down the information a number of ways to help you figure out the script's length and how long it may take for you to voice. The first category, speech count, tells you how many words an average person is able to read on a word per second, word per minute, and word per hour basis. This information is particularly helpful if you have a large word count and don't know how long it will take for you to record the script. Line counts are also helpful, as are word counts and reading time. Knowing how long it will take you to voice a given script can help you to quote for projects faster and more easily. To discover more about quoting and getting paid for your work, flip to Chapter 15.

Should you charge for audio editing?

Shorter recordings, such as voice mails or commercials, may not be of much consequence editing-wise where your time is concerned, but what if you were requested to edit longer projects? Shouldn't there be a fee for editing levied, too? Indeed there should! Think about the time you need to record the script and then double that time to gain an appreciation for the length of the editing process.

Although the answer may seem obvious, many voice actors working today have adopted the mindset that the recording of a voice-over and the editing of that voice-over are one in the same. This is simply *not* the case, and if you were to believe that, you'd be doing a lot of work for free! Review Chapter 16 for more information on quoting for your work.

If you were to go to a professional recording studio, you'd discover that it often charges separate fees for editing, mixing, and mastering. Editing in general takes twice as long (if not longer in some cases) as the time it takes to record the voice-over itself.

Asking any questions you have about the script

You need to cover all the questions you have about the script before you sign off on voicing it. These questions may include what direction to take your read, how to pronounce unfamiliar names, or when to request clarification on how the client wants you to send the finished work.

You also may need to ask how certain words are read. For instance, if you have to read numbers out or read web addresses, you may want to double-check on how to do that. When considering how to say a domain name, is it "www dot" or "triple w dot?"

Sometimes your questions may be more technical in nature when it pertains to the recording itself. For example, if the job is for a telephone system, you may need to break the files down into prompts, giving each part of the telephone system its own file, such as the auto-attendant, interactive voice response(IVR), any messaging-on-hold, and voicemail boxes.

Finalizing the Agreement

As with any business contract or arrangement, make sure you have a work agreement as well as a schedule for payment, including the estimated delivery date. On some online marketplace sites, such as Voices.com, you can include work agreements when you're finalizing terms.

Some professionals are hesitant to use contracts because they feel clients will feel offended or sense a lack of trust. In actuality, using a contract protects both the voice actor and client from misunderstandings or unmet expectations. The key is to present the contract as a customary and beneficial tool to the client instead of as a legal weapon for ensuring payment. It's all how you present it. The agreement describes the work you provide to the client, when to expect delivery of the audio files, the level of service you provide, and how payment is arranged for your services.

Viewing the job offer

After a client selects you to record the voice-over, your next step is view the job offer. Larger projects are often broken up into smaller, more manageable pieces with their own deadlines. These are often referred to as *milestones* and include

✔ A deliverable (what's to be sent to the client)

✔ A payment (the amount you're paid for delivering the goods)

✔ A deadline (when the due date is for the deliverable)

Accepting the work agreement

A *work agreement* describes your services and outlines the price, turnaround time, delivery method (for instances where it may not be a file upload), number of edits, file format, and so on. After a client has accepted your work agreement, you can move ahead with recording the voice-over. Not all clients will expect a work agreement, but you, as the professional voice actor, should be prepared to present your clients with one.

Signing a nondisclosure agreement

If you've been in voice-over for any length of time and are doing well, you may have run across situations where your client has made you sign a nondisclosure agreement (NDA) or advised you not to share that you are the voice of the campaign, product, or company.

Although you may have had to sign one, have you ever thought about why you were asked to and what the motivation behind that request was?

In the voice-over industry, a lot of high-profile work goes without credit in a public sense. Perhaps allowing people to guess at who did the voice does more for a company than actually confirming who voiced the project because it kept the brand and commercial alive in discussions on the topic.

In some instances NDAs are used to keep something under the radar, including the script's contents, in order to protect someone or a particular group. For example, the expert panel discussion at a voice conference where a friend had recorded voice-overs for a branch of law enforcement specific to prison guard training. By not revealing the contents of that script or potentially the artist's name, an entire profession is protected because that information isn't disclosed.

Sometimes NDAs are used from a competitive standpoint, hiding the identity of the voice actor, producing an incognito voice-over as a result. One example is how the Republican Party, during John McCain's run for the presidency in 2008, chose to conceal the identity of the campaign voice "Joan," stating that her identity was a corporate secret.

You may find that you're not bound to an NDA legally, but many times, there is still an air of, "We'd rather you didn't promote the fact that you recorded this," which makes you hesitant to claim the work as your own or mention it in detail on your resume. While there are no technical or legal restrictions, you may feel bound by your desire to keep working for the client and agree to not list them among your recent customers. By not openly revealing who did the voices for something, a company may be trying to maintain an air of mystique, or perhaps, magic.

If you find none of these examples to be the case but you still weren't credited for the work (assuming it would've been reasonable to do so), there is reason to follow up and see if it was an oversight. Recently, we reviewed an audio-book that on first glance had hidden tracks. To our delight, we excitedly wrote about the extra material that we considered to be a bonus and contacted the voice actor to congratulate her on her work, only to find out that she, although featured narrating four tracks on the CD, had no idea that her work had gone without credit on the CD packaging and on the publisher's website. This product had also been nominated for a Grammy! After this realization, she decided to follow up with the producers to inquire to see if it was indeed an oversight. Considering her talent and involvement in the project, we sincerely hope that it was an oversight.

Planning for Contingencies

Inevitably, you won't be able to do every job that comes your way. But what do you do when you're sick, on vacation, or too busy to take on a voice-over job with a tight deadline? Instead of just passing on the gig, how about applying some thought to creative solutions that will still help you to serve that client and be perceived as helpful.

This section covers specific instances of when you need a contingency plan for getting the job done. But in general, follow these tips:

- ✔ Make a list of backup actors you can refer just in case the need arises.
- ✔ Create a client account at Voices.com in case you need to outsource the voice-over job.
- ✔ Instead of simply turning your client away with nothing, make a recommendation or cast someone in your stead.

  This process helps clients achieve their goals and meet their present needs. They'll appreciate it and find value in your creative problem-solving skills.

What to do if you're sick

Being sick isn't fun, especially if it means that you have to pass on work opportunities. If illness affects the desired timber of your voice or quality of performance, it really is in the best interest of your vocal health (and your business) to use your time wisely to rest, heal, and build up energy reserves.

Some voice-over actors may say that their voices are still in demand when they're sick; however, if you do record and speak when your voice should be resting, you may find that you set yourself back in the healing process, thereby prolonging or worsening your illness.

Some actors give discounts if they are in poor voice but still want to do the job. The thinking behind this is that you aren't at your best and you also won't be able to replicate that sound as easily again. The choice is up to you, but keep your voice and health in mind when making that choice!

What to do if you're on vacation

Everyone needs to take a break, right? If you have plans to go away for a vacation, there are a couple of things you should do well in advance of your trip that will make your getaway more relaxing and less inconvenient for your regular clients.

One idea is to write an email newsletter that you send to your client list. Many voice actors do this a couple of weeks in advance of the date they're leaving. By letting your customers know you'll be unavailable well in advance, you can give them a much needed heads-up and also the opportunity to record before you leave. This results in grateful customers and can also lead to an influx in work for you prior to your vacation.

For those of you who have regular gigs and need to deliver regardless of where you are (even if you're vacationing), consider these recommendations:

- Make contact with a fully equipped recording studio in the city you're visiting.
- Bring a portable recording studio with you (laptop, microphone, and so on).
- If recording in your hotel room, insulate the "studio" area well using pillows or heavy blankets, such as a comforter or duvet, to block out extra noise. You can drape blankets over yourself and your recording area to further insulate the area.
- Ensure that your Internet connection is sufficient to deliver large files.

In the event that you take your gear on the road, which is becoming more common among voice acting professionals, you can squeeze in emergency recording sessions from just about anywhere, given you have the right tools with you and can record in a suitable environment. Hotel rooms are great places to record, what with all those pillows and comforters you can use to soundproof with.

Some voice actors manage to record remotely while on vacation and use their vehicles as mobile recording studios. You may not have thought about it before, but the inside of a car can block out a lot of noise, and its upholstery can help create a good buffer zone between you and your microphone and critters in the great outdoors.

What to do if you're too busy

On some days you may be booked with back-to-back sessions. If you also teach, produce, or consult, in addition to voice acting, this could be even truer. In a given day, you're auditioning, promoting your voice, recording work, and juggling any number of other responsibilities. So it's likely that a day may come where you're simply too busy to take on a project.

Instead of simply saying no and leaving the client stranded and without a voice, refer another voice actor who you believe could do the job instead. In order to do so, you need to have built a network of your peers (other voice actors you trust) who can step in and do the job just as well as you could. We recommend that you find one or two people who you know have a voice and capabilities similar to your own. The client may want to work with you because of your voice age, voice type, or accent. Of course, you'll also want to have a few people's names on hand who have voices decidedly not like your own in voice type, gender, accent, voice age, and so on, in case your client asks you to manage or produce a project with multiple voices. Something else that may be helpful in this instance is to have a voice sample of theirs on hand and to know how much those voice actors charge for their services. This way, you have their rates right on hand and will know who might be the best fit for a client in a pinch.

Taking a job that you can't reasonably fulfill by the client's deadline sends the wrong message, wastes the client's time, and also gives the client a poor impression of your talent. In that regard, be selective and only take on work that you're confident you'll be able to complete on time. Should the opportunity arise to refer a fellow voice actor, pay it forward and present the opportunity to someone who you know can do the job.

Working On Multiple Jobs at Once

If you find yourself in a situation where you're juggling multiple jobs at the same time, make sure to use good judgment and only schedule in work that you know you're capable of doing in a professional and timely manner. Other tips include

- Finding a good way to budget your time
- Keeping an online booking calendar for your clients to view your schedule
- Discerning which projects can be recorded and which ones can't
- Having a list of actors you can refer the extra work to
- Always allowing yourself a buffer by adding at least two hours on top of how long you believe it should normally take

These sections discuss important points to remember when working on multiple jobs at the same time.

Managing your workload

While recording for clients should take priority, don't forget that you still need to be auditioning for some part of the day and getting your name and voice out there. You may want to allocate certain parts of your day for specific purposes, such as auditioning, client work (this could mean recording a voice-over or editing) and working on your own business.

Something else you could try to help you manage your workload better is to group like activities. If you have a few telephone voice-over jobs to record, why not do them all at once? You'll be in the groove and the work may get done faster.

Similarly, if you have a number of character-related jobs to do, consider setting aside time to record character voices and take advantage of the creative mental space you're already in. Your voice will likely be warmed up, which can help you more easily use the full range of your instrument in fun and challenging ways.

Prioritizing projects

Tackling projects isn't difficult when you can factor in which ones need to be completed quickly in comparison to others that may be less urgent. Prioritize your jobs by which ones are smaller and easy to do, and get them out of the way first. If you're trying to complete a larger project, devote significant chunks of time to that project to ensure it's completed on time.

If you really are in a pickle and there's simply too much work to do all at once, consider getting some help. Maybe it's help with the marketing of your business. For most voice actors, it could be enlisting the services of an audio engineer who can help out with editing to save you time.

Outsourcing editing

Are you finding that audio editing is becoming a hindrance to marketing yourself and recording work for your clients? Many voice actors are outsourcing audio editing to capable audio engineers who can get the job done for a reasonable price and in a timely fashion. When outsourcing audio editing, you can save time, money, and your health.

While outsourcing in general terms isn't new, a number of actors are realizing how much time they can reclaim in terms of spending it with family, pursuing other opportunities, or getting a good night's sleep. Some voice actors have found ways to incorporate this time-saving strategy to make life a little easier on themselves. Working with an audio editor halfway around the world maximizes productivity, because their waking hours are spent editing a project while the voice actor carries on with other tasks or sleeps.

Time is money. If you find that your time could be better spent doing something else (like recording for more clients), you may find that outsourcing, although it means paying someone else to do the audio editing for you, may in fact save you money in the long run and even afford you the opportunity to earn more money because you can take on more projects.

Regardless of how your audio editing gets done, just be sure that it gets done in a manner that doesn't drag you down. Some voice actors choose to do their own editing because they enjoy it; however, being the artistic people that voice actors are, artistic license also plays a role in the desire to maintain control over the final cut. So long as you're not stressed over deadlines, audio editing is something that can be enjoyed and not outsourced.

Chapter 15

Getting Paid for Your Work

· ·

In This Chapter

▶ Earning money from voice acting

▶ Quoting for your work

▶ Getting paid

▶ Managing invoices

· ·

*V*oice actors, in the eyes of many, are living the dream. Who doesn't want to get paid for something most people think is as easy as speaking into a microphone? Talking couldn't be that difficult after all, right? Although voice actors do speak into a microphone and get paid for their efforts, voice acting is much more. If you want to achieve any measure of quantifiable, financial success, you need to know the ins and outs of assessing a project, quoting for work, and getting paid for recording a voice-over.

This chapter covers making money with your voice, including how to quote for a variety of projects in a number of different ways, how to run your business like a business, and how to manage invoices.

Making Money Doing Voice Acting

You may not be completely sure if voice acting can turn into a viable way to make money. We're here to tell you that you can make money. You just need to have an understanding of how you can create revenue streams and grow your voice acting business.

Getting paid for your work requires that you understand how voice actors are paid. Fees in the voice acting world are largely determined by the usage and the size of the audience hearing the recording. A longer voice-over recording doesn't necessarily earn more than a shorter one. What matters is how the recording is being used and how many people will hear it.

For example, a commercial airing in New York City commands significantly more money than a commercial airing in Poughkeepsie, even though they may both be the same duration in length. Likewise, a voice-over recorded for a larger brand may garner substantially higher fees than one for smaller companies. In the world of business and advertising, voice-overs can range from hundreds of dollars per job to five figures in the realm of movie trailers and the like.

Many voice actors face challenges in knowing what rates to set, where to draw the line for fees, and how to charge for what. Because no certain rates are imposed on people in many areas of the world, you have the freedom to set your own rates; however, you have to be careful to quote fees that are competitive and still make a career in voice acting viable for you and those who depend on you.

In the Australian voice acting market, everyone, whether union or non-union, quotes from the union rate card as a base. Non-union Australian voice actors are able to command the same rates for their work as union actors.

This chapter provides you with the knowledge and confidence you need to step into the arena and make a decent living as a voice actor working from a professional-grade home recording studio. Please note that the rates you charge are your own to set.

Quoting Your Pricing

A client wants to hire you for a voice-over job. To ensure you get paid what you deserve, you need to quote the client with the amount the project will be. *Quoting* is simply looking at the requirements of a project and determining how much to charge for the work. When quoting, you need to know how the client will use the voice-over, how long the client will use it, and also where the client will use it. The waters for quoting can be quite murky if you don't know what to look for.

The goal for this section is to ensure that you can assess the work being quoted on and confidently present a fee that covers your costs while meeting budgetary constraints. When you quote, you want to be sure that you have accounted for your time, resources, and skill while meeting the client's budget and expectations. These sections can help get you on the right track.

Determining your method of quoting

You can choose many different ways to quote for work. No matter which method you use, the fee ultimately should come out about the same. The following are different ways you can quote.

Different ways of quoting exist mainly because of the scope of a project or usage of the audio. For example, you would quote a commercial based upon the market, whereas you would quote an audiobook based upon a per-finished-hour basis. When you're starting out, quoting on a per-page basis is helpful, which is better than charging on a per-word basis. You can make more money if you charge per page.

When working with your client, we recommend you charge 50 percent upfront with the remaining 50 percent due immediately upon receipt of the finished work.

✔ **Market size:** This method is most commonly used for commercial radio and television spots that air to the mass public. Markets are determined by the audience size that will be hearing the voice-over. The market size largely determines how much you'll charge for the recording. This kind of quoting differs from projects outside of broadcast television and radio. Commercials are about how many ears you're impacting as opposed to how many words or for how long you are recording.

To clarify these two distinctions, you can break down the markets into three categories:

- **Major:** A *major* market refers to large centers such as New York City, Los Angeles, Chicago, Toronto, Vancouver, or Montreal.

- **Regional:** A *regional* market covers a particular geographic area encompassing many cities.

  Major and regional markets have target audiences with a potential count of more than one million. Furthermore, Internet/news media applications, documentaries, trailers, IDs, and in-house advertising are considered *major* markets, also sometimes referred to as *national.*

- **Local:** A *local* market serves a smaller population, and a message broadcast locally may not reach much farther than the city itself or its immediate surrounding area. If your project is distributed, broadcast, or displayed in a nonmetropolitan area with a population of fewer than one million, for internal training use, corporate videos, or telephony, then it's considered a local market.

Some union rates apply in major cities, such as New York, Chicago, and Los Angeles. Get the most recent rate page at http://www.voiceoverresourceguide.com/la/08union.html.

✔ **Per page:** Use the per-page quoting method for lengthy scripts for an audio book, e-learning programs, medical narration, and technical tutorials. This method gives the client the ability to ballpark how much your services will be. Also, if the client suddenly adds another chapter to the book or another course to the e-learning program, you can refer to your initial quote that your services will be billed per page.

You want to have a standard method for measuring what constitutes a page. We suggest you determine that one page is a Word document, Arial font, size 12-point, double spaced. Setting a standard can eliminate any confusion and also let the client know in which format you would prefer the finalized script to be delivered.

✔ **Per hour:** Having an hourly rate for edited material on hand is important. This rate includes voice-over and audio editing. The kind of work that falls into this category includes but isn't limited to long-form narration for e-learning, audiobooks, and documentary narration. If the work is comparable to audiobooks, the going rate is between $200 and $300 per finished hour, so for a 20-hour project at $250 an hour, you would quote $5,000.

✔ **Per word:** Shorter scripts such as voicemail messages, one-liners for a website greeting, or even a few sentences for a public service announcement may be best quoted by the word. Using this method makes is easy to perform a word count in Microsoft Word to discover the total number of words in the script, and then quote accurately using your per-word rate.

If you have a long project with enormous word counts, how do you know whether to charge per hour or per word? Here we show you how a per-word quote compares to a per-hour quote for a long project, when the script exceeds 100,000 words:

Script length: 126,000 words

Average words you can speak per minute: 150

Divide 126,000 by 150 to get the total number of minutes it will take you to record, which is 840 minutes.

Figure out how many total hours it will take to record by dividing the total minutes (840) by the total number of minutes in an hour (60) to get 14 hours that it will take you to record.

• So compare your per-word rate of 126,000 words or your per-hour rate of 14 hours. Doing this math can help you to know how long it will take to record so that you can accordingly schedule your sessions and give an estimate for how long it will take you to complete the project. The word count itself is a critical factor in estimating how long it will take you to record.

Recognizing billing cycles

When you quote, you may want to consider different billing cycles. A *billing cycle* determines how long you give a client to pay for services rendered. Billing cycles are commonly used for broadcast voice-overs, such as commercials. Following a billing cycle ensures you're paid on time for your work in the cases where you have an ongoing arrangement, such as you may encounter in radio, where you're paid in monthly retainers. You can set your own billing cycle, or you may need to yield to your client if he has a system in place.

Some different types of billing cycles you may encounter with your clients include the following:

- **13-week cycle:** Most broadcast commercial campaigns run in 13-week cycles, roughly three months.

- **Seasonal license:** Designed for advertisers to run targeted campaigns around a specific calendar event, such as Christmas or back to school.

- **One-year renewable license:** An annual contract designed for committed advertisers.

You may also want to consider a full buyout. A *buyout* is the purchase of the entire holdings or interests of an owner. In the context of voice acting, a full buyout is royalty-free with no additional charges. Unless otherwise stated, most clients assume that they own the rights to the finished product after they've paid you in full for your work.

Saving time with a rate sheet

A *rate sheet* is a quick reference guide that details how much you charge for any given service. Figure 15-1 shows an example of a rate sheet. A rate sheet like this can save you time when trying to determine how much you should charge for work.

You can easily create your own rate sheet, based on what you determine to charge. You can keep your rate sheet private or make it publicly available on your website for prospective clients to consider when evaluating what you have to offer. Having a rate sheet on hand saves time because you won't ever be at a loss for what to quote if you go by your rate sheet.

RATE SHEET

Find professional voice over talent and audio producers at Voices.com

Category	Time	$
Radio Commercial: Local / Regional	:15, :30 or :60	200
Radio Commercial: New York, Los Angeles, Chicago	:15, :30 or :60	300
Radio Commercial : National Network	:15, :30 or :60	1000
Radio Station Promotion / Station Imaging	:05, 15 or :30	200
Public Service Announcement on Radio	:15, :30 or :60	200
Television: Local / Regional	:15, :30 or :60	300
Television: New York, Los Angeles, Chicago	:15, :30 or :60	500
Television: National Network	:15, :30 or :60	2000
Radio Station Promotion / Station Imaging	:05, 15 or :30	300
Public Service Announcement on Television	:15, :30 or :60	300
Television Animation	1 hr recording session	300
	Per additional studio hour	100
Non-Broadcast Corporate, Industrial and Educational	1 hr recording session	300
	Per additional studio hour	100
Interactive Media / Multimedia	1 hr recording session	300
	Per finished hour of audio	500
Audiobooks	1 hr recording session	125
	Per finished hour of audio	500
	Per page rate	125
	Per word rate	0.01 - 0.05

- Radio and television rates for unlimited airings in a 13-week cycle.
- Rates are in US Dollars for finished dry voice only. Any post-production required is $100/hr.
- All rates are for reference only. Some voice talent may charge their own fees.
- Questions? Contact us at support@voices.com

For More Information
Contact your account executive
to learn how we can help you
succeed!

Corporate Headquarters
Voices.com
150 Dufferin Avenue, Suite 800
London, ON Canada
N6A 5N6

Service & Support
North America 1-888-359-3472
International +1-519-858-5660
Email support@voices.com
Web http://www.voices.com

Figure 15-1:
A rate sheet
shows what
you charge
for different
projects.

Illustration courtesy of Voices.com

Negotiating your quote

Many clients are willing to negotiate rate; however, they appreciate being quoted an actual dollar figure for their project that falls within their stated budget range. Should your quote be higher than the range the client has selected, be prepared for your prospective customer to ask you to renegotiate your quote. Set your rates with a margin of flexibility in mind.

If a job is paying less than you think it should, you can quote what you would expect to be paid and appropriately explain to the client why you've quoted in the manner you did. They may reconsider and pay you what you've asked or meet you in the middle.

Sticking within the client's budget range when you make your quote and renegotiate is often the safest way to go, though. Don't be afraid to quote higher up in the range. From personal experience, we've hired voice actors who quoted in the top range and were more than comfortable doing so. Why? Because we were casting based on the voice and interpretation, not the price.

You'll find that where a brand is concerned, there are fewer things more important than finding the right voice, even if that voice actor is quoting in the upper range or possibly higher than the client's budget. Bearing this in mind, anything is possible, but you'll need to take the chance to find out!

Receiving Payment: Cash, Moolah, Dinero

Getting paid is the single most important aspect of being a freelance voice-over professional, so make sure that you take your time and do things right. This section walks you through the steps you need to do in order to receive payment for your services.

Opening a business bank account

Having a separate business bank account is important for many reasons. You want to keep your business and personal bank accounts separate so that you can keep track of your business earnings and expenses. Keeping them separate can make tax reporting much easier if you haven't comingled money from your business and your personal life.

To set up a business account, follow these simple steps:

1. **Acquire an Employer Identification Number (EIN) by contacting the IRS.**

   Call the IRS Business and Specialty tax line at (800) 829-4933 or go online (`http://www.irs.gov/Businesses/Small-Businesses-&-Self-Employed/Employer-ID-Numbers-%28EINs%29`) to get your EIN. You need to do this before going to the bank.

2. **After you have your EIN, go to the bank and set up a business account.**

   Bring your business documentation, such as your business name registration, incorporation documents (if you have incorporated), and your EIN. Chapter 14 talks more about setting up your business.

Setting up a PayPal account

Many people choose to connect their business bank account with a PayPal account. PayPal is a third-party service that lets you send money to anyone with an email address set up with a PayPal account. The service is free for consumers and works seamlessly with your existing credit card and checking account. PayPal is fast, easy, and secure, which means you can easily accept online credit card payments from your clients for voice-over work. After you have set up your free PayPal account, you can start receiving payments right away.

PayPal offers three types of accounts, which we discuss here:

✔ **Personal:** Members who want the ability to send money from other PayPal users or accept debit and credit cards can use this type of account. eBay Tools and Merchant Services are limited for personal PayPal accounts.

✔ **Premier:** These accounts are for members who have a high transaction volume, need to accept credit card payments, or want to access special features not offered with the personal standard accounts. Premier accounts include all the benefits of the personal accounts, as well as the special features.

✔ **Business:** These accounts allow you to do business under a company or group name, accept all payment types for low fees, and accept payment from customers without PayPal accounts. Business accounts include all the benefits of Premier accounts, as well as special features.

To further compare these three options, visit the PayPal website at (`www.paypal.com`). After you're a member of PayPal, you can take advantage of advanced PayPal techniques, create invoices, and build trust and credibility with the PayPal logo, a graphic known and respected worldwide.

Acquainting yourself with SurePay

Most voice actors at Voices.com use SurePay to get paid for voice-over work. SurePay is Voices.com's escrow payment service that enables a client to make a full deposit upfront and have the deposit held until finished audio files are delivered through the Voices.com website. The SurePay system manages payments made by VISA or MasterCard, or through PayPal for you. You can control your payout preferences via the Preferences link in your Voices.com account.

The process starts when you get a job offer from a client. If the client accepts your work and you reach an agreement, the next steps include the depositing of funds in an escrow account, the recording of the voice-over, the delivery of the files, and the approval of work completed. After the client approves the work, the funds will be released to the voice actor either through PayPal or by check.

If you decide to use Voices.com, contact Voices.com for more information about SurePay or visit www.voices.com/surepay.html.

Managing Invoices

In order to ensure you get paid for your voice-over work, you need to keep detailed records, invoice your clients, and then manage those invoices. When managing the invoices, you want to make sure your clients pay in a timely fashion, depending on the terms that you set. The following sections identify what you need to do to manage your invoices to get paid and what you can do if your clients don't pay in a timely fashion.

Handling purchase orders

A *purchase order* is a document that gives you permission to bill a client. It's a companion document to an invoice. Larger clients that have accounts payable departments often issue purchase orders. The accounts payable department issues a purchase order to you, giving you permission to bill the client for the services described in the purchase order. A purchase order has a number often called a *P.O. number*; print that purchase order number on your invoice when you bill the client for work after you've completed the project. That way, your client (or more specifically, its accounts payable department) can quickly match up the invoice that you submitted with the original purchase order resulting in much faster payment.

The purchase order can be as simple as a one-line statement that says "voice-over services" or you can go into more detail, such as what is being recorded, how long it is, and how it will be used. Figure 15-2 shows what a purchase order looks like.

Your Company Name
Your Company Slogan

PURCHASE ORDER

Address
City, State ZIP
Phone 123.456.7890 Fax 123.456.7891

The following number must appear on all related
correspondance, shipping papers, and invoices:

P.O. NUMBER: 100

To:
Name
Company
Address
City, State ZIP
Phone

Ship To:
Name
Company
Address
City, State ZIP
Phone

P.O. DATE	REQUISITIONER	SHIPPED VIA	F.O.B. POINT	TERMS
				Due on receipt

QUANTITY	UNIT	DESCRIPTION	UNIT PRICE	TOTAL
				$ -
				$ -
				$ -
				$ -
				$ -
				$ -
				$ -
				$ -
			SUBTOTAL	$ -
			TAX RATE	8.60%
			SALES TAX	-
			SHIPPING & HANDLING	-
			OTHER	-
			TOTAL	$ -

1. Please send two copies of your invoice.
2. Enter this order in accordance with the prices, terms,
   delivery method, and specifications listed.
3. Please notify us immediately if you are unable to ship as specified.
4. **Send all correspondence to:**
   Name
   Address
   Phone: Fax:

AUTHORIZATION

Authorized by   Date

Figure 15-2:
An example
purchase
order.

Illustration courtesy of Voices.com

Issuing an invoice

An *invoice* notifies the client to pay a certain amount due. An invoice should include the following information (Figure 15-3 shows a sample invoice):

✔ Your company name and mailing address as well as the client's company name and billing address.

✔ Services rendered such as voice-over recording, editing, editing and mixing, as well as the total price.

✔ A date that the invoice was issued and the terms for remitting payment.

Invoice

DATE:
INVOICE #:
TAX ID:

Bill To:

SALESPERSON	P.O. NUMBER	TERMS	

QUANTITY	DESCRIPTION	UNIT PRICE	AMOUNT
		$ 99.00	$ -
			$ -
			$ -
			$ -
		TOTAL	$ -

Make all checks payable to **Pipes Studios**

All fund in U.S. Dollars

If you have any questions concerning this invoice, contact Pipes O'Brien, 555-555-5555, sales@website.com

THANK YOU FOR YOUR BUSINESS!

Figure 15-3:
An example
invoice.

Illustration courtesy of Voices.com

A proven payment strategy is to require a 50-percent payment when you begin the work with the remaining balance due prior to delivery of the final product. You need to invoice twice then. You may also choose to invoice in quarters, depending on how complicated the project is.

When you get paid, keep these basic strategies in place to avoid many payment issues:

- ✔ If the client pays the deposit via PayPal, you can get started right away, working on the project.
- ✔ If you're waiting for a check in the mail, particularly for final payment, wait for the check to clear at the bank before sending the CD master.

Grasping payment terms

When you issue invoices, you want to make sure the payment terms are clear so your clients know how long they have to pay. For example, if the invoice is due upon receipt, that tells the client that he needs to immediately cut you a check. If the invoice says, *net 30,* the client has 30 days to pay from the date printed at the top of the invoice.

Make sure to use *net 30* on your contracts. What this means is that your client has 30 days to pay the full balance that it owes you. Because many companies routinely pay between 30 to 90 days late on all invoices, never make your terms net 60 or net 90.

If you have a schedule for your client's payments, clients can remember to pay. If you break up the payments into periodic invoices, you can increase your cash flow with a number of smaller payments rather than a single large payment after the work is complete.

Collecting on Overdue Invoices

If a client is late in paying an invoice, you need to take immediate action to ensure you get paid. After all, you're expecting payment for your services, and you probably need the money to pay expenses and live everyday life. When you encounter unpaid invoices, we suggest you take the following action:

✔ **Send a friendly email or call.** You should always send something first to the client in writing stating the overdue status. Clients appreciate both email and mail reminders. You can also call to remind the client. Telephoning is effective because the client has no choice but to listen to you. Even if the client doesn't answer, the worst-case scenario is you either leave a message on voicemail or you speak to the receptionist, who will no doubt grow tired of hearing from you and send your request to the billing department to have the invoice paid immediately.

Sometimes a friendly email or phone reminder is all it takes for a payment to be sent. Your clients are busy, and they may have simply forgotten to make the payment. In other instances, people may be on vacation, and the payment may be sitting on someone's desk.

You can let a client know that you mean business without being invasive or argumentative. Reinforce the reasons why you expect to be compensated and be very clear that you fulfilled your end of the agreement. You're a professional and deserve to be paid on time and at the rate you arranged with the client. Remember, this is your bread and butter, and if you need this payment to make essential living expenses, demand that your client follows through and compensates you accordingly.

✔ **Go to collections:** If your client hasn't taken the hint or refuses to budge, collections agencies can help you hound the client until the client pays for your services. These agencies charge a commission fee and subtract it from the money that they have acquired for you from your client. These fees vary depending on the agency, so contact at least three agencies to receive quotes for your predicament. You may wish to do this as a last resort for outstanding payments of a substantial amount that are more than 90 days late. Small claims court may be a better option, depending on your situation.

✔ **File a claim in small claims court.** If you find that your efforts to secure payment are falling on deaf ears, consider taking the client to a small claims court. This option is best for individuals who are both working in the same municipality or region because you're closer to each other, which improves your chances of receiving what you're owed. Though going to small claims court may be time consuming, it's worth your investment when you receive the payment for your services. You don't need a lawyer to represent you, only your evidence and conviction. After a client receives notice that you're suing him, the client usually immediately pays you to save face or to quickly end the affair. Note that small claims courts usually have limits. Having a written agreement with the client prior to working together pays off here because you can bring it to court as evidence.

Seeing your name on the Top 100

The Featured Voice Talent are the most active community members at Voices.com. The Top 10 are listed on our home page and the Top 100 are listed on a separate page dedicated to the Top 100. The categories include New Voices, Most Listens, Recently Hired, and Top Favorites.

✔ **New Voices:** These are the newest Premium and Preferred voice actor members who have registered at the website or recently renewed their accounts. It's a way for them to gain some immediate exposure as well as a way to make a quick return on investment.

✔ **Most Listens:** Voice actors who receive the most plays or downloads of their audio files at Voices.com are recognized on this list. You can view three different Most Listens lists, including all time, this week, and this month.

✔ **Top Favorites:** People in this list have been most favored by clients. You can view three different lists, including all time, this week, and this month. Clients who are logged in to their accounts can favorite voice actors by clicking the "Add to Favorites" link in the search results, audition submissions, or on a voice actor's website at Voices.com.

✔ **Recently Hired:** This category identifies voice actors who have been hired within the past several hours by clients using the SurePay escrow service. This list updates as audio files are accepted and approved by clients hiring voice actors. You can view three different lists, including all time, this week, and this month.

Chapter 16

Nurturing Your Business

. . . .

In This Chapter

▶ Getting organized for success

▶ Hiring an agent

▶ Being your own agent

▶ Creating a winning team

▶ Considering a union

. . . .

*Y*ou've made the decision that you want to become a voice actor. Now what? In order to be successful in this endeavor, you need to develop a plan to help nurture your business. Being prepared and organized can help you reach success. If you don't know what you want, then you don't know where to go.

Planning for this success makes sense. This chapter shows you how to nurture your business and prepare for success by sharing tips for how you can build your business by managing your customers and organizing contacts, using an agent or going on your own, and having a strong team.

Applying Joe's advice

Voice-over industry announcer and icon, Joe Cipriano, shared some wonderful thoughts when commenting on a `Voices.com` blog post pertaining to achieving your goals. Encouraging and straightforward, Joe said, "Work on your goal at least one hour a day. Whenever I identify a new goal, I utilize this same strategy. It's very difficult to keep to that relentless schedule of focusing on your dream or goal and doing something to move it forward each and every day. But I have found that if you have that commitment and attitude, you will succeed."

So you can take Joe's words of wisdom and apply them in your voice acting business in the following ways:

✔ **Identify a goal.** Pinpoint what you want to achieve. Be very specific.

✔ **Commit to working toward your goal.** Pledge to yourself that you will do whatever it takes to reach your goal.

✔ **Work toward your goal for at least one hour a day.** Create time in your day for working toward achieving your goal, making incremental advances to get you closer to the mark.

✔ **Have a good attitude.** See each step in the journey as something that will build you professionally and help you achieve your goal.

✔ **Be prepared for success.** After you achieve your goal, you'll start to see the results of doing so. Be ready for opportunities that may come your way.

Keeping Everything Organized

To run an efficient voice-over business, you need to have the tools of the trade to manage your customers.

Before you start contacting potential clients, you need to develop a system that stores contact information, such as names, phone numbers, and email addresses. This practice, customer relationship management (CRM), is a software system that manages your potential and current customers. Look into a simple CRM system early on (many of them are free) that allows you to track the following:

✔ Client names, addresses, and contact information

✔ Tasks and events

✔ Marketing activities

✔ Sales opportunities and invoicing

✔ Projects and other work-related documents

The following sections identify the different ways CRM can help you operate your voice-over business.

Managing your clients, day to day

Developing and maintaining your CRM database is essential in order to run your everyday business operations. A CRM system provides a way that you can manage all your contacts, your calendar, and your communications in one central location. For example, you can keep a file on each client that you have worked for or have been in contact with for future opportunities. Storing the client's information not only makes it available to you when you need to contact clients, but it also keeps track of your business relationships and enables you to cater to each client on an individual basis.

Having a system to manage your business's most valuable asset, your clients, can prove to be well worth the investment of your time. After you get one, you need to decide the best way to host your information. We discuss your hosting options in the following sections.

Installing it on your PC

You can choose to install your CRM software on your personal computer. Having it there does have some great benefits. You know that your clients' contact information is readily available as long as you're near your computer. Furthermore, software installed on a local machine is generally faster.

On the downside, you need to get in a routine of backing up your data to a CD-R or to another computer. In the event you get a virus or your computer crashes, you can rest assured that all vital contact details, notes, and documentation have been saved to an external source. Software such as Act, Goldmine, and Daylight are all great CMS products.

Although contact management software, such as Microsoft Outlook for PC users or Apple Mail and Address Book for Mac users, aren't full-blown CRM solutions, they're good starting points if you're new to the business. The bottom line is that you need something to keep yourself organized.

Accessing your database from anywhere

If you do a lot of traveling or you like the idea of logging into a system, you may want to consider a web-based, also called a *web-hosted,* CRM solution. The single most significant benefit of hosted software is that you can access your information anytime from anywhere in the world, no matter if you're in San Francisco or Sydney, South Carolina or Saskatchewan. If you're at a client appointment, in a studio, or at a coffee shop, you can quickly create a new customer contact, jot down the time of your next meeting, or send a quote for your services.

Hosted CRM providers back up your data on a daily basis and store your business information on bank-level secure web servers. Hosted software solutions, such as Salesforce.com, NetSuite, Sugar CRM, Zoho Office, or 37 Signals' HighRise, are good investments to consider, allowing you to access your CRM database wherever an Internet connection can be made.

Going with a web-based, dedicated work calendar

Nothing irks a client more than a missed deadline or skipped meeting, so you want to make sure you keep a detailed calendar. Your calendar is the most important organizational tool that you have. It can save time and is a record of your successes for extended periods.

A web-based, dedicated work calendar can make sure you meet all deadlines and attend all client meetings. You can access the calendar from a smartphone or any other computer as long as you have Internet access. Several free web-based calendars are available, including Google, Apple Calendar, and 30 Boxes.

To avoid confusion, we suggest you keep separate calendars for home and work, and both electronic and hard copy if you need a physical reminder. Keeping separate calendars for work and home can help you to maintain a work-life balance, keeping all related things in one place. Some calendars do let you identify events as work or home related, such as with Apple's Calendar. Be sure that you have set up alerts on your calendars so that you know when something is coming up. A hard copy is good for people who need to write things out so that they can more clearly remember their commitments.

Another benefit of a web-based calendar is that you can keep notes there so you have a firm grasp of the project, which can eliminate potential misunderstandings. If anyone makes any errors or the project exceeds its original specifications, you can easily refer to your notes and politely inform the client as to how you originally quoted. Manage your bill payments and ensure that the client pays pay on time (if not, you can charge interest). (Refer to Chapter 15 for other ways to manage your invoices.)

Keeping a task list

A task list allows you to prioritize your daily, weekly, and even monthly activities so you're working most effectively and not feeling burned out after a day of business. A simple method to assign the three designations on your to-do list:

- **High priority:** *High priority* tasks may include following up with a client who is interested in working with you, finalizing a script, booking a studio session, delivering finished work, or sending an invoice.

- **Medium priority:** *Medium priority* tasks may include submitting auditions, sending out emails to prospective clients, working on your website or web page, or even following up with existing clients that you haven't heard from in a while.

- **Low priority:** *Low priority* tasks may be researching new equipment or looking into getting an agent. These tasks are often engaging, but also can distract you from earning a living because they take up precious time that you could be using to get work done or pursue revenue-generating opportunities. Never let something that should be a lower priority overtake items on your list that deserve to be higher priorities.

Organizing your contacts

A great way to organize your contacts is by how likely they are to do business with you in the future. Assign a customer status for each client so you focus your time on those clients who prove to be most profitable. The three most common categories are as follows:

- **Prospect:** A new contact to whom you have yet to make a formal introduction in person, on the phone, or by email.

- **Lead:** After you connect with a client, you can upgrade her status to that of a *lead,* sometimes referred to as a *warm lead* or a *hot lead.* At this stage, you may set up an appointment, send a proposal, submit your voice-over demo, and send your rate card.

- **Customer:** When a client agrees to do business, she is now officially a customer. If a financial transaction has occurred, the party in question is a paying customer. You need to designate as such in your contacts.

 No matter whether you're dealing with a prospect, lead, or customer, make sure you treat them all with the highest respect. You never know when a prospect or lead can turn into a paying customer. These sections provide a few suggestions on how you can move your prospects and leads into the customer column.

Mining your database

Knowing your prospects and leads and giving them what they want are the fundamental principles of marketing. This principle is simple in theory, but increasingly challenging to put into practice. Discovering what your prospects and leads are thinking isn't easy, but with some investigating and effort, you can see the fruits of your labor. Here are some suggestions:

✔ Research the company's website for information.

✔ Keep in touch by email or telephone to make inquiries regarding their needs.

✔ If they're past customers, you can send them newsletters and occasional promotional materials, which may spark their interest and lead to work opportunities.

Staying in touch

Friendly follow-ups go a long way in ensuring that you continue to win the business of your customers. Be consistent and persistent in your follow-up campaigns. Try out these ideas:

✔ Verify the customer received your product and that it was successfully implemented. Refer to Chapter 21 for additional information.

✔ Ask for a testimonial. Doing so can help build your credibility for future employment opportunities. Refer to Chapter 9 for how to get and use a testimonial.

✔ Try sending holiday cards, thank you cards, or cards that mark the anniversary of the day you first did business.

✔ Make quick phone calls to let clients know you're available for future projects. They can keep you in your clients' awareness.

Tracking your work and being accountable

At the end of the year, you want to be able to look back and quickly reference the work that you've done. One great way to do keep reliable records of your work is to use digital filing cabinets. For each job you have booked, you can archive relevant information, such as communications with the client, the script, quotes and invoices, and the audio you produced for that client.

You also want to keep track of your work so that you can declare it as income at tax time. You can use accounting software, such as QuickBooks or Simply Accounting. QuickBooks even comes as an online version with a free mobile app, giving you anytime-anywhere access to your accounting information. Excel spreadsheets are also good options.

Furthermore, we recommend that you keep a daily journal so that you can chronicle and track your progress. You can then periodically refer back to the private journal to see how you're doing.

If you want help from others on ways to be accountable, you can start a blog or post updates about your progress to family and friends via social networks, such as Facebook and Twitter.

Marketing your services

A good marketing system allows you to inform prospective clients and current customers about your services and what you can do for them. This system tracks which marketing initiatives are working and which aren't. Most marketing systems are tucked away in a CRM database, but you can also create a basic marketing system using an Excel spreadsheet. You can do so by having a section on each customer record called a lead source. A *lead source* is the original marketing initiative that caused the customer to do business with you.

Lead sources include

- ✔ Your website
- ✔ Your profile on a voice acting site, such as `www.elance.com`
- ✔ Direct mail or postcard
- ✔ Conference or event
- ✔ Cold call
- ✔ Referral or word of mouth

You can find out which lead source each of your clients used by simply asking "Do you recall where you first heard about my services?" When they reply, immediately add the information to your tracking system. Each customer ideally has a lead source, but some may not, which is okay. You can later look back at your best customers and see which marketing initiatives really paid off. Then, next month and next year, focus your efforts exclusively on those initiatives(Chapter 9 covers marketing in more detail).

Getting an Agent

Having an agent is one of the most attractive relationships in business for voice actors. An agent is another person, or even a team of people, who help you get work. An agent has his own connections and can send you for casting calls or promote your voice throughout his network.

This section walks you through some expectations an agent has of you, how you can find an agent right for you, and how to get the attention of those in a position to represent you and help you get work.

Knowing what an agent can do for you

Before you go looking for an agent, you need to know what an agent does and what an agent expects of his voice actors. An agent manages relationships between voice actors and the end client, including the auditioning process, casting to a degree, and the billing related to the job. An agent's role is to qualify voice actors for opportunities to reach a successful end. Agents can have relationships with companies they directly work with as well as pursue opportunities through online marketplaces where they can promote their voice actors.

Most agents work hard to maintain good relationships with their voice actors as they strive to get them work. That being said, you may not hear from your agent as often as you may like, but don't be too discouraged by that fact. So long as you're happy with the stream of opportunities you receive and work you book through your agent, working with an agent is usually smooth sailing.

Among their other responsibilities, agents only submit auditions from voice actors on their roster who they feel best meet a prospective client's overall needs. When an opportunity arises, they refer to their roster of actors, consider their options, and then settle on a select person or a select few that they believe stand the best chance of being hired to interpret copy and perform the voice-over.

Finding an agent

Locating an agent who can represent you and promote your voice and increase the amount of auditions you get is more than just flipping through a phonebook or doing a quick online search. This person or people can ultimately help you make it or break it in the voice acting business.

So how do you locate an agent? Try the following tips:

✔ **Ask a friend or colleague for a referral.** Sometimes word of mouth referrals are the best option. If you know people who have agency representation, ask them if their agent may have an opening. If your friend thinks you're a good fit, she can personally recommend you to her agent for consideration.

✔ **Attend conferences, workshops, or mixers where an agent may be present.** You can introduce yourself, discuss your skills with the agent, and network (see Chapter 9 for some networking tips).

Approaching agents

After you find some prospective agents, you need to follow up on your research and see if you're a good fit for their agency and vice versa.

At a conference called VOICE, Joyce Castellanos shared some tips on what works and what doesn't when trying to get a talent agent. She has worked for more than 25 years as an audio director/producer for promo departments at NBC, Disney Channel, Warner Marketing, and The WB Television Network.

If you're in the process of pitching your voice to agents and want some direction, keep these insights in mind and carefully think them through before you pound the proverbial pavement for representation. Here are some of Joyce's tips for what works when approaching talent agents. We've added some explanatory information to help you.

✔ **Introduce yourself by email or phone.** Introduce yourself depending on the agent's preference. Do some research to see which mode of communications the agent prefers.

✔ **Have professionally recorded demos at the ready.** An agent may want to listen to your demo on the spot. Make sure you have something representative of your work with you whether it's a CD or something online. For more information on demos, go to Chapter 6 and 7.

✔ **Know what you can offer to the agent or agency.** Research the voice actors that the agent already represents and see if you can fill in a hole on the agent's roster.

✔ **Express what your needs are.** Let the agent know what you're looking for and what your expectations of a voice actor–agent relationship are.

✔ **Describe how you would fit in on the agent's roster.** After you research the agent's roster, identify where your voice can fit in and highlight particular areas where you can shine and be an asset to the agent.

✔ **Conduct yourself honestly.** Always tell the truth and act with integrity. Honesty is the best policy, which includes anything from how your business is doing to the kind of auditions and work you're willing to do. For more on how to determine what you will and won't audition for, go to Chapter 10.

✔ **Have enough personality to shine.** Be yourself! Share who you really are with the agent so that she can appreciate your unique gifts and attributes.

✔ **Be honest about where your talents lie.** Know your voice and capabilities. Be sure to represent yourself well when describing what you can do. Agents will likely book your signature voice. Read more about how to find your signature voice in Chapter 2.

✔ **Don't sound needy.** One of the last things an agent wants to hear is how badly you need her representation. Voice actors who get represented by agents are usually able to book their own work in addition to booking with agents.

✔ **Don't second guess yourself.** Interacting with agents can be intimidating, but that shouldn't affect how you see yourself. Be confident in your abilities and approach getting an agent as another part of your overall business and marketing strategy.

Going Alone As Your Own Agent

Although many voice actors dream of having an agent, landing an agent can be difficult to do. Some other voice actors prefer not to have an agent. In fact, most if not all voice actors start their careers by being their own agent. During that beginning time, you develop your business acumen, artistry, and audio production skills.

Some voice actors find that even if they have an agent, they end up booking more work on their own than they do with their agent's help. We have heard many instances where voice actors get frustrated because their agent isn't sending them as many auditions as they'd hoped or the agent isn't putting their demo forward for consideration when the voice actor may actually be a good candidate for the job.

If you choose to be your own agent, you need to remember that you represent yourself and get more opportunities you believe you're qualified and suited for. In order to do that well, you need to think like an agent. These sections help you figure out what you're responsible for as your own agent as well as how to know whether to audition and to enjoy the auditioning process.

Thinking like an agent

If you are your own agent, you may not be quite sure what it really means. As your own agent, you need to see your voice through the eyes of someone who is trying to make money, not necessarily just as an artist. An artist sees things subjectively, whereas an agent will, if she wants to get the booking, objectively see things through the client's eyes.

Being your own agent means that you bear the responsibility of promoting your own voice, so you need to be selective with regard to the kinds of opportunities you submit yourself for. This is especially true when you're using websites, such as www.elance.com and www.voices.com, or trying to get work through an online casting call via social media or by other means.

Voice actors applying for work via the voice-over marketplace do a lot of unsupervised, self-directed auditioning. In some cases, this independence and liberty may result in some actors auditioning for jobs that they're unqualified to do, which negatively affects their audition to booking ratio.

In order to think like an agent, keep these two tips in mind:

✔ Be honest with yourself and only apply for work that you can do.

✔ Read and follow instructions.

Deciding whether to audition

As your own agent, you can be selective and only apply and audition for jobs that pertain to your expertise. When you're selective and apply for work you're able to do, you make a much better first impression and are more likely to be hired by the client.

You don't need to audition for every casting call that comes your way. If you feel that a particular audition, although it technically matches your expertise, isn't in line with something that you're confident doing, you are at liberty (and encouraged) to pass on it. Use your time wisely and determine whether the opportunity can yield some form of value for your business.

Making the auditioning process more fun

Thinking like an agent makes auditioning more interesting for you and also helps you to book more of the jobs that you audition for. When you think like an agent, you'll save time (which can also equate to money) and energy, and get a better shot at booking the projects you're auditioning for. As your own agent, you need to do the following before you audition:

✔ **Know your voice and your abilities.** Understanding what you're good at and being honest with yourself as a voice actor is important. If you need clarity in this area, a voice coach can help. Discover some coaching options in Chapter 3.

✔ **Have and exercise objective discretion.** Know where you draw the line in the sand. What jobs do you audition for and which ones do you pass on? Chapter 10 goes into greater detail regarding how to select opportunities that best reflect you and your business.

✔ **Understand what is being asked of you.** Thoroughly read the casting specifications and only answer the job if you understand the requirements and can meet them. Again, refer to Chapter 10 about reviewing job postings.

✔ **Commit to your choice.** After you decide to audition and map out your approach, you need to stick to your interpretation in order to deliver a confident performance. Chapter 11 guides you on how to make artistic and technical choices when auditioning.

✔ **Submit your best possible audition and let it go.** After making minor edits (if necessary), submit your polished audition and move on to the next one. Refer to Chapter 12 for more on submitting auditions.

Applying for work from the perspective of someone else representing you can be an interesting and enlightening experience. As your own agent, you'll be maintaining a website or completing your profile on a marketplace site as best you can, considering opportunities as they come along, and deciding which opportunities are most aligned with you as a voice actor, whether technical, artistic, or as a person. The freedom this brings can be amazing. Some voice actors have agents and never hear from them all year long, let alone get submitted for work. As your own agent, you're advocating for yourself and can open doors of opportunity that wouldn't have been made for you otherwise.

Building a Winning Team with Professional and Advisory Support

Even though as a voice actor you're a freelancer, you're not alone. Consider yourself a businessperson. Every person in business is supported by their peers and colleagues within the industry. The reality is that you are in business, and the service you provide is voice acting. That being said, you won't be an expert in some areas of business in general, so having the right people in place to fill in the gaps where you aren't experienced can make an amazing difference.

This section covers how you can build a winning team of qualified people to help you grow and succeed in your business. We focus on three of the more important areas. Your winning team can also include

- ✔ Voice coach (check out Chapter 3 for what to look for in a voice coach)
- ✔ Agent (refer to the earlier section, "Getting an Agent" for some help
- ✔ Peer support group (refer to Chapter 1 for online communities and support)
- ✔ People in your social network (see Chapter 9 for more on social networking)
- ✔ Tech or web person (see Chapter 9 for more information on web support)
- ✔ Vendors and partners (see Chapter 15)
- ✔ Lawyer and business advisers (see the next sections)
- ✔ Role model or mentor (check out Chapter 9 for more guidance)
- ✔ Spouse or significant other (Family matters! See Chapter 2 about discovering voice-over to glean how your other half can help you explore your voice.)

Finding legal representation

Having a good attorney who is reliable and understands the entertainment industry is like having a secret weapon. Your attorney can help you develop your standard agreements and review agreements that you'll inevitably receive. Attorneys who specialize in business or entertainment law have seen hundreds of contracts so they can provide you a professional opinion on how best to proceed. Although the ultimate decision whether to sign a contract or enter into an agreement rests with you, your attorney's advice can steer you in the right direction and save you countless headaches down the road.

When searching for an attorney, do your homework to make sure you're comfortable with this person:

- ✔ Ask friends and family members for referrals.
- ✔ Consult a professional organization that can refer you to someone who would best meet your needs.
- ✔ Check with industry organizations, such as an actors' union or guild, to see if they can recommend a few attorneys and provide you with their contact information.

When meeting with your lawyer candidates, interview them and ask lots of questions, such as

- ✔ **How do you like to communicate?** Some prefer phone, while others email. Every phone call or email you send to your attorney has a price.

- ✔ **What is your fee structure?** Some attorneys charge by the hour and some in 15-minute increments. Find out ahead of time, so you can keep your communications brief. On the other hand, other attorneys are available on *retainer,* which means you pay a monthly fee, and the attorney is on call and can answer any questions you may have, review contracts, and provide general advice on-demand. Either way works; just know the details upfront.

- ✔ **What do you specialize in and how can you best help me?** Different kinds of attorneys can help with different aspects of life and business. Look for lawyers who work in business law. You may even want to consider looking for an entertainment attorney to see what he can offer to you as a voice actor.

You're not shopping for just any service provider. Rather, you're looking for someone you can rely on and who in all likelihood will be your attorney for many years to come.

Hiring an accountant

If you want to become a professional voice actor, hiring an accountant may not only save you time, money, and stress, but an accountant can also make sure that you're in good financial shape. Even if you have a background in finance, delegating this aspect of your business allows you to focus on the creative side of what you do and build your business through serving your customers and reaching out to prospective customers.

Your accountant should be someone who is personable, generous with his time and advice, and who has a lot of patience. From setting up your accounting system, to teaching you how to issue an invoice and how to account for the check when it arrives in the mail, an accountant keeps you financially healthy.

When it comes to tax time, your accountant can help you reduce the amount of tax you pay or possibly find tax credits, which can result in a refund. The services of an accountant, such as a Chartered Accountant (CA), Certified Professional Accountant (CPA), or Certified General Account (CGA), easily pay for themselves.

Connecting with business advisers

You also want to surround yourself with other business advisers. These people can be your champions who celebrate your many successes as well as speak truth and wisdom into your life when you need a reality check.

Some of the business advisers that can be important to a voice actor include

- **Banker:** Your banker at your local financial institution can be one of your greatest allies. Keep an open line of communication and share what's going well in your business by sending a quick email. If cash is tight, your banker will be much more likely to provide some financial relief and help you get through a rough patch if she has a history with you. When business is booming, your banker can provide you with the capital required to grow or pursue a new opportunity.

- **Small business administration personnel:** The folks at your local small business administration office are good people to know. They can review your business plan, discuss challenging situations, and help you make connections in the local business community.

- **Business coach or mentor:** For personalized attention, a business coach may be right for you. A business coach or business mentor provides general business advice, encourages you, and helps you avoid costly mistakes.

Business advisers should be a part of your overall career or business plan. As they say, success in business is "not what you know, but who you know." Business advisers are the people who can open doors and connect you to others who can help you grow in your career.

Looking at whether a Union Is Right for You

Just like in the working world, unions exist in the entertainment industry to protect voice actors and supply them with benefits. Some unions are by invitation only, while others allow voice actors to pay an initiation fee that enables them to join their organization. They just have to pay union dues each year thereafter.

Unions can provide health, insurance, and disability benefits, and they serve their members in legal matters where contracts and financial compensation are concerned. The union works as an advocate for its members and is a useful body to belong to when looking for solidarity. The union is a structured, accepted means of conducting business as an actor on the stage, in film, television, radio, or behind the microphone or otherwise.

If you're interested in knowing more about unions, the following sections can help. Here we explain what unions a voice actor can join and what you can do if you want to join.

Getting up to speed on the union

At their core, unions embody the utopian idea that everyone should behave in a particular fashion, observe the same guidelines, assume the same political leanings, and strive to achieve a common good as is defined by the union. As a reward for doing so and by hitting a specific financial goal, members can achieve access to health coverage, a pension, and other worthwhile benefits.

Unions exhibit traits of strength, unity, and purpose through strong membership. Without a strong membership base and reasons for everyone to abide by the ideals set out by the leadership of the union, no matter how great a union's past, it can still fail because an organization is only as strong as its weakest link.

Identifying the unions you can join

The most recognized entertainment unions include the following:

- ✔ Screen Actors Guild-The American Federation of Television and Radio Artists (SAG-AFTRA): Go to www.sagaftra.org for more information about the union, about joining, and about other details.

- ✔ Alliance of Radio and Television Artists (ACTRA): Check out www.actra.ca for more information.

- ✔ Actors Equity Association (also called Equity or AEA): Refer to www.actorsequity.org for additional information.

SAG and AFTRA recently merged, and the new union is referred to as SAG-AFTRA. Prior to their merger in 2012, the two were the dominant players in the North American marketplace. Now that they are merged, SAG-AFTRA jointly provides services for different kinds of actors and artists. Many voice actors were members of both unions before the merger so it made a great deal of sense to bring these two entities together.

Part V
Establishing Your Home Recording Studio

In this part . . .

This part includes some more advanced and yet important material. Here you can discover how to create your own professional, yet cost-effective, home recording studio. We introduce you to the basics of audio recording, and we explain important pieces of equipment you should invest in to make your studio complete.

We also discuss the important skill of editing. Editing is a big part of making your voice-over recording sound polished, including editing out mistakes, long pauses, and breaths. We also cover other topics, such as mixing and mastering. As a voice actor, your customers will have certain expectations regarding what you can do for them in the capacity of an audio engineer. Although you may not be an engineer, having some of these skills tucked away for when you need them is helpful.

Chapter 17

Creating Your Own In-Home Recording Studio

*N*ew technologies and the Internet have removed many practical obstacles that used to thwart the paths of professionals in any number of fields. More advanced tools and processes are available now than ever before. Equipment has become more affordable, and millions of people around the world enjoy the benefits of working from home. Most professional voice actors are in many ways living a dream because they're able to work from home while doing what they love.

When you start a voice-over business, you need to make a modest investment of say $2,000 in your equipment given you already have a modern computer; however, that being said, you can't just buy anything and expect that it meets your needs and the approval of those in a position to hire you. Depending on how tech savvy the people are or clients are, they'll know in one look at your profile, or listen, what kind of equipment you used to record your voice. Perception can make or break your studio because people in the know are going to notice.

If you don't have a studio at home, you can record at a local studio, but with a home studio, you're positioned to record whenever you need to do so, and you don't have to check in with a studio all the time for availability. In the long run, you'll save time and money by having your own studio.

Furthermore, having your own studio at home is also one of the best and most convenient ways to develop your audio engineering skills. Chapter 18 on recording and Chapter 19 on more advanced audio engineering skills, such as editing and mixing, can provide you with more direction and information about the use and operation of your recording equipment. In this chapter, you discover how to set up your home studio and all the tools you need to stock it.

Constructing Your Home Recording Studio

Building a home studio is a great way to work from home and record at your convenience. You can set your own hours and have the flexibility to record custom auditions for clients. Although purchasing a home studio is a considerable financial investment, in the long term, it saves you time, resources, and money, particularly when you have to record revisions for a client.

In this section, we guide you on selecting your room and making it your own space.

Selecting a room

You don't want to choose just any old room in your house for your studio. Typically, a spare bedroom or home office is a perfect location. The room should have the best possible recording conditions, so take into account these considerations:

- ✔ Walk around your house or apartment and listen for street noises, loud air conditioning units, or other ambient sounds.

- ✔ Find a room that's quiet and free from these noises (if you can), or choose a room where you can easily block out those noises.

  A second floor typically works better because you're more isolated from foot traffic, floor squeaks, appliances, and other noises common to a family home.

- ✔ Choose a room with several electrical outlets and one that provides space for your recording equipment.

Soundproofing your room

There's actually a whole science dedicated to soundproofing and room treatment called *acoustics.* Short of filling another book, here we stick to the critical points as they relate to soundproofing your home recording studio.

The primary goal of soundproofing is to prevent unwanted noise from bleeding into your recordings. These unwanted noises can range from a rumble of trucks outside, sirens of emergency vehicles, or kids playing in the background. Even more subtle is the buzzing of an air-conditioning unit or the furnace humming in the background.

There are actually some very low-cost techniques for minimizing external sounds. These techniques include the following:

✔ **Hang blankets on your walls.** The blankets help absorb unwanted sounds.

✔ **Utilize dressing dividers and hang thick blankets, such as comforters or duvets, over them.** Thicker blankets absorb more sound than a thin blanket, such as a bed sheet.

✔ **Create a portable studio.** This *studio* is simply a box with foam lining the inside. You then place the microphone inside the box, which eliminates a lot of external sounds and gives you a nice clean recording. You can buy a completed portable studio from Harlan Hogan or for instructions on building your own, search online for "how to build a portable studio" or "how to build a porta-booth."

Making it comfortable

You'll be spending a good deal of time in your studio, so you may as well make it comfortable. Personalize your studio so it's a place you really enjoy spending time. Some voice actors like to decorate their studios with photos of family members or add a few house plants. Others enjoy building a studio that feels like they're in a production house.

However you decide to decorate, make sure that the design and decorations are conducive to audio recording and absorb noise — not create more of it.

Here are some additional tips:

> ✔ **Buy a good sitting chair and ergonomic equipment.** You're bound to spend long hours in your studio, whether sitting or standing, so make sure you're comfortable. A number of voice actors go the extra mile to have special padding under where they stand to help them with posture and to increase their stamina for recording standing up.
>
> ✔ **Use bright lighting.** Bright light helps you to read your script and minimize eyestrain.

Considering Start-Up Costs

Most people can build a decent home recording studio for a minimum of $2,000. To give you an idea of the equipment out there, professional recording studios are worth tens of thousands of dollars. The most expensive recording studios cost well over 1 million dollars to construct. But you don't have to spend that much! On average, a professional-grade home recording studio costs in the neighborhood of $2,000 to $10,000.

Regardless of industry sector or creative background prior to the start of an imminent voice career, the purchase of a professional-grade home recording studio is the largest, most tangible investment that will be made in the life of your voice-over career. With the advent of new, more efficient technologies, the costs associated with building a top-tier audio recording studio have plummeted, making some aspects of the previously unattainable multimillion-dollar studios of a decade ago available today. Now, you can find that you can "plug and play" with the aid of simplified digital audio recording devices, specifically using USB microphones and cables.

For a quick analysis of start-up costs based on a professional home-based recording studio, check out Table 17-1. This table shows you the high-end costs; some of them you may not immediately need when you build your in-home studio. Others you may have already purchased.

Table 17-1	Budgeted Start-Up Costs
Category of Expense	*Cost*
Accounting services	$500
Advertising and promotion for opening	$500
Cash	$1,000
Deposits for utilities	$250

Category of Expense	*Cost*
Estimated taxes	$250
Insurance	$150
Legal costs	$500
Licenses and permits	$50
Office supplies	$50
Print design and printing	$500
Rent deposits	0
Unanticipated expenses	$500
Website	$500
Total start-up costs	**$4,750 (USD)**

Buying secondhand equipment

A voice actor entrepreneur's highest expense when getting started is the equipment to build his home recording studio. Ideally, a professional-grade home recording studio has a computer, recording/editing software, a professional microphone, a microphone stand, headphones, mixing board, speakers (to hear the balance of your mix with), and a proper room to record in. But this all comes at a cost, so what about secondhand equipment?

When you're in the market to buy gently used recording studio equipment, the odds are in your favor that you'll get a great deal and equipment in good condition. How can you tell if the equipment is worth the asking price and if it will happily meet your needs? Here are some tips:

✔ **Seek out photographs of the object you're interested in.** If you're networking locally with someone, set up a meeting to evaluate the equipment in person, including a test-drive of what the piece can do for you and how it operates.

✔ **Check for scratches, dents, loose items, and quality.** Brand names the likes of Shure, Neumann, and AKG are high-end, whereas a microphone from an all-purpose electronics store in the mall may be less professional.

✔ **Ask where the item was purchased, how much it was purchased for, and when it was purchased.** Knowing these variables gives you the leverage you need to decide whether the price for the equipment is fair or way off base. You can also request a copy of the original receipt.

✔ **Ask for original boxes, warranties, and user guides.** This documentation proves that you're purchasing from the original owner.

Some manufacturers offer transfer of ownership, papers allowing you to benefit from free software and hardware upgrades or promotions in the future. The serial number would be registered under the purchaser's name, making you eligible to receive bonuses and free upgrades by virtue of your business dealings. Your return on investment will be evident in good usage of your equipment. As long as you are learning how to use it, you will get something out of it.

Stocking Your Studio

If you love technology and appreciate gear, this part of your voice acting journey to stock your home recording studio may be one of the most exciting tasks to date. In this section you can find out what you need to get your voice acting studio up and running, starting with a modern computer onward.

Recording with your computer

One of the biggest trends in recent audio production involves merging digital recording with computer technology. The recording of audio onto a computer hard drive allows you to edit and manipulate your sound files. This data can be stored as a sound file such as .wav or .aiff.

When recording and editing your voice-overs by using your computer, you can realize several advantages:

- Record long and uninterrupted narration
- Digitally edit and remove unwanted background noise or embellish the audio track with music and sound effects
- Add digital effects to your voice, such as reverb or echo, and master your entire demo for sonic clarity

PCs

If you've purchased your personal computer in the last three years and you're running Windows 7, your system should be more than adequate to record an audio file with a microphone, and then save the recording as an MP3 file.

Look for these specifications:

- Intel Pentium 4 or equivalent processor
- Windows 7 or higher
- 15GB of available disk space
- 2GB of RAM (4GB or more recommended)

Macs

Apple is committed to the digital revolution with the latest updates of its iTunes and GarageBand software. A lot of other great software is available for the Mac platform. The all-in-one iMac desktop computer is a great starting place if you're in the market for a new computer. The misconception that the Mac is simply too expensive or that Macs are only for students and artists is wrong. Apple even introduced the Mac Mini, a scaled down version of the Mac that allows previous PC owners to make the switch, but still keep their monitor, keyboard, and mouse.

Look for these specifications:

- ✔ Processor: 1.83 GHz Intel Core Duo
- ✔ Operating System (OS): OS X 10.6 or higher
- ✔ 15GB of available disk space
- ✔ 2GB of RAM (4GB or more recommended)

Many studios run much older systems with slower processors, but they aren't always compatible with the latest audio interfaces. To determine the capabilities of a Mac you currently own or of one you're considering purchasing, click on the Apple icon in the upper left-hand corner of the screen, and select About this Mac, and you can see the processor speed and the amount of RAM you have installed. Click on More Info for a detailed list of all the features of the computer. If your present computer doesn't have enough memory or RAM, don't worry! RAM prices are at an historic low with 4GB of RAM for many Mac computers being much less than $100.

If you're simply plugging your microphone straight into your computer, you need to use a *preamplifier,* also known as a *microphone preamp.* A preamp is a sound engineering device that prepares a microphone signal ready to be processed by other equipment. The preamplifier can give a boost so to speak to the sound as it makes its way through the *signal chain* (also called *signal flow*).

Recording with an audio interface

An *audio interface* is a piece of hardware that increases and improves the sonic capabilities of a computer. When choosing your audio interface, consider these points:

- ✔ **The method in which it connects to your computer:** For example, USB or FireWire.

- ✔ **The quality and features of the preamplifier(s):** A preamplifier is necessary to use with any condenser microphone. The preamplifier helps to boost how your voice sounds as it goes through the microphone, the microphone cable, and into your computer. Some preamplifiers are built in to the audio interface, while others are external and can be purchased separately.

> ✓ **The quality of the analog to digital converters:** The quality of the converters affects the quality of your voice. Lower-quality converters lack detail and definition and can mask the qualities producers want from your vocal performance.

In this section, we give you a few specific audio interfaces that are our recommendations.

Mbox Pro and Mbox Mini

Another product to be aware of is the Mbox available in either the Pro edition or the Mini version. The Mbox is a professional-grade audio interface that allows you to capture sounds and record at the highest quality. The Mbox Pro has eight inputs and eight outputs, comes with two jacks for headphones, and connects to your computer using a FireWire cable. The Mbox Mini comes with only two inputs, two outputs, and a single headphone jack, and connects to your computer via a standard USB cable. The best part of the Mbox is that both versions come with the industry's standard Pro Tools recording software.

Griffin iMic — USB Audio Interface

The iMic universal audio adapter adds stereo input and output to your Mac or PC through a USB port. You can connect any microphone or sound input device to your MacBook, MacBook Pro, or other Mac or PC with a USB port. iMic's audio is better than a desktop's built-in soundcard because it uses USB for the audio signal.

The Apogee One and Duet

In the under $500 category, two good channel models are the Apogee Duet and the new Apogee One.

> ✓ The Duet is a two-channel audio interface complete with breakout cable and 48-volt phantom supply for both channels. The preamps are excellent, as are the digital converters.

> ✓ The Apogee One is a single-channel audio interface with a built-in microphone and an input for an external microphone. It provides the quality of the more expensive Apogee Duet, but it doesn't provide phantom power, which is often referred to as "48+" or 48 volts. (See the nearby sidebar "Phantom power.")

Apogee has worked closely with Apple, and its products are very well made and executed. They integrate seamlessly with GarageBand and Apple Logic Studio, and connect to your computer with a regular USB cable, which means less time spent configuring software and more time recording for clients.

Phantom power

Phantom power is a direct current (DC) voltage that is sent through a microphone cable to power the microphone itself or an associated device. Phantom power is necessary on all condenser microphones. The microphone you choose determines whether you need phantom power. For example, the BLUE "Blueberry" and the Neumann TLM 103 microphones do require phantom power, so be sure your audio interface supports phantom power.

Other interface/hardware suggestions

Other suggestions include

- ✔ M-Audio Interfaces
- ✔ Roland's Edirol AudioCapture
- ✔ Lexicon Lambda

Selecting a microphone

Whether you're using a Mac or a PC, you need a microphone to record your voice into your computer. While we can't give a definitive answer to anyone who asks "What microphone should I get?", we can provide you with tools to help you decide for yourself. Be sure to also get a microphone stand so that you can properly mount your microphone in your studio.

Usability

The best microphone is the one that you can use with the fewest technical problems. If all other things are equal, choose the simplest setup that you can that enables you to record as quickly as possible — hence the saying "plug and play."

Frequency response

Some microphones like the RE20 (the stereotypical radio microphone) are large diaphragm microphones designed to pick up lower frequencies such as a deep male voice, a bass drum, or even a bass guitar.

The small diaphragm or small capsule microphone is designed to pick up higher frequencies such as the female voice, the brightness of an acoustic guitar, or shimmering cymbals. You may have seen these as the overhead microphones on a drum kit or above an orchestra.

The most used promo microphone is the Sennheiser 416, a small diaphragm microphone that suits many voice types.

Polar patterns

Every microphone you'll find on the market has a property called *directionality* (also called *polarity*). Directionality relates to how sensitive a microphone is to the sound being produced around it. Polar patterns are divided into four main categories:

- **Omnidirectional:** Picks up sound from every direction
- **Cardioid:** Picks up sound from directly in front of the microphone
- **Hypercardioid:** Even more narrowly picks up sound from directly in front of the microphone
- **Bidirectional:** Uses a figure-eight pattern and picks up sound equally from two opposite directions such as the front and back of the microphone

Decide which type of directional pattern, also known as a *microphone's polar pattern,* best suits your needs. For voice-overs, a more focused directional microphone is likely best. The polar pattern you should be looking for is a *cardioid* or a *hypercardioid.* This type of polar pattern minimizes room tone and ambient noise because it's designed to pick up sounds within close proximity of the front of the microphone.

Pop filter

A *pop filter* is considered a standard accessory for voice artists. The pop filter acts as a screen that helps to reduce the impact of the air from your mouth onto the microphone capsule, which results in the minimization of mouth noises.

Shock mount

A *shock mount* is a mechanical fastener that holds your microphone in place, suspending it by elastics. One of the benefits of a shock mount is that the microphone is isolated from stand vibrations. For instance, if there is a low rumbling under foot, the shock mount can absorb it.

Testing

Experiment with a friend's microphone or borrow a handful of microphones from the music store and test them out. If you're looking at a high-end microphone, you may consider renting a few mics for a couple hundred dollars overnight to test a few pieces of equipment before investing a couple thousand dollars on the right microphone for your voice.

Our favorite microphones

Some time ago we posted an article asking voice actors to comment about their favorite microphones and why they loved them. If you're looking for some first-hand recommendations from people who love their mics, we encourage you to read this article at `http://bit.ly/hotmicrophones`.

Many reviews are available online where people describe their experiences with various microphones. A quick online search can lead to more information quickly on a particular microphone of interest.

Price

The best microphone for your voice won't necessarily be the most expensive one on the market. From one perspective, the best microphone is the one that is affordable and gets the job done, which is why many of these criteria could be considered "nice to haves," and not "need to haves."

Having said that, the microphone, along with the preamp, are the pieces of technology that are between you and your computer, so get the microphone that makes your voice sound best but also fits in your budget.

Recording and editing software

In this section, you will discover the different options out there for recording and editing software. Some, like Audacity, are free to use, and others, like Pro Tools, require more of an investment.

Audacity

Audacity is a free, easy-to-use audio editor and recorder for Windows, Mac OS X, GNU/ Linux, and other operating systems. You can use Audacity to record live audio, convert tapes and records into digital recordings or CDs, edit Ogg Vorbis, MP3, and WAV sound files, cut, copy, splice, and mix sounds together, change the speed or pitch of a recording, and more.

GarageBand

GarageBand lets you easily perform, record, and create your own music. Whether you're an experienced or aspiring musician or just want to feel — and sound — like a rock star, the new version of GarageBand can get you there and even record multiple tracks at the same time. GarageBand is for Mac only and comes free with most Mac computers.

Adobe Audition

Designed for demanding audio and video professionals, Adobe Audition offers advanced audio mixing, editing, and effects-processing capabilities. Its flexible workflow, combined with exceptional ease of use and precise tools, gives you the power to create rich, nuanced audio of the highest possible quality.

Pro Tools

Pro Tools is the professional recording, editing, mixing and mastering software for Mac and PC users and is considered the industry standard. The manufacturer, Avid, offers Pro Tools HD for professional grade studios and also provides the Pro Tools Express version bundled with the Mbox audio interface for the more budget conscious. You'll have everything you need to create and produce music with professional results regardless of whether you choose Pro Tools HD or Pro Tools Express. Whether you're looking for an all-in-one audio/MIDI solution with an integrated control surface or simply a highly portable Pro Tools system, there's a powerful solution designed to satisfy your creative needs.

You may be afraid of Pro Tools, perhaps in part to its complexity and price, but it's good to know that it provides both a hardware and software solution. Many of you won't have a need for the multitracking capabilities that Pro Tools provides; however, if you do get into any kind of production work, this is the industry standard.

Grabbing the Last-Minute Accessories

Most voice actors use additional tools to help them make cleaner recordings. Others employ the use of headphones to help them gain a better appreciation for how they sound. In this section, you discover a number of extras that help complement your studio and enhance your performances from a technical standpoint.

Downloading iTunes for the Mac and PC

If your audio recording program only exports a WAV file, you need an audio conversion program. The easiest way to convert files into MP3s is using iTunes. Many people use iTunes as a file converter and may even store session files in there.

Filtering pops with a pop filter

If you're looking for more noise reduction or need something that gives you the portability of a voice booth, you may want to get a *pop filter*. This piece of equipment sits on the mic stand and acts as a portable booth, weighing all of 11 pounds. The microphone mounts right into the center of it, and you can use it in any room to turn it into a studio environment. We recommend the sE Electronics Reflexion Filter as a pop filter. It acts as if you're standing in a whisper room or recording studio.

If you have a lot of external noise (such as road traffic), the sE Electronics Reflexion Filter won't block it out, but it's very good otherwise for recording in a quiet room.

For simpler editing software solutions, try Amadeus for the Mac and Adobe Audition for PC. Both are easier to use and don't cost as much as the audio recording industry-standard Pro Tools. Audacity (can be used on both Mac and PC) is free to use and perfect for voice actors who want to get started without spending any money on an audio program.

Listening with headphones

Not everyone uses headphones when recording, but in some instances you may need to wear headphones. These include

- ✔ If the director requires it
- ✔ If you need to hear the production as you voice, like in promo
- ✔ If you're voicing to a music track

Some voice actors see headphones, or *cans* as they're sometimes called, as a distraction that takes away from their ability to perform. When you have a set of headphones on, you may experience the tendency to focus more on how your voice sounds processed than on your artistic performance. Not only can headphones be a vocal distraction that keeps you from excelling in your performance, but they also can inhibit your ability to move and use your whole body as a voice actor. Remember that the headphones are plugged into something and therefore make it harder for you to let loose in the booth. Another benefit to not wearing headphones is that you won't have more than necessary being piped into your ears.

Backing up your work with an external hard drive

If you're weeks into a recording project, the last thing you want is to redo all that hard work because you didn't back up your work. Right? Right. So invest in an external hard drive to back up your computer!

You have some good options for backing up your work. You can buy another hard drive for as little as $99 that connects to your computer with a USB cable. External hard drives come with back-up software that makes the process pretty easy. Then, save your important files to the external hard drive. Look for a hard drive that has at least 1 terabyte (TB); One TB is equal to 1000GB of storage (enough space to store at least a dozen large projects).

When you're done with the project, you can always burn a DVD for archival purposes to free up space on your hard drive.

In the unfortunate event of a catastrophe, such as a flood or fire, at your home studio, your external hard drive will be lost with your computer. With that in mind, you may want to consider off-site storage by using a web-based service, such as DropBox or Box.net. These services allow you to store files on their secure servers for a small monthly fee.

Whatever option you go with, do something. Back up your work. You'll sleep better at night because you do.

Chapter 18

Understanding the Recording Process a Little Better

*T*he fun part is finally here. You've been working for a long time preparing to finally record your demo. You've been dreaming of standing behind the microphone and letting all the voices in your head come out. Recording your voice is both an art and a science.

Recording your demos well takes some preparation and understanding of how the recording process works. In this chapter, we explain the recording process, introduce you to some common terms used by audio recording professionals, walk you through how to position the microphone and music stand, and decipher the actual recording process.

Eyeing the Recording Process: What Exactly Happens

Have you ever captured your voice on a recording? Maybe you remember recording your voice on a tape deck as a child or hearing a playback of what you sounded like while singing Karaoke. Even though you may have played around with recording your voice, you probably don't know what actually happens during the recording process and how it actually is recorded.

This section shows you how the voice enters the microphone and gets recorded, how you can create a recording session, and how you can keep recording sessions simple.

Indentifying the signal flow

In order to fully understand what happens in a recording studio when you're recording your voice-over work, you need a basic foundation of what recording engineers call signal flow. *Signal flow,* also referred to as *signal chain,* is basically the path by which sound travels from source to destination. In creating a voice-over demo, the source is your voice, and the destination is an MP3 file. (An MP3 file is a digital audio file format recorded on your computer. Check out Chapter 21 for more information.)

The following list breaks down, step by step, what happens with typical voice-over signal flow:

1. **You speak to create a vocal sound from your mouth.**

2. **The microphone detects the vocal sound.**

3. **The microphone passes the signal along the microphone cable.**

   The microphone cable is plugged into a mixing board or digital interface, which is plugged into a computer. (A *digital interface* basically is a hardware box that plugs into your computer and routes sound in and out of your computer. Sound going into the digital interface is an *input* and sound going out from your digital interface is an *output.*)

4. **The computer records the signal using recording software.**

   During playback, you can listen to exactly what was recorded. The signal is routed to the audio interface and out to your headphones or speakers where your ears actually hear your voice-over recording. If you don't have an audio interface, the signal will be routed directly to your computer speakers. The computer software records what the microphone hears and then saves that information in your session. In order to share your recording with someone else or upload it to your own website, you need to export your recording as an MP3 file, which Chapter 21 explains how to do.

Opening a new recording session

A *recording session* is the term that both describes the event (you've marked this time off on your calendar) as well as the project folder containing all the recordings, the client's script, and the link to launch the recording software.

Regardless of which computer software you'll be using for the recording, you need to start a new session when you start to record your voice-over.

You create a new session file, which is like a folder that contains all the other files that relate to your recording, such as music, sound effects, vocal tracks, settings, and more. In other words, you want to keep all the related material with this voice-over job together, in one place. For now, remember that when you want to start recording a new job, you need to start a new recording session.

For best results, make sure you use the same microphone and microphone positioning when you record for each session that's part of a larger project. Doing so creates a consistent sound for your voice-over work when recording for that specific client. Furthermore, you end up saving a lot of time during setup because you're familiar with your equipment and your computer software and the settings for that specific project.

To help you store all your settings and preferences for a specific job, we suggest you keep a *session template.* This template keeps everything — background music, vocal tracks, and all other settings — in one easy-to-access place. To create a session template, you set up a new session and configure (*configuring* a session means that you set your preferences as to the numbers and names of tracks that you have by default, any effects or plug-ins applied to those tracks, as well as any other settings that you want to have established by default so that you don't have to re-create these properties from scratch each time you start a new session) it for a normal recording session.

Your template should include the following:

- ✔ Vocal track
- ✔ Alternate vocal track
- ✔ Music track
- ✔ Sound effects track (optional)
- ✔ Other processing or special effects, such as an equalizer

After you get the perfect session, which is to say you have the settings and preferences established just the way you want them, save it as "Template Session – Dry Voice-Over." You can save it as a particular kind of recording session template. You may have one template for certain kinds of reads (perhaps a different one for podcasting, one for audiobook narrating, one for commercials, and so on, depending on the production elements involved.) The differences between these kinds of templates include the number of tracks, the types of tracks (is this a music, sound effect, or voice-over?), any plug-ins you've added, and specific presets made to those plug-ins.

You also want to include on your template the saved settings for your plug-ins, such as the equalizer, compression, and others. These saved settings are called *presets*. By default, many plug-ins already have a number of presets ready for you to pick and choose from. Presets, in addition to elements from the preceding list, contribute to a perfect setup for your session template.

For your next recording session, open the template from the file menu and save it as the client's name. Make sure you use "save as," which maintains all the settings in your new session without overwriting the original template session. Repeat this process for each new session and you can save a lot of setup time.

Whether you have one template or an entire library of session templates, this time-saving tip can save you hours of repetitive setup, allowing you to get recording faster than you ever thought possible.

Defining Important Studio Terminology

When you enter a recording studio, you inevitably will hear lots of technical terms and jargon. You may have even heard a few terms tossed around by your radio buddies or computer geeks you know. Maybe you've said a few yourself without even realizing what the word really means. Getting a strong understanding of all these terms can be overwhelming at first, but fret not.

In this section, we run through some of the key terms you'll likely come across in the recording studio, either with the related software or in your discussions with a recording engineer in a studio or with another voice actor in person or online.

Voice coach and performer, Marc Cashman, provided us at one point with a brilliant glossary of terms. We include them here for you to help define some of the jargon you may hear people say in the industry and may need to use yourself.

- **Back bed:** The instrumental end of a *jingle,* usually reserved for location, phone numbers, legal disclaimers, or any other information the advertiser needs to add.
- **Background:** Known also as *background noise,* it's usually music or sound effects that are placed behind the voice-over.
- **Board:** See *console.*

✔ **Boom:** An overhead mic stand.

✔ **Booth:** An enclosed, soundproofed room where voice actors usually work.

✔ **Branching:** Recording one part of a sentence with variables within that sentence as a means of customizing a response. Often recorded for multimedia games and voicemail systems. Also known as *concatenation*.

✔ **Butt-cut:** When sound files are placed together tightly with no dead air in between, particularly for a commercial voice-over demo, but it also applies to most demo types.

✔ **Cans:** Another word for *headphones*.

✔ **Channel:** Refers to the physical input or output of your software. Channels can be assigned to any available output, such as your speakers in the recording software system. Stereo systems have a left channel and a right channel.

✔ **Compression:** Reduces the dynamic range of an actor's voice. Engineers apply compression to cut through background music and sound effects.

✔ **Console:** A large desk-like piece of equipment where the audio engineer monitors, records, and mixes a voice-over session.

✔ **Control room:** Where the engineer and producer (and many times, the client) are located. This room is usually separate from the *booth*.

✔ **Cross talk:** When one mic picks up copy spoken into another mic. The sound is said to spill over or bleed into the other actor's mic.

✔ **Cue:** An electronic or physical signal given to an actor to begin performing.

✔ **Cue up:** Matching to time and speed, lining up an actor's voice to the visuals or music.

✔ **Cut:** A specific segment of the voice-over recording, usually referred to during editing.

✔ **Decibel (dB):** A unit for measuring the intensity of sound. Zero is no sound; 130 would cause acute aural pain.

✔ **De-esser:** A piece of equipment used to remove excess *sibilance*.

✔ **Dialogue:** A script calling for two people talking to each other.

✔ **Distortion:** Fuzziness in the sound quality of a recorded piece. Distortion usually happens because the original recording tends to be too loud. This usually happens if you go over the meter threshold as indicated often by a red light on the recording meter. When looking at the waveform, you can notice that the tops of the waveform are cut off like a plateau and no longer have peaks.

- **Earphones:** Also known as *cans, headphones,* or *headsets.* Worn during the session to hear your own voice as well as cues and directions from the engineer or producer. Also used to converse with the client during an ISDN or phone-patch session. A phone-patch session allows your client to hear you and provide artistic direction as you record by listening in on his or her telephone. ISDN is similar to phone patch in that your client can hear and direct you; however, the session is conducted using an ISDN line.

- **Engineer:** The person who operates the audio equipment during the voice-over session.

- **Equalization:** Also known as *EQ,* equalization is used to emphasize or de-emphasize certain frequencies, which can alter the sound of a voice.

- **Faders:** The vertically moving objects located on the lower section of a mixing console. Faders are used to increase or decrease the volume level of a particular track.

- **Fish-bowl effect:** When the actor in the booth can't hear what the engineer or producer is saying or vice-versa.

- **In the can:** A phrase connoting that a part of the copy or the entire spot is acceptable and done.

- **Jingle:** The short tune or song used in commercials. They're generally catchy and help make a marketing message memorable.

- **Mic:** A common, shortened form of the word *microphone.*

- **Mix:** The blending of voice, sound effects, music, and so on. Final mix usually refers to the finished product.

- **Monitors:** The loudspeakers in the control room.

- **Multitrack:** A machine capable of recording and replaying several different tracks at the same time.

- **Music bed:** The soundtrack that will be placed behind the copy or mixed in with it.

- **On mic/off mic:** Either speaking or not speaking directly into the microphone. An actor is always on mic when recording, unless shouting, and then turns his head slightly to speak off mic.

- **Patch:** To make an electrical/digital connection for recording and/or broadcast. Also referred to as a *phone patch* or *land patch.*

- **Phones:** A short word for *headphones.*

- **Pick-up session:** An additional session to complete the original. It may include making copy changes or character changes in a spot before it finally airs. A pick-up session usually happens after the client changes his or her mind before committing to air the spot.

✔ **Plosives:** The consonants that when produced create a burst of air. Basic English plosives include *t, k, p* (they're voiceless plosives, meaning that there is no vibration of the vocal folds required to produce those sounds) and *d, g,* and *b* (which are voiced plosives, meaning that it takes vibration of the vocal folds to produce those sounds).

✔ **Pop:** When voice sounds are registering too hard into the mic. Usually caused by *plosives.*

✔ **Pop filter:** A foam cover enveloping the mic or a nylon windscreen in front of the mic. Mitigates popping. Also known as a *pop stopper.*

✔ **Post-production:** Also known as *post.* The work done after the voice actor has finished recording the session and includes mixing in sound effects and music.

✔ **Regions:** A piece of audio data. An audio region can be a voice-over, sound effect, or piece of music. In most recording programs, regions are captured from an audio file and assembled together to create a playlist. When editing, you can edit a region into smaller parts or trim out the beginning or end. Audio regions are assembled as playlists for playback.

✔ **Reverb:** A variation of echo. It's an effect added to your voice in post-production.

✔ **Rough mix:** The step before the final mix. This is when the producer and engineer fine-tune levels of voice, music, and sound effects.

✔ **SFX:** Short for *sound effects.* Also referred to as *EFX.*

✔ **Session:** The event where a voice actor performs a script for recording purposes. A *session* is also the file name that includes all the parts of your recording, such as music, sound effects, vocal tracks, settings, and preferences. In your recording software, you likely open a recording session from the "File" menu and click "New."

✔ **Sibilance:** The snake-like hiss that you hear, particularly when saying words that contain the letter *s* or soft *c.*

✔ **Stand:** Where the printed script is placed in the booth.

✔ **Studio:** The facility where all recording and mixing for a commercial takes place.

✔ **Talkback:** The button connected to the microphone in the engineer's *console.* It allows the engineer or director to talk to the voice actor in the booth.

Grasping what hertz means in voice acting

We attended a voice-over workshop where the term *hertz* was explained in terms of the human voice. Hertz, named for the German physicist Heinrich Hertz, measures the number of cycles per second. Where the human voice is concerned, this means the number of times the vocal folds vibrate per second.

✔ A healthy male voice's fundamental frequency usually falls between 110 to 120 hertz.

✔ A healthy female voice's fundamental frequency usually falls between 200 to 210 hertz.

✔ A child voice's fundamental frequency usually falls between 300 to 400 hertz.

The higher the vibrations per second, the brighter the sound. To give you an example, you may be familiar with A440, also known as *concert pitch*. As an orchestra prepares to tune, the principal violinist will play this pitch to help others in the ensemble tune their instruments.

✔ **Time code:** A digital read-out on the engineer's *console* referring to audiotape and videotape positions. Used in film dubbing.

✔ **Tracks:** Every recording session has at least one track. After you hit record and you see a waveform show up in the software, you're seeing a track. A track can be made up of a single region or many regions in sequence.

✔ **Waveform:** A graphical representation of a recorded sound. The shape of the waveform tells you about the sound's characteristics, such as frequency and amplitude.

✔ **Windscreen:** A *pop filter* or *pop stopper*.

✔ **Wrap:** The end, as in "That's a wrap."

Consider yourself prepared for the next recording session where you have an engineer in the room or you're getting help from a technical wizard.

In the event you hear a word not on the list, never be afraid to ask for clarification. Industry people usually are genuinely helpful, and many are glad to discuss technical terms at length.

Positioning the Microphone and Script Stand

Getting the microphone and the stand in the right spot can make or break your recording. A well-positioned microphone is at mouth level, about two hand widths away from your mouth. The closer you are to the microphone, the more intimate the recording will sound. The farther away you are from the mic, the more room sound you'll inevitably pick up, which isn't desirable.

You also want to find a good spot for your script stand so you can easily read the words off your script and not be craning your neck to read the next word.

These sections explain about finding the sweet spot on your microphone and how to use a music stand to position your script, whether it's a piece of paper or a digital copy displayed on a tablet. Take the time to set up so that you're comfortable as you record!

Finding the sweet spot on a microphone

For most voice actors, the *sweet spot* is the exact point or area of the microphone where their voice sounds its absolute best. When you've been around microphones long enough, finding that sweet spot where you sound amazing will become second nature to you. If you haven't worked much with a mic, you know you've hit the sweet spot because it's where your voice sounds its most robust or fullest.

You may need to practice before you find your sweet spot; over time you'll know instinctively where to stand in front of the microphone to voice in the sweet spot. Even though each microphone is different, playing with your voice can help you to know how your voice sounds best and where to speak into the microphone.

When you're in the recording studio with an engineer, trust the engineer to know where to place the mic and how its placement is unique for each voice-over actor in the session. It's the engineer's job after all. When you do find your sweet spot, it's even sweeter.

When speaking into the mic, remember these tips to help your voice sound better:

- ✔ **Smile through your words.** If you smile while speaking, your mouth creates a way for softening words that begin with plosives such as the letters *p, t, k, b, d,* and *g.*

- ✔ **Put a pencil in front of your mouth.** The pencil acts as a barrier for the puff of air that leaves your mouth when saying words that begin with plosives.

- ✔ **Cut the air in half by speaking with your face turned down a bit.** Doing so can minimize the amount of air headed toward the microphone. You can also speak across the microphone instead of directly into it to minimize the impact of plosives.

Using a stand to hold your script

Generally speaking, placing the script stand between you and the microphone is best. Have the stand at a comfortable height in front of you so you'll be able to read right off the script, and the microphone will naturally pick up your performance. Don't put off the stand to the side, or you'll be constantly turning your head away from the microphone to read the words from the script.

If you're reading a script on a computer screen or off a tablet, position it so that you can see the copy well and maintain a clear line of vision between your script and your eyes. Whatever you do, don't take your eyes off the script when you're reading. As a voice actor, you have the benefit of always having the script in front of you and not having to memorize lines like an on-camera actor. Use this to your advantage by aligning your script well with your recording setup.

Hooking Up Your Equipment

Setting your studio up properly is paramount to getting the sound you want to have. In this section, you discover what equipment to use to hook up your equipment.

Digital input/output interfaces allow the user to transfer digital audio data that is stored as samples between two pieces of digital equipment, thereby avoiding extraneous conversion back to analog and reconversions to digital.

Digital I/O interface standard must send:

- ✔ The sample date
- ✔ The sample rate and timing information
- ✔ The bit-depth (word-length) used

To connect audio recording equipment in a professional recording studio, here is a list of cables to use:

- ✔ **AES/EBU standard (Audio Engineering Society/European Broadcast Union):** The serial transmission format standardized for professional digital audio signals. A specification using time division multiplex for data and balanced line drivers to transit two channels (left/right) of digital audio data on a single twisted pair cable using 3-pin XLR connectors. With this balanced configuration, AES/EBU data can be sent over long distances. It carries 24-bit audio and has multichannel capabilities.

✔ **S/PDIF (Sony/Philips Digital Interface Format):** A consumer version of the AES/EBU digital audio cable standard based on unbalanced coaxial cable and RCA connectors. Transmits up to 20-bit audio with extra bits holding track ID information.

✔ **Optical:** Optical digital interface is utilized on some professional gear, but mostly on consumer products. It consists of a fiber-optic cable with a light transmitter and receiver on each end by using a similar format to S/PDIF (see the preceding bullet).

✔ **TDIF and ADAT Lightpipe:** Tascam Digital Interface (TDIF) and the ADAT (Alesis Digital Audio Tape) Lightpipe are proprietary formats for transfer of digital audio in a multitrack situation. The TDIF interface uses specially shielded cables with regular DB-25-pin connectors, while the ADAT interface uses optical connections. Third-party company boxes allow interface between these connections and S/PDIF or AES/EBU equipped devices.

Your Work Pays Off: Time to Hit Record

It's your big moment. The moment all your hard work comes together to put into practice and record your voice. By this time, your equipment is set up, your mic is in position, and your script is in front you. All that's left is to start recording.

To make the actual recording in your recording software, do the following steps:

1. **Record enable the track that you want to record.**

   By clicking the "record enable" button, you're telling the software where you want your voice recorded to. For example, say your session template has three tracks, one for your voice, one for your *slate* (which is simply saying your name in a professional manner), and another for music. If you want your voice-over recorded on that first track, then click the "record enable" button on that particular track, and your voice-over will be recorded on track 1.

2. **Click the "record" button on the controls, usually identified by a red circular button.**

   As soon as you hit record, the cursor will begin to scroll across the screen and visually display soundwaves, which represent the sounds captured by the microphone.

   That's it.

We recommend that you record a short take first, such as simply reading out one of the lines you have to perform, just to be sure the software is recording correctly.

These sections explain how to record your first take, how to record multiple takes, and how to listen back to your work. Listening back to your recordings is a great way to identify mistakes, learn from them, and develop your voicing and editing skills.

Doing your first take

After you test the setup, you're ready to do your first take. A *take* is the recording of one specific piece of voice-over copy from start to finish.

To do your first take, stick to these simple steps:

1. **Read through the copy aloud first to be sure you're able to get through it without making any mistakes.**

   You must rehearse aloud because that's how you're going to do the actual recording.

2. **When you're ready, hit that big record button, take a deep breath, and perform the script.**

   Don't worry about getting everything right the first time. Just try to get through the entire script.

3. **After you finish performing the script, click the stop button in the recording software.**

4. **Immediately click "Save" to be sure you've saved your first take.**

Congratulations! You've just done your first take, which is a huge milestone.

Doing multiple takes

We understand if you didn't perfectly read through the entire script the first time. That's where the magic of multiple takes comes in. A *multiple take* is reading the script more than once in the same recording.

You can do multiple takes in two different ways without erasing what you've previously recorded:

✔ **In sequence:** You record one take after another. If you're new to recording software, this method is definitely easier.

✔ **In parallel:** You record multiple tracks. In other words, you can have a few different tracks for your voice-over recording in the session template and pick and choose from each what you want to include in the final mix.

Listening back

After you record your takes, you can have some fun and listen back to what you just recorded. Listening back, sometimes called the *playback,* is your first chance to hear your performance.

Advancing your skills with multitrack recording

Multitracking is the concept of a layered audio composition. Multitasking allows you to individually control and manipulate each sound within your voice-over recording. By recording with multitrack software, you can produce the foundation for music, sound effects, and other voices participating, which results in a fully produced sound.

For example, a musician's tracks can include individual tracks for percussion, guitar, keyboard, and vocals. Many multitrack software programs include at least eight tracks for you to work with and have a theoretical maximum of 256 tracks (although most computers usually don't have enough power to allow that much capacity). These multitracks can be your theme music, announcer introduction, segments, and sound effects.

To create a multitrack in your recording software program, do the following:

1. **Adjust the Gain control on your audio interface.**

   Within the recording program, set the recording level of your voice.

2. **Test your distance from the microphone to determine where you sound the clearest.**

3. **Do a short test recording.**

   Be sure that the recording meter never goes into the red because doing so may cause unwanted noise or distortion.

4. **Plug in headphones to your computer or audio interface for the best quality recording.**

   Otherwise the recording will pick up sound from your speakers.

5. **Begin recording.**

   Remember to keep your original microphone position. If you make a mistake, you can always do a second take and fix it when editing.

6. **Listen to the results.**

7. **When you finish and like your final recording, save your work.**

   We encourage that you save as you go, so that you don't lose anything if your program shuts down for whatever reason.

To play back, you simply use the controls in the recording software to rewind the recording back to the beginning by hitting the << button. Make sure you listen to the whole recording from start to finish. If you've recorded multiple takes, listen to them all, one after another.

When you listen to the playback, evaluate the recording and trust your ears. The human ear is an incredibly sensitive instrument, capable of picking up on even the most subtle nuances in a recording. Did you like the performance? Did it sound natural? If your performance was good, how was the recording quality? For example, did you hear any background noise, such as dogs barking or the furnace or air conditioner running? Do you notice any distortion or feedback? Were any plosives particularly startling? Are there any breaths, coughs, times you cleared your throat, or other mouth noises that you need to edit?

If your ears are telling you that the recording needs to be improved, you have a couple of options:

✔ You can either record another take, hoping that you can nail the performance.

✔ You can edit the audio. For more about editing, check out Chapter 19.

Chapter 19

Editing and Mixing: Getting More Advanced

*W*elcome to the world of audio post-production. It's a land of technical tools, tips, and tricks where you can fix blunders that occurred during the recording (to a degree) and create a mix by blending the various sounds such as your vocal track, music track, and sound effects into an inspiring audio production.

Editing generally involves correcting mistakes, removing breaths, clicks, and pops, but can also include speeding up or slowing down certain words. *Mixing* is the art of balancing all the sounds of your recording so the vocal track is the most prominent, and the other sounds complement the voice, instead of compete with it. A good mix is a pleasure to listen to, and everything can be heard clearly without any one sonic element taking over the show. You'll know you have a good mix on your hands if the recording sounds equally good on your computer speakers, as it does in your car or home stereo system.

In this chapter, you discover the ins and outs of editing and mixing. It's really quite amazing what can be done with sound!

Getting to Know Your Editing Tools

Audio post-production is now more a process of elaboration and embellishment than a process of necessary correction and repair. Although independently produced voice-overs are sounding better, the production can be greatly enhanced to sound more like a polished broadcast. The objective is to make your voice-over flow seamlessly from one section to the next.

Most recording and editing programs have similar tools that allow you to edit the audio you have just recorded. We cover those tools in this section. In Chapter 18, we introduce some of the most popular audio recording and editing software packages, but regardless of which recording software you choose, the editing tools are pretty standard and work in more or less the same way.

Undo

Making mistakes is easy, so our favorite editing tool is *undo*. You can fix mistakes that you made during the editing process. Undo simply reverses or reverts back to a previous state. Knowing that you have an undo editing tool up your sleeve can give you the freedom to get a lot more creative and not worry so much about making your changes permanent. In the tech world, this process is referred to as *nondestructive* editing because your changes don't compromise or destroy your original recording.

You can always go back and undo your mistakes, usually up to 99 steps back. In most software programs, you can find the undo feature under the Edit menu or for a shortcut, just type control-z on your keyboard.

Redo

Okay, we've opened a can of worms here. We know. But if we're going to mention undo (see the preceding section) and how amazing it is, we'd be remiss if we didn't mention *redo*. Sometimes you may hit the undo shortcut a few too many times, and you need to undo your undo — called a redo.

Undo's and redo's are helpful tools to have at your disposal before getting into the heavy duty slicing and dicing (or chopping if you're so inclined) with the tools in the next sections.

The selector

The selector is used to highlight the section you want to edit. Clicking and dragging the cursor across any audio waveform in a track selects that range for editing. After you select an area, you can cut, copy, paste, or apply special effects to only the selected area.

The grabber

The grabber, often symbolized by a hand, is a very useful tool. With this tool, regions can be moved or rearranged along the timeline of a track. The *timeline* is the horizontal axis that has timestamps printed out in one-second increments. With the grabber, you can often double-click to select the region and move an entire section forward or backwards in the timeline. Remember to click-and-hold the selected region with your grabber tool to move it.

The trimmer

With this tool, regions can be quickly shortened or expanded to a desired length. If you've ever cropped a photo, you'll get the hang of trimming audio quickly. To trim a region, simply click the cursor at the right or left of a region and drag toward the center. As you drag, the edge of the region is trimmed off until you release the mouse button. To extend a region or expand it beyond its current area, click the cursor on the appropriate edge of the region and drag outwards. The more you drag, the more audio is uncovered until the region is restored to its original length.

The zoomer

By clicking the zoomer tool, the cursor turns into a miniature magnifying glass. To use the zoomer, follow these steps:

1. **Click and drag the magnifying glass over a portion of a track that you want to view in greater detail.**

   As you drag, a dashed box appears that indicates the range that you zoom in on.

2. **Zoom in closer than you may think you need to make the cut.**

   Use zoom for editing, cutting, or other "surgical work."

3. **Edit the waveform at what's called the *zero crossing*, where the waveform line crossed from a positive amplitude (the crest) to a negative amplitude (the valley).**

   The zero crossing is where you should make your edit to avoid awful clipping sounds. Now, if you're done editing and somehow you've found yourself staring at a white screen, you've zoomed in way too far. Zoom out by double-clicking the magnifying glass. Alternatively, look for the 100% zoom setting that should get you back to a normal view.

 Editing is the process of removing sections of audio that you don't want due to a mistake, laugh, cough, sneeze, or other element. Editing is very subjective and only you as the producer can discern whether something should be edited out of the recording or left in. Your finished recording should flow seamlessly from one sentence to the next.

Editing a Voice-Over

Editing audio is very important. Editing skills allow you to cover up small mistakes, clean up the recording from clicks and pops, odd background noises, and more. The end result is a much more polished and professional audio recording. In this section, you're introduced to rudimentary editing techniques, some of which may be a review if you're somewhat familiar with editing in general.

The basic editing techniques are similar to those of a word processor:

- Recording
- Selecting
- Copying
- Cutting
- Pasting

When editing audio, pay attention to these first steps:

1. **Identify the region of audio that you want to edit.**

2. **Select the region of audio.**

3. **Perform your edit to that specific region.**

4. **Listen to your edited section to be sure you made clean edits.**

The beauty of digital audio recording is that you can start and stop the process at your leisure and combine the best parts of each recording into your final masterpiece.

Editing dialogue

Dialogue editing, the editing of your voice-over recording, is required when the tracks need to be cleaned up. Often editing is required if noises occur between lines of dialogue or to delete long pauses between the characters speaking.

Your first attempt at cleaning up the situation is of course to edit the voice-over. Editing is often faster and sounds more consistent than setting up the microphone and recording the line of script again, especially if days have passed between the initial recording and the editing session, because you can actually sound a little different due to a variety of factors:

- ✔ Your vocal health
- ✔ Air humidity
- ✔ Barometric pressure
- ✔ Environmental differences
- ✔ Microphone placement

You may consider editing the dialogue or rerecording the script in the following scenarios:

- ✔ **If a single word is mispronounced:** Check to see if you recorded the word elsewhere and try to copy the good version of the word and paste it over the bad version. This may not always work, but sometimes you can be amazed at how easy the edit was.

- ✔ **If entire sections are done incorrectly:** What if you mispronounced the name of a city or person throughout the entire script? It's best to go back and rerecord the script. Hopefully the script isn't too long.

- ✔ **If there are simply too many mistakes:** Consider rerecording the script if, despite your best efforts, the edits make the recording sound choppy with a lot of starts. And. Stops. You don't want that. Your client will likely ask you to rerecord it anyway, so save yourself the embarrassment and get it right the first time.

✔ **If you hear a lot of moisture in your mouth during the playback:** The mouth makes all kinds of strange noises and not all of them are flattering. Lip smacks or mouth pops sound unprofessional to say the least. And for a listener, they will be extremely distracting. This usually occurs because you have too much saliva in your mouth.

Fear not! There are some remedies to reduce the amount of saliva in your mouth, especially right before jumping into a recording session.

✔ The simplest solution is to drink some water and wash down the excess saliva.

✔ Green apples soak up saliva. Eat an apple before recording.

Editing out breaths

During recording sessions, you can sometimes be heard breathing through your nose. Many different opinions and creative processes exist when it comes to interpretation and performance, but the trend is to remove the breaths from the recording.

Editing breaths out of auditions may be a reasonable thing to do, especially if you're having some respiratory issues or have a cold. You can remove the breaths to make the audio sound cleaner, but the end result could be that the voice-over loses an aspect of its humanity and may sound unnatural.

If the breath "sounds" right or feels like it should be there given the context of the copy and character, you could leave it in. This is a matter of preference and discernment. Some extra work may be involved with removing breaths that don't align well with the read or character, but the process may be what makes the difference between a polished presentation and one that didn't fall in line with the context of the script.

Replacing automatic dialogue

Automatic Dialog Replacement (ADR) is simply rerecording specific lines that couldn't be salvaged in the edit. The sound and performance of the lines must be matched to the original performance. For a successful retake, attempt to re-create the original take by recording in the same tone of voice, through the same microphone, positioned in the same way.

Is audible inhalation a no-no?

One morning we received a question from a voice actor who asked, "I've run into voice-over artists locally who tell me that all auditions should be 'de-breathed,' not just lowering the volume of breath noises, but cutting them out completely. What do you recommend?"

Professional voice actor Jodi Krangle, responded to this question in this manner: "What an interesting question! For narrations, I don't suggest ever leaving breaths in at all. And when I remove breaths, I also remove the space, but not too much, so it still sounds natural. You can imagine a breath might be there, but you don't need to hear it. The breaths don't take away from the content that way.

"When it comes to commercials, breaths can sometimes be left in, but I find that they're mostly removed then too. Time is at a premium with most commercials, and breaths take up space. If I'm recording a commercial in a different studio though, I've noticed that sometimes (the producers) leave them in for a truly "conversational" read. So it's really a subjective kind of decision on the part of the producers.

"As for character voices? Breaths are a whole other ballgame from what I understand. It's all about the acting. If the character breathes in a certain way or in a certain place, it's part of the acting. If it's not part of the acting, it probably shouldn't be there."

Focusing on Sound Editing

Sound design puts an auditory stamp on your voice-over and shapes the overall consistency of the recording's theme. This section helps you identify what elements of your recording need to be fixed or embellished before the editing stage.

Including sound design

Just as a set designer would design the backdrop and props for a theatrical set, a sound designer does the same thing but with sound. A sound designer's objective is to create a realistic sonic landscape that builds a believable world for the listener to take in.

Capturing room tone

Room tone is the sound a room makes. Yes, rooms make sounds! Right now, as silently as you can, close your eyes and focus on listening to the sound of the room you're in. Can you hear a distant hum or buzz? Maybe it's a windy day and you can hear leaves rustling in the trees outside. Or, perhaps you're in a basement and you can hear plumbing or the mechanical elements in your house creaking.

A neat experiment may be to capture the room tone in an audio recording that you let run while you aren't in the room. When you come back in the room, stop the recording and then listen back to get an idea of what sounds are being produced and captured in the room.

One tip is to record a bit, say 30 to 60 seconds, of the room tone on a separate track in your recording software. Why would you want to do this? Good question. Well, if you've done a lot of editing of the vocals, you can reduce some of the choppiness of the edits by placing some of the room tone under the edited vocals.

Creating ambiance

You may want to include other sounds in your audio production that give the listener the feeling that he's in another location. Ambiance consists of sounds present in your recording environments that create a feeling. Similar to a beautifully crafted, descriptive sentence that transports your imagination to another time and place, you can create this type of ambiance in your recordings.

For example, a voice-over that's recorded at a baseball game has an ambiance with cheering fans, vendors selling treats, or the crack of a bat hitting a ball. These are production decisions made after you've completed the recording and you're looking to embellish it through sound design.

Using sound effects

Recording intelligible dialogue is the number one priority of your audio recording. Adding sound effects should augment the original recording. A few examples would be doors slamming, cars passing by, or birds singing in the trees. The purpose of sound effects is to create the illusion that the auditory environment is real, rather than fabricated.

Placing an emphasis on selected sounds can create tension, atmosphere, and emotion in your recording. It can also impart personality to demo. Sound effects can exaggerate or diminish the listeners' perception of a voice actor and the characters that they may be portraying. Clocks ticking can make a character sound busy or impatient; whistling can make a character sound relaxed or free-spirited. Carnival noises can make a character sound silly.

Sound effects fall into two main categories:

- ✔ **Specific sound effects:** An element with a specific hit point such as a door slamming or car crashing

- ✔ **Background sound effects:** Ambiance, birds, traffic, air conditioner, machinery, and so on

Sound effects come from many sources:

- ✔ Production reels
- ✔ Commercial libraries
- ✔ Your own library
- ✔ Synthesizers and samplers
- ✔ Location recording
- ✔ Foley studio

Mixing Your Voice-Over

Mixing is balance engineering. The mix is the time for combining art with technology. In the mix, not only do you need to balance the volume of the various tracks, but also you're placing them in space by putting your tracks in the left or right speaker. This technique is known as *balancing*.

Balancing the width or pan of your mix doesn't have to be constant. Consider the listener's perspective for stereo instruments, such as a piano. When listening to a piano, you hear the higher notes coming out of the left speaker and the lower notes out of the right speaker. If you're going to get creative with this type of balancing, remember to maintain either the audience perspective (what the instrument would sound like if you were sitting in the audience) or the player perspective (what the instrument would sound like if you were the one playing).

For voice-overs, it's almost always centered. Because it's only a single track of voice that's recorded, it should be placed in the center and not panned to the left or right.

Keep all lead instruments or vocals in the center for proper balance. The bottom line is that creating consistency and predictability gives your listener a sense of comfort.

Close your eyes when listening to your mix. Focus on just what you're hearing. After sitting in a chair for a long time, you become accustomed to hearing your mix from that position. Get up and take a step back, even to the back of the room. Notice how it sounds different. Make the small adjustments you need to so everything sounds well-balanced.

In this section, you discover how mixing your audio, be it an audition, a demo, or even a big project for your newest client, involves balancing the voice-over, music, and sound effect tracks for optimal clarity and impact.

Planning your mix

The best way to start your mix is to think ahead with the end goal in mind. You most likely have a vision of what you want your finished recording to sound like. Your goal is to maintain that sound from the beginning to the end of your production.

Building your mix

Start by setting your lead vocal volume to a good level. Because your voice is the central focus, all other elements in the mix are secondary. Gradually adjust the volume faders until all the elements within your demo are set at appropriate levels. This is called a *static mix*. Keep the focus on your voice. Your voice should be the loudest and clearest element of your mix.

 Enhance the sonic quality of your recording by isolating individual tracks using the solo button. By pressing Solo, all other tracks will be muted, allowing you to only hear the track you've designated. Two special effects that you can apply to either a selected region of audio or to your entire production are covered in this section.

Volume faders

Volume faders control the volume. Each track in your mix has it own fader that controls the volume level.

Fade in, fade out

When you wrote your voice-over script, you left room for mixing. In fading in and fading out, you can mix in your intro, the section that announces your name, and the kind of demo that you're voicing. It's most effective if this is the voice of an announcer, distinct from your own. Some professionals prefer to introduce themselves while others employ an actor of the opposite gender to record their intros.

For example, if you're producing a podcast, you can try fading your background music in when a new segment begins. Lower the volume level of the music when you are speaking so that your listeners can hear every word you say. At the end of the segment, fade your background music out. Use musical transitions between the various segments of your recording. These musical transitions are known as bumpers, stages, or sweepers.

Getting Acquainted with Production Techniques and Tools

Any device that processes audio can be considered a signal processor. Elements that can be processed are the frequency, amplitude, pitch, time, and phase. In some recording studios, you'll see racks of audio processing equipment. Why do they need so much equipment? Many pieces of audio equipment are dedicated signal processors, which means they only can perform adjustments to one of the elements of sound, but they do it really well with a lot of precision and control. Multi-signal processors allow you to manipulate two or more elements.

Nowadays, you don't have to invest in an entire room full of audio equipment or have a dozen dedicated signal processors. Most audio recording software programs have a standard set of signal processing capabilities. Plus, you can often add on other functionality by installing a plug-in.

Regardless of whether you're creating a studio with a lot of signal processing hardware or whether you're taking the simplified route and sticking with software exclusively, you can achieve amazing results.

Frequencies

Frequency is the number of sound waves per unit time. Check out Table 19-1 for a chart of frequency ranges.

Table 19-1	Frequency Ranges and Their Characteristics
Frequency Ranges	*Characteristic*
Very Low	20 Hz–200 Hz
Low Middle	200 Hz–1000 Hz
High Middle	1000 Hz–5000 Hz
High	5000 Hz–16000 Hz
Very High	16000 Hz–20000 Hz

Audio bandwidth

You can pack a lot of sonic information in the mid-range (from 800 Hz to 4000 Hz), because that's where the human ear is most sensitive.

Controlling frequencies

An *equalizer* is any device, hardware or software, whose primary function is to modify the frequency response of the audio. *Equalization* is the process of altering the frequency response of a signal so certain frequencies become more or less pronounced than others. Equalizers give control over the harmonic and enharmonic partial content.

Equalizers can be considered to be musical. For example, the low "E" on a keyboard is exactly 80 Hz. A tuning fork used to tune instruments in an orchestra rings an "A" note and is exactly 440 Hz. Think of how the concert master tunes before the orchestra begins to play. The pitch the violinist plays is A440.

Equalization was originally invented to compensate for signal loss in telephones and radio when hearing the person speaking on the other end was difficult. By boosting the signal around the 1000 Hz mark, the human voice became clearer and more audible. This is why your friends and family all have a similar sound when speaking over the phone; the frequencies have been boosted in such a way as to make it easier to hear.

Also known as equalization or EQ, filters are used to increase or decrease the volume level in a specific range of audio frequencies. The most common filters are the simple bass and treble controls found on inexpensive stereo systems, which act on a broad range of frequencies. Other more sophisticated filters are designed to surgically boost or cut very narrow bands of the audio spectrum.

When it comes to mixing, a general rule is to decrease rather than increase frequencies wherever possible. Decreasing undesired sounds is always less obtrusive, and increasing too much can make a track too loud and lead to digital distortion when encoding. The end result will be a clearer sounding audio recording.

Graphic equalizers

There are professional and consumer graphic equalizers that visually display the curves on a screen. When you make adjustments to a graphic equalizer, you're adjusting the center frequency. Professional equalizers have 27–32 bands.

Roll-off filters

Roll-off filters cut out all the frequencies above or below the cut-off point. Filters are often used in live sound, but also have their place in the recording studio. You filter out unwanted sounds by sorting out the frequencies that make up the sounds. Essentially, you're deciding which frequencies you don't want to hear and are eliminating them.

A *high-frequency (HF) roll-off* removes all the frequencies above the cut-off point. A low-frequency (LF) roll-off removes all the frequencies below the cut-off point, known as the *cutoff frequency.* The cutoff frequency is 3 decibels (dB) below the maximum output. The cutoff frequency is sometimes called a *breakaway point* or *turnover frequency.*

You may use an HF roll-off filter to eliminate an unwanted high-pitched hiss. On the low end, you may use an LF roll-off filter to eliminate rumbling street noise. Setting the roll-off filter at 80Hz is likely going to get rid of a lot of that rumbling you hear in an amateur recording.

Be conservative when using roll-off filters because they're blunt instruments that all but eliminate all sounds above or below the frequency of choice. The side effects are that your audio production sounds likes it's missing a floor or doesn't have any weight to it. On the other end of the spectrum, your recording sounds like it doesn't have air to breathe because you cut it all out.

The recommendation then is that if you are going to roll off low frequencies, never roll off more than 160 Hz and below. On the high end, you can likely roll off 16,000 Hz or sometimes read as 16 kilohertz (kHz) and above without really noticing.

Shelving filters

As the simplest form of filtering, shelving increases or decreases all frequencies above or below a fixed frequency. A bass shelving filter, also called a *low-pass filter,* increases or decreases everything below its fixed center frequency, the cutoff frequency. Likewise a treble shelving filter, also called a high-pass filter, increases or decreases everything above its fixed center. A single control typically adjusts the amount of amplification (increase) or attenuation (decrease), also known as boost or cut.

Say that you renovated your kitchen and have just put all the dishes away. The plates are in their place and the cups too. Then you realize that you want more room for your plates and you'll need to raise the shelf of your cups. With your cups still on the shelf, you raise the entire shelf at once, which raises all the cups too. That's similar to how the shelving equalization method works. All cups, I mean, frequencies are affected and raised by the same amount.

If you increase a shelving filter by 15 dB at the 10 kHz mark, you cause every other frequency above 10 kHz to also be amplified by 15 dB.

Because you're using a shelving filter, you've raised all the frequencies at once. These filters are useful for making broad changes like reducing boomy bass and wind noise. The output of your recording software can easily be overloaded by too much bass or treble, so it is recommended that you use these filters to cut or decrease high and low frequencies to prevent digital distortion.

Bandpass filters

Bandpass filters can be used to increase or decrease audio on both sides of a center frequency. Bandpass filters are commonly used as mid-range filters, because they have little effect on either high or low frequencies. The familiar graphic equalizer is just a set of bandpass filters tuned to different center frequencies.

More sophisticated versions, called *sweepable bandpass filters,* have an additional control allowing you to change the center frequency. Bandpass filters are useful for increasing the intelligibility of a speaker without increasing hiss or background noise. A variation of the bandpass filter is the notch filter, which increases or decreases all frequencies except those around the center frequency.

Parametric filters

Think of a parametric filter as a surgical editing tool for very precise equalization adjustments. A parametric filter is a bandpass filter with an additional control to adjust the width of the frequency band being affected.

The peak method for applying a parametric filter is created when the center frequency is amplified (increased) or attenuated (decreased). Three factors make up the bell curve:

- ✔ **Amplitude:** The amount of boost or cut to the frequency

- ✔ **Center frequency:** The specific frequency that you select

- ✔ **Quality factor:** Sometimes just labeled "Q," the ratio of center frequency to bandwidth; the higher the Q, the narrower the bandwidth

Sibilance is a high-frequency characteristic accentuated by high-frequency peaks. *Sibilance* can occur when you say words that begin with an "s." It's more common among female actors because the tone of their voices is of a higher frequency. To avoid this, move yourself off-axis, meaning that you're not directly in front of the microphone, but rather off to the side slightly.

Reduce dynamic ranges

A compressor's basic function is to reduce the dynamic range of an audio recording, which is the difference between the loudest and softest sounds in a recording. By reducing the volume of the loudest sounds, a compressor lets you raise the level of the entire audio track, making it all sound louder than it originally was. Compression can be a big help in achieving intelligible audio tracks with a more uniform volume that will sound great on any stereo system.

A compressor consists of a level detector that measures the incoming signal, and an amplifier that controls the gain by the level detector. A threshold control sets the level at which compression begins. Below the threshold, the compressor acts like a straight piece of wire. But when the input level reaches the threshold, then the compressor begins reducing its output level by an amount determined by the ratio control.

The ratio control establishes the proportion of change between the input and output levels. If you set the compression ratio to 2:1, then when the input signal gets twice as loud, the output signal will increase by only half. If you set the ratio to its maximum (10:1 or more), the compressor becomes a "limiter" that locks the maximum level at the threshold. While a compressor can level out a recording, high levels of compression can also introduce artifacts including "pumping," in which there is an audible up and down change in volume of a track, or "breathing," which sounds like someone inhaling and exhaling as the background noise level goes up and down.

Done properly, compressing the dynamic range will normalize the audio until its loudest point is at maximum level. The overall signal level is now higher, which makes for clearer audio, and also reduces encoding distortion. The only downside of normalizing is that it increases the noise as well as the audio signal, so it should be used carefully. It should be your last step before exporting your finished production, and you may not need it at all.

Increase dynamic ranges

As the level of the audio signal gets louder, the expander's amplifier turns up further, making loud signals even louder. An expander can be used to reduce noise in a process called *downward expansion*. In this case, you set the threshold just above the level of the background noise. The expander will then raise the volume of everything above the threshold, but won't change anything below the threshold, thereby lowering the perceived background noise.

Creating space with reverb and delay

When mixing, you can give the listener a feeling that the sound is present or absent through the use of time and time delays. For example, a sound will be perceived more present if there are no time delays, no echo, or no reverberations. Alternatively, a sound is perceived more absent if there's a lot of echo. A sound that echoes appears to be coming from far away.

Echo

An *echo* is an example of sound being altered in time. The sound travels from your mouth and slaps up against the wall (of the canyon or building) and then returns to your ear. At a canyon, you may even hear multiple echoes because of the time it takes for the sound to bounce off each side of the canyon.

Reverb

A more subtle example of the time effect is how an instrument sounds in a music hall or amphitheatre. The big open space with tall walls is designed to bounce the sound around and then out to the audience.

Each of these effects can be reproduced in the studio environment artificially through the use of reverb equipment or reverb software. Reverb is measured in the time it takes for the signal to decrease in amplitude by 60 dB. This is called RT60. There are two main elements which make up RT60: time and amplitude.

In your recording software, you'll likely be able to adjust the RT60, which may be called the *time decay*. Increasing the time decay gives the listener the perception that the recording was done in a larger space such as a stadium or a concert hall.

Here are some facts about reverb:

- ✔ Reverb has multiple random reflections over time
- ✔ Early reflections of sound within a room first determine the perception of space
- ✔ Reverb is frequency dependent, meaning that higher frequency sounds are perceived to sound louder in a reflection than lower frequency sounds
- ✔ Each room has a unique density of reflections

Too much reverb can really clutter up a mix. Going crazy applying reverb to each track, your voice-over, and music soundtracks make your mix sound busy and tiring to listen to. Less is more.

Automatic double tracking (ADT)

Reverb is multiple delays of the signal. A single slap delay was popular in music when Elvis started producing #1 hits in the 1950s. Elvis's vocals had a 98 millisecond (ms) delay that gave them a touch of depth and sound as if he sang the song multiple times exactly the same each time. Yes, he had an amazing voice, but maybe you didn't know he had a technical trick helping him: a common production technique called ADT or automatic double tracking.

Instead of recording the same vocal track over multiple times and then layering the voices, ADT adds a 15 to 35 ms delay to simulate the effect of multiple singers.

Delay processing

Delay is a controlled audio processing element and can be heard if the sound bounces around and you hear different arrival times. In digital processors, the parameter pre-delay defines the initial perception of space.

Digital delay line (DDL)

Delay lines are distinct echoes heard at the exact same spacing as the beats of the music. A popular music technique, these delay lines can be easily calculated by figuring out the tempo of the song, measured in beats per minute and how long of a delay you want, such as a sixteenth note (short delays) or a quarter note (longer delays). The result is that repetitions happen in sync with the music.

Whatever the depth of sound you're trying to create, or lack thereof, stick with it throughout your entire production. If you decide that your entire recording should sound like you're in an air-tight scientific lab, you'll have no echo or reverb. Whereas if your recording should sound like you're on stage giving a speech, it will have a touch of reverb to simulate that you're in a performance hall. Either way, make your choice and stick with it.

Pitch processing

Phase shift is the time relationship between two signals. You can use phase shift to your advantage for a production technique called *phase tuning*. The way you make this work is by applying the rule of 3X. Set up your first microphone say 3 feet away. Then your second microphone should be 9 feet away. You can create a neat effect if you have two of the same type of microphone recording the same subject at the same time.

Phase shift

Digital processing plug-ins re-create the manual work of setting up microphones at exact distances to create the phase tuning effect. Phase shifters are an example of this. Check your plug-ins and try it out. Sometimes, it's best to try an effect to hear how it sounds.

Phaser

A *phaser,* a popular guitar pedal effect, uses equalization to achieve phase shift by sweeping through multiple notch filters. It sounds like a whooshing sound that's passing over the audio recording. Some people have even said that a phaser can have a dizzying effect. Be seated before trying!

Noise reduction

Music masks noise that exists at a lower level within the same bandwidth. If you reduce the bandwidth of an audio signal, the perceived noise is also reduced. A *noise gate* is a plug-in that shuts out all sound below a set volume threshold. Sounds above the threshold are allowed through the gate untouched. Sounds below the threshold aren't allowed through. This tool can work wonders if you have a low-level hum or drone in the background that is audible between vocal passages. If you're running into such an issue, experiment with a noise-gate to see if it helps.

The *noise floor* of an audio device is the noise power generated by the device itself in the absence of any other equipment. This is measured as the signal-to-noise ratio: the loudness of the signal versus the loudness of the noise. In an ideal world, there would be no noise, but all devices and pieces of equipment make some noise, albeit often in miniscule amounts. Still, it's an important factor to consider both in the initial building of your studio, the setup of each recording session, and when listening back to your recording. You just need to come to terms with the fact there will always be a little noise. If you think it's louder than it should be, then perhaps a little troubleshooting is required to isolate and ultimately reduce or at least minimize the noise.

Chapter 20

Recording the Finished Product

· ·

In This Chapter

▶ Decoding artistic direction in voice-over recording

▶ Being your own director

▶ Evaluating the finished product

· ·

After you book a job, the fun actually begins. Taking a script and running with it can be one of the most thrilling aspects of working as a voice actor. The client or director has asked you to breathe life into the script, and now is the time for you to shine. Now is the time to actually record.

As a voice actor, you get to shape how the voice-over sounds and vocally build characters to be believable, interesting, and engaging. Your voice is the vehicle for the words, and the client has hired you to do justice to what the author or copywriter has written. With your help, their words can be lifted from the written page and spoken aloud to give a new dimension of meaning and understanding in the audio medium. Chapter 5 helps you interpret a piece of copy and bring the words to life.

You're ready for the recording studio now. This chapter helps you interpret and decode artistic direction, figure out how to handle unclear direction, determine how to give yourself some direction when recording, and understand what to do when listening to the finished product.

Cracking the Artistic Direction during Recording

After you get a job and are ready to record, you may receive some contradictory information from the director. *Artistic direction* basically is how the director wants you to sound while reading the copy. Not all jobs come with artistic direction, and in those instances, you need to infer what you should do based upon the script and other clues the client provides you. You can also obtain this information by simply asking for direction regarding how they want the voice-over to sound.

When artistic direction is fuzzy, you need to be able to decipher what the director really means when he asks you to do something. Most of the time, your director provides clear instructions. However, sometimes the artistic direction isn't straightforward. In these sections, we identify different ways that you can help yourself in those situations and better understand the artistic direction you may (or may not) receive during a recording session.

Receiving conflicting or contradictory direction

Your director may tell you something that is unclear and pulls you in different directions. When this happens, be sure to ask for clarification if you can on what the director's expectations are. If you're unable to get clarification, try to figure out what the director wants and give a read that best reflects how you feel it should be read, given the target audience. Consider the following examples with some suggestions on how to address these confusing directions a director may give you:

✔ "We want your read to be happy, yet sad," or "You need to sound strong, yet vulnerable," so how do you take it? Finding a happy medium between those two extremes or using subtle vocal nuance can help.

✔ "Read the text in a relaxed manner, but you need to put 45 seconds worth of copy into a 30-second spot." Don't you just love trying to cram copy into the time allotted? Doing so is kind of like running a verbal gauntlet. You need to keep the recording within the confines of the set time limit, but you still have a responsibility to deliver the text as it has been written.

Speaking slightly faster than you normally speak can help to shave seconds off of what may ordinarily be a longer read. Some spots don't have as much discrepancy between the time allotted and how long it really takes to record; however, sometimes meeting this request and recording a certain amount of text in allotted time is unrealistic.

When you encounter this request, we suggest these few ideas:

• Ask the client or director if the script can be edited down slightly to meet the allotted time.

- Let the client or director hear first-hand by reading the script through (without breathing!) to show him how unreasonable this request is. After hearing the rushed, unnatural read, most clients and/or directors make changes to the copy so that it better fits with the time for the spot.

- Record two versions. Make one recording where you've read the script verbatim with the time constraints. Make another recording, edited and pared down, to make the recording fit in the time allotted, while sounding natural.

When making comments about the copy, gently make a suggestion in a friendly way to improve the text, especially if you know the client well. Just be careful with what you say and to whom you say it. A lot of work went into writing the script, and many of the people in the room or on the line (if you're recording remotely) may have been personally involved in the writing effort. Tread lightly. The director and other individuals involved with the client may not be willing to make any changes to the script. Be professional, but don't let people take advantage of you.

Deciphering ambiguous direction

Your director may give you some ambiguous direction, such as "Be a tree," or "Sound more purple," This kind of direction can often result in numerous takes with you grasping at straws, trying to figure out what the director wants.

For example, maybe you're recording for a voice-over for a grape juice commercial and the director tells you that your read isn't "purple" enough. How do you make your voice sound like a color? Think grape? Oftentimes, just even putting yourself in the place of whatever it is that you're supposed to sound like according to the direction can get the take at least somewhat closer to what is being asked for. You need this skill also for self-direction. Refer to the later section, "Directing Yourself When You Record Your Voice" for advice.

When you receive this type of direction, look at it as an opportunity and try the following suggestions until you can get the money take (a *money take* is the final recording they end up going with):

✔ **Let loose, explore, and play with your voice.** Be creative and try different things. Don't clam up or feel self-conscious. Remember that the goal of the casting director or director is to get the absolute best possible performance out of you. Finding that "voice" within you is just as important to him as it is to you because his job often depends on producing great performances.

✔ **Ask questions for clarity.** If you've just delivered a line based on the direction, you can ask something like, "Just like that?" or "That felt good. Do you want to go with this take?" The director may realize at that very moment that yes, it's what she wanted and that you nailed it! (Refer to the next question for more information about asking questions when you want more clarification from your director.)

✔ **Take a deep breath and keep everything in perspective.** If you need to, excuse yourself for five minutes, go to the bathroom, and breathe deeply. When you're frustrated or don't feel appreciated, remember that you're doing something you enjoy. You could be doing something much riskier to earn money.

Directors who don't know how to express what they want often give you the opportunity to do so. We hope (as much as you probably hope) that they're patient and good humored. Not all directors have patience for voice actors who don't understand their vision. At some time in your career, you probably will face differences of opinion and even physical challenges where your voice is concerned when recording a job. Just monitor how you feel and remember that nothing lasts forever. The recording session will eventually end; the longer you're there, the more the client will have to pay you for your time.

Handling questionable and offensive vocal direction

Some voice actors unfortunately have received not only odd, but uncomfortable and embarrassing vocal direction, particularly relating to race and sex. If you find that you're in a situation that makes you feel icky, remember that you do have rights, and we hope you exercise them to both remove yourself from the situation and stand up for yourself.

When you let the people in charge of the session know that you don't appreciate being treated in a particular way, they may apologize and you can start on a fresh page with them. However, if this behavior continues even after you have made your discomfort with the behavior toward you known, see if someone else can come in and direct the session in a more professional manner.

Looking for clues when the artistic direction is lacking

When you're recording a job, you ideally will have some kind of artistic direction that explains what the client wants. Sometimes, though, you may not receive specific direction about the delivery and other aspects to the job.

If you don't receive any direction, you can take the initiative and figure out what the client wants. Put on your detective hat and start looking for clues by trying to answer the following questions:

- ✔ **Who is meant to hear this message?** Knowing who the target audience is can give you more insight on how to communicate to that demographic. The answer to this question may also give you a better understanding of the text and what is being asked of you.

- ✔ **What does it mean?** Do you have a firm grasp on what you are saying? You need to completely understand the text and what is being asked of you in order to effectively communicate the message to the intended target audience.

- ✔ **Why is it relevant to the people hearing the message?** Think about why those people intended to hear the message should care. Why should they listen to you? What's in it for them? Understanding why the message is being shared with that particular demographic will translate in a more informed and believable read.

- ✔ **Who would the person on the receiving end want to hear from?** The messenger, or voice role in this case, is important to consider when positioning the read and selling the message to the target audience. If you were part of that listening audience, what sort of person or professional would you want to hear from? For instance, if it's a commercial about spending time around the dinner table as an investment in your family, you'd probably want to hear it coming from another parent instead of a family therapist or psychologist.

- ✔ **How can I best communicate the message?** Taking all the information from this list into account, you need to figure out the best way to interpret the script, which character role to use, and how to understand the motivation for why the audience would care to hear and act on your message. Experiment with a few different takes and go with what you consider to be the most believable take that the audience would relate to best.

Keep in mind that some clients or directors may not know what they need and are open to hearing all kinds of voices and interpretations. If the direction is lacking, give the client an opportunity to outline his requirements on a deeper, more creative level by using adjectives. Ask the client to write down the adjectives that describe how he wants the voice-over to sound.

Although having that kind of information can be useful, you still may not get the guidance you seek. In that case you need to rely on your instincts, experience, and ability to self-direct, given the answer you come up with from the preceding list of questions.

Getting clarification on artistic direction: What some pros say

Before you're ready to record (or audition), you may want some clarification from the client or director. Here are some tips from professional voice actors that may help you.

✔ **Julie Williams:** "It's helpful to know the demographic and psychographic of the audience you're talking to, but if the script is well written, you don't need the client telling you who to 'imitate' or the sound they want."

✔ **Paul Plack:** "Feel what you're saying, and you will present the message they intended. If it has potential to be a satisfying job and is missing only a few clues, I'll go online and use a search engine. Often, you can piece together a mental picture of who you'll be talking to and the company's approach in other media in as little as a minute or two. If you get it right, you may wind up with a repeat customer."

✔ **Paul Hernandez:** "There are quite a few job postings out there that don't give you much to go on in the way of direction. In the book *Word of Mouth* Susan Blu talks about 'The Basic Process,' which is a way to prepare yourself to read the copy by asking questions like Who are you reading to? Who is speaking? Why are you doing this? It's a great way to get creative and come up with your own take on the copy. Also I too like the idea of searching the web to get a feel for what the company is all about."

After you do a very quick analysis of the script and the answers to these questions, you're ready to record (or audition) with more than just an educated guess, proving that a little thought goes a long way.

When clients post jobs at `Voices.com`, they receive additional guidance from the job posting form and are shown through examples how to describe and communicate their needs to potential applicants in order to get the best responses possible. Keep in mind that not everyone who uses the site knows exactly what he or she is looking for. If the client had a preference or knew what kind of voice and attributes he wanted ahead of time, he would have indicated so in the script.

Directing Yourself When You Record Your Voice

Even when you receive artistic direction from the client and director, you still may need to self-direct yourself, especially if you're working on a smaller project and recording it by yourself. You're ready to press record, and you've evaluated your character and studied the script. You're confident and positioned behind the microphone. In this section, we explain some studio basics for acting on your own and expectations that may be applied to you as a voice actor working in the 21st century.

Understanding what self-direction is

One of the biggest challenges today in voice acting isn't getting work. It's *self-direction,* where you put on the director's hat and make creative decisions that influence your read. Being able to direct a session on your own is a fundamental skill voice actors need to develop in order to give a solid performance.

Before the phenomenon and boom of the professional-grade home recording studio, voice actors used to go to studios to audition and to recording studios to complete work they were hired to voice. Recording at the studio was far less technical and more social and interactive. It also provided a more conducive environment for coaching and directing during the recording process.

The voice actor's role has changed dramatically over the years, mainly because recording technology has become more economical and easier to use. As a result, voice actors are required to take on additional roles and responsibilities, such as becoming an engineer, business person, manager, and director.

Being your own director

It's showtime. Acting as your own director and recording your voice for the finished product are really no different than recording an audition (refer to Chapters 11 and 12), except this time is the real thing. The only difference is that you're on your own, so get comfortable and put all your hard work leading up to this point into practice. You're prepared to do a great job, and if you're well-rested, focused on your performance, and warmed up, your voice won't let you down.

To self-direct, take care of the same preparations as if you had a director, including the following:

✔ **Set up your microphone and stand for the script:** The position of your microphone and stand are important because they're part of the signal chain that helps your voice make it through to the computer to be recorded. (Refer to Chapter 18 for how to do so.)

- ✔ **Interpret the script:** When you read a script, you need to prepare yourself for a role and not just regurgitate what is written on the page. (See Chapter 5 for how to interpret a script.)

- ✔ **Determine who the audience is:** As a self-director, knowing your audience is even more important because no one else is there to fill in the gaps information-wise. (Flip to Chapters 4 and 5 for understanding your role as a voice actor as it pertains to your audience and uncovering helpful tools.)

- ✔ **Create and develop your character:** Knowing your character means that you have a good understanding of what your character would do in any given situation. You understand your character and can make solid judgments on how he or she would say something, why he or she would say it, and how he or she would best communicate the message.

  Knowing this information applies to all applications of voice acting, not just animation or commercials; every job that you take on is another role you will perform, even work that you may perceive to be corporate, including telephone system voice-overs, podcasts, or business presentations. (Refer to Chapter 5 for how to create and develop your character.)

- ✔ **Speak to your audience:** You need to know your role so that you can competently and confidently speak to your audience. This means understanding who you are in terms of whether you are an announcer, an instructor, and so on. (Check out Chapter 4 for how to speak to your audience.)

When you're self-directing, you need to draw upon all the information you have at your disposal, including what role(s) you are playing, who you are speaking to, why the audience should care, and so on. You also need to consider the brand you're recording for and what its values are.

To direct yourself well, you need a quiet space where you can experiment with different takes and listen back to them. One of your best allies is the script because it's chockfull of clues, particularly in audiobook narration. The author gives you an amazing amount of direction that you can interpret on your own. The best part: The author is consistent with this direction, providing you an almost foolproof guide on how he or she intends for you to voice the script.

Depending on the length of the assignment, make sure you have allocated enough time to record the entire script in a single sitting. Why? Believe it or not, your voice changes slightly from day to day. External factors, such as the amount of rest you received, the weather, and the time of day you record, all affect the consistency of your recording.

To combat these challenges, schedule your sessions for long recording projects, such as audiobooks, one day after another until the project is done.

Listening to the Finished Product

When you've finished recording the script and following the client's directions, you want to listen to the finished product. Consider the final listening to the finished product as proofreading where you can double-check to ensure the work is ready to submit.

When you're listening to the finished product, stick to these steps to ensure the final product is ready:

1. **Follow along with the script.**

   You want to make sure you read the script just as the client wanted and you didn't accidentally skip a paragraph. Believe us, even the best voice actors have inadvertently done it. You can catch omissions simply by listening through your takes.

2. **If you identify any missed material, record it.**

   Try your best to match your voice, speaking at the same speed and register you had performed earlier in the session, so that what you voice after the fact fits in nicely with what you had recorded earlier.

3. **If you identify material that needs rerecorded, rerecord it.**

   If you notice a word or phrase that isn't as clear as it needs to be, or an outside noise (such as a neighbor dog barking), rerecord that part of the script. The great thing about audio editing is that you can move one part of your recording and place it wherever you want to in a file.

4. **After you complete the recording, have edited any mistakes, and mixed the audio to your satisfaction, export the recording into the format as requested by your client.**

   If the client hasn't specified a particular format, deliver the audio as a WAV file, which is a high-quality, uncompressed format. (Refer to Chapter 21 for more information about file formats, including WAV files. Check out Chapter 19 for editing and mixing instructions.)

5. **When you complete the exporting processes, play the audio file.**

   Sit back and listen to the recording from start to finish without starts and stops. In fact, stand up, walk around, and then return to the studio for one final listen.

Be careful of falling victim to *listening fatigue,* which occurs when you've been editing or mixing for hours on end. After sitting in the same position and listening to the same bit of audio, your ears tend to get foggy and you can miss little nuances. To overcome listening fatigue, take a break and then return to the session with fresh ears.

Listening fatigue is similar to the effect of driving at high speeds on the highway for hours and then driving in city traffic. You feel like you're driving slowly, even though you're probably going faster than the speed limit.

Chapter 21

Delivering the Final Product

. . . .

. . . .

Recording great voice-overs is just part of what it takes to be a successful voice actor. Knowing about the technical side of things, such as using file formats, delivering files to your customers, and receiving approval of your finished work, is very important.

Utilizing your business acumen is also necessary for getting valuable feedback from your customers in the form of either a feedback rating and review or a testimonial that you can use for future marketing purposes to obtain more work.

In this chapter, we discuss some of the most common file formats used in digital audio production today. You want to make sure you're sending the files in the format that your client desires. After your client reviews the files, you want to ensure he or she is pleased with your work. You also want to acquire a taste for giving and receiving feedback as a professional voice actor.

Identifying Best Practices for Sending Audio

Applying the best practices for sending audio recordings demonstrates that you're a professional who knows what you're doing. Best practices are generally accepted as the "best way" to do something. In this section, we look at the best practices for sending audio files, which include saving the audio in a common file format, naming the files appropriately, and sending the files over the Internet.

Handling file formats

Many types of audio file formats exist, but as a voice actor, you only need to be familiar with a handful of them. You're probably familiar with the common ones, such as a WAV file or an MP3 file. You may have even heard of an AIFF. In the following sections, we discuss just the file formats that you need to know about and how and when you may come across them.

Note that we list the file formats in this section from the highest quality file formats through to lesser quality file formats. The lesser quality are still useful and can do the job.

WAV

Without a doubt, WAV, which stands for *waveform audio file format,* is the most common professional audio format — professional in the sense that it's uncompressed and most widely used. Microsoft and IBM jointly developed the WAV file format, which explains why it was built into Windows 95 as the de facto standard for sound on PCs. The quality of a WAV file is superior to MP3 (see the later section on MP3s), but it takes a lot longer to download, because of its size. Most broadcast-quality audio is saved as a WAV file. You can always encode a WAV file as an MP3, but you can't change an MP3 to a WAV file.

AIFF

AIFF stands for Audio Interchange File Format. Apple developed AIFF, which explains why it's the standard audio format for both storing and transmitting sampled sound on Mac computers. AIFF file extensions tend to appear as .AIF or .IEF.

When using AIFF, you can't compress the audio file, and an AIFF tends to be rather large. That being said, a version of the file type called AIF-Compressed, referred to as AIF-C or AIFC, supports compression ratios as high as 6:1.

MP3

MP3, which stands for MPEG-1 or MPEG-2 Audio Layer 3, is a common audio file format for consumer storage (think your music collection) as well as the de facto standard of digital audio compression for the transfer and playback of music on digital audio players. Although its quality isn't as high as a WAV file, if the MP3 is encoded at a high enough *bitrate* (a measurement of the quality of the audio), the quality is more than acceptable, even broadcast-ready in some cases. The higher the bitrate, the better the sound quality. Most audio files you encounter on the web are MP3s because the files are much smaller than other formats and can be quickly downloaded.

OGG

The Ogg Vorbis (OGG) format is comparable to other formats used to store and play digital music, such as MP3. Unlike those formats, however, Ogg Vorbis is license-free, so commercial video games often use it.

When you save an OGG file, you can select one of three basic encoding options:

- ✔ **VBR (target bitrate):** It allows you to specify the target bitrate in kilobits per second. This option maintains audio quality by varying the bitrate, depending on the complexity of the audio being encoded. This method can maintain higher audio quality, although file size isn't as predictable as with fixed bitrate encoding.

- ✔ **VBR (quality index):** This option is similar to VBR (target bitrate), but it lets you specify quality on a scale of 0 to 10.

- ✔ **Fixed (bitrate varies):** This option measures the quality level as needed to ensure that the bitrate stays at the specified rate. This method makes a consistently sized file, although the quality may not be as high as with variable bitrate encoding.

Naming files

When you name a file, be sure that the name directly relates to the contents of the audio file. That may mean that you include the name of the client you're working for and your name. Use hyphens or underscores to separate words in the file name. An example of this may be:

    yourname-client.mp3

Properly naming the file can help you keep track of what the file contains and who the client is. For more complex jobs, your client may ask you to use a specific file naming convention to identify which files are which. If the file name is important to your client, she often spells it out for you before you start on the project. If you don't receive any instruction, you may want to double-check with your client about how she wants the files named.

If you're working on a project with hundreds of files, using this clear file-naming convention not only comes in handy, but it's also a necessity. For example, telephony work, e-learning modules, and some audiobooks can have complicated file naming conventions because of the sheer number of individual files you have to record.

Zipping files

If you have large file attachments to send, you can shrink files to manageable sizes by zipping them. Zipping a folder with files in it is also a great way to send multiple files in one package.

To zip, follow these easy steps:

1. **Create a folder for the files that you want to send to your client.**

2. **Copy or add all the files that you want to send into that folder.**

3. **Right-click (on a PC) or Control-click (on a Mac) to open up a menu of actions that you can take on that folder.**

   On a PC, select "Send To" and "Compressed (zipped) Folder." This may be different depending on what version of Microsoft Windows you have.

   On a Mac, it says "Compress your folder name here," which is Apple's way of saying "zipping."

   You may want to double-check that all the files you have zipped are together in the .zip file. After you see they are there, you can attach the .zip file to an e-mail and send it.

Sending Files: The How-To

How you landed the job and how big the files are will determine how you send the audio files. Check with your client to determine if she has any requirements for how you deliver your files. These sections identify some of the many ways you can deliver files to your clients, including email or third-party services.

Emailing files to your client

For small projects that involve a small number of audio files (say less than five), you can simply email the files to your client. Doing so is as easy as composing a new email message and then attaching the files to your email.

Include in your email message something like "Please confirm receipt of these files." You're not asking for the client to approve the files, but you simply want acknowledgement that the client received them.

If you don't hear back from your client, follow up by email (or by phone if you're working on a tight deadline) to verify that the client did indeed receive the files. Just because the email message is in your sent box doesn't necessary mean your client received it. A spam filter may have caught the message, or it may have exceeded a file size restriction on the receiving end.

Every email service provider has file size limitation and may result in your email bouncing back as undeliverable. For example, Gmail has a file attachment limit of 25MB (megabytes) per email. Other email services have similar constraints, which is why zipping your files can come in handy (see the previous section about how to zip files). If you receive an undeliverable message, you may want to try another means to deliver the files. As a general rule, if the file size exceeds 25MB, you should deliver the files through a file-sharing service or by FTP (as we discuss in the next sections).

Using a file-sharing website

In recent years, file-sharing websites have been all the rage. They solve a pretty significant challenge online. They allow you to deliver large multimedia files quickly and easily — and at low cost.

A file-sharing website, sometimes called a *file-hosting service,* offers a convenient way to upload, organize, and share multimedia files, such as audio, video, photos, and large PDFs. You can organize files into folders just like you do on your personal computer and then share either a single file or an entire folder with your client.

Considering most services offer a free entry-level package, we see no reason why you shouldn't set up an account at one of the following sites:

- ✔ **Google Drive:** Previously known as Google Docs, Google Drive (https:// drive.google.com/start) allows you to store files conveniently online so that you can access them from anywhere at anytime. You can easily share these files with others by sending a link to where they can download the file from.

- ✔ **Microsoft SkyDrive:** With this file-sharing website (http://windows. microsoft.com/en-CA/skydrive/home), you can easily store and securely share files with others. You get 7GB of SkyDrive Storage. You can also install a SkyDrive app on your computer.

- ✔ **DropBox:** DropBox (www.dropbox.com) creates a new folder on your computer, whether a PC or Mac. You can save files or other information in specific folders on the site. You can share a DropBox folder with someone else, which allows that person to access the files you want to share.

✔ **YouSendIt:** This site (www.yousendit.com) provides the ability for you to take your files with you. YouSendIt also lets you access or send files from home or on the road using any mobile device or computer.

Uploading your audio with FTP programs

For larger projects, the file transfer protocol (FTP) is the way to go. With FTP, you can transfer data and program files, in this case an MP3 file, from your personal computer to your web hosting service. Your client can then access the files from the web hosting service. Access is restricted between you and the client. Accessing the service requires a username and password, which the web hosting service provides.

If you're working for a large client, it may have an internal FTP. You can get web hosting with FTP for as little as $4.99 per month, so it's quite affordable. Just realize FTP is for the technically inclined and requires a bit of setup, depending on the service you use.

To get started with FTP, you need an FTP program, which communicates to your web hosting company. Dozens of FTP programs are available on the market; many of them are *open source,* which means they're free! In no particular order, here are some of our favorites.

✔ **Cute FTP:** (www.cuteftp.com): Cute FTP claims to be the world's favorite FTP client. After you connect, you can transfer data between your Windows-based PC and the web server of your choice.

✔ **Fetch FTP:** This FTP service (http://fetchsoftworks.com) is a Macintosh program that allows you to send files over networks, such as the Internet, using the FTP. You enjoy all the standard features of a modern FTP program with the benefit of an easy-to-use interface.

✔ **Captain FTP:** Captain FTP (www.apple.com/downloads/dashboard/networking_security/captainftpwidget.html) is a powerful, secure, and user-friendly site that allows you to share files to authorized users. It offers simple navigation and several features to make sharing files that much easier. Localized versions are also available in English, German, French, Japanese, and Chinese.

Recording live sessions with ISDN

Integrated Digital Services Network (also known simply as ISDN) is at its core a Digital Service Line (DSL). For a number of decades, voice actors working from home have used an ISDN line to send real-time, two-way studio quality audio to a second studio. ISDN allows for a producer or director to direct the voice actor from afar over the ISDN line as if he were in the studio with the voice actor. Some telecommunications providers offer ISDN lines, and you pay for the time spent on the ISDN line. In order to have an ISDN line, you and the studio both need to have hardware (a little black box) in order to have a successful session in terms of connectivity.

Securing an ISDN line costs between $3,000 and $5,000. Having a line in your studio can be quite expensive, but if you're regularly booking high paying jobs that require ISDN, the line can pay for itself and then some. However, you may find that most clients don't require you to use an ISDN, particularly if you're focusing on *business-to-business work,* meaning that you're directly working with the end client. Ad agencies and big studios may demand that you have an ISDN line, but not everyone does, so check with your client before you make the investment.

Because an ISDN line is considerably pricey, along with installation and maintenance services for ISDN, the shift to other digital technologies is inevitable. Alternatives to ISDN lines include AudioTX Communicator and Source-Connect, which we discuss in the next sections. Although these technologies aren't completely on par with ISDN reliability and quality, they're certainly gaining ground and becoming more popular as their technologies improve.

ISDN and the Internet eliminate the commute

With today's technologies available, voice actors have significantly less commuting back and forth between home and recording studios (which also makes for cleaner air and less money spent on gasoline). When ISDN was becoming more widely used in the 1990s, voice actor Beau Weaver and several of his peers wanted to use the new technology and work from home studios.

They asked Don LaFontaine to use his influence and help make the transition from having to be physically present in a recording studio to auditioning and working most of the time from home. If Don told the industry that he wanted to have an ISDN hookup in his home to work, then everyone else would be able to follow suit,

and look where the industry is today. (Don is known for being the voice of the movies, having recorded more than 5,000 movie trailers over his 33-year career. Don inspired generations of voice actors, and his legacy is that he was a great artist, mentor, and trailblazer.) Since then, sessions with ISDN have saved clients and talents time, money, and mileage, and have dramatically changed the lifestyles of the working voice actor. With the combination of the fact that nearly all voice actors have personal computers with high-speed Internet access and the decrease in prices for equipment, the home studio boom was triggered and the market expanded. (Refer to Chapter 17 where we discuss some ins and outs of setting up your own home studio.)

AudioTX Communicator

AudioTX Communicator provides broadcast-quality audio over ISDN, IP networks, and the Internet. You can send files such as MP3s and more. This is a software-only ISDN audio code that works with all other ISDN codecs. AudioTX Communicator can send and receive live, professional-quality audio files over any IP network or the Internet.

Source-Connect

Source-Connect enables worldwide real-time audio connections similar to how ISDN bridges studios for the recording of live sessions without the significant cost of investing in ISDN and its usage fees. In fact, flawless recordings with broadcast-quality audio are what make Source-Connect with no ongoing monthly fees the choice for many voice actors. Source-Connect is a plug-in that you add to your recording software and allows you to affordably record, collaborate, or monitor sessions from your professional, home, or portable studio, anywhere in the world. You don't need any expensive ISDN lines, hardware, subscription, or usage fees to use Source-Connect.

At present, Source-Connect is compatible with both Macintosh OS X and Windows XP, but it only works with higher-end, multitrack recording programs, such as Pro Tools, Cubase, and Sonar.

Delivering your work to Voices.com

For jobs you've received at `Voices.com`, you need to deliver your audio files through the Voices.com website because your client will expect you to do so. To load your files on the website, follow these steps:

1. **Log in to your account.**

2. **Navigate to the job.**

3. **Click on the tab called "Files."**

4. **On the Files screen, click on the link to "Add New File."**

5. **Browse your hard drive for the finished audio file that you exported from your recording software and attach it.**

6. **Give the file a name and description.**

   If you have more than one file to upload, you can do so by clicking on "Add another file."

7. **When you're finished, click the "Upload file" button to send the files to your client.**

With Voices.com, you can upload an unlimited number of WAV and MP3 files per job, but each file can't exceed 250MB each. If for some reason you run into a technical issue, such as the file not uploading, call the toll-free hotline (888-359-3472) or email customer support.

The main benefits of Source-Connect include the following:

- ✔ It uses the highest quality audio encoding technology.
- ✔ It only requires a broadband Internet connection.
- ✔ A restore feature insures flawless recordings regardless of Internet congestion.
- ✔ It works with ISDN systems
- ✔ It synchronizes two recording studios for easy overdubbing

Doing What It Takes to Get Approval

Seeking approval from your clients before invoicing them and making sure they're happy with your work is important. The customer is always right, right? After reviewing the files, your client may ask you to make revisions to the tracks, whether because you incorrectly said something or the client had a change in the copy after the deal was struck.

Sometimes when you seek approval from a client, she may request you make a small revision to the files. A *revision* is when you make an alteration to an existing recording, whether slight or significant. Alterations may include the pronunciation of specific words, the interpretation of a script, or changes made to update the script over time. These sections identify what it means to make minor and major revisions to the tracks before the client can ultimately approve them. After you get final approval, you want to ask the client for feedback.

If you happen to be using a marketplace website, more than likely you'll deliver the finished audio through its website. If you're using Voices.com, our site automatically sends an email to your client to inform her that you have uploaded the files and that they're ready for her approval. After a client approves the files associated with her job by clicking on the "Approve File" button, she is prompted to release the funds from escrow, and Voices.com is able to pay you for your work. If you're using a different marketplace website, check with the company to see how it handles seeking approval from clients.

Doing small edits

Many of the revisions you may have to make can be classified as minor revisions. You generally need to make smaller revisions to recordings that that client intends to use for long periods of time, and can be regarded as ongoing updates to the script.

When a client reviews the files, if she notices a word pronounced incorrectly or unclearly, she can ask you to rerecord the voice-over at no charge. You're responsible for giving the client what she paid for. However, if the recording needs to be recorded again due to a script change, that type of revision is a major revision, which we discuss in the next section.

When you make minor revisions, you may only need to rerecord certain portions of the script and not the entire script as a whole. What you'll want to do is listen to the original file and try to match what you sounded like then for consistency.

Making major revisions and knowing whether to charge or not

Sometimes your client may request that you make major revisions to the recordings. Major revisions include changes to the script, which can lead to additional charges for your services.

How do you know when to charge for revisions? These few guidelines can help you determine what to do:

- ✔ You can charge for revisions when the client introduces new copy outside of what was originally presented.
- ✔ You can charge for revisions if the client wants you to rerecord an entire script.
- ✔ You don't charge if you're responsible for a mispronunciation.
- ✔ You don't charge for a revision if something is in your recording that shouldn't be there (extra words, extraneous noises, and so on).
- ✔ You don't charge for a revision if the audio quality you produced was poor.

Most voice actors, when individually assessing situations, know when it's right to charge for a revision and when it's better to be gracious and let the word or two be changed without incurring another fee for a minor revision. Go with your gut. If the revision won't take you long and you have a good working relationship with this client, do what you need to preserve this relationship. On the other hand, don't let a client take advantage of you.

You want to communicate with your client whether the revision she requests warrants an additional charge or whether the revision is simple that you can do in a short amount of time. Be careful, because you don't want to give the impression that your time and effort have no value. If you do decide to include minor revisions that result from a client changing the script for free (or your editing the copy to flow better), inform the client in a gracious way that you have done this as a value-added service. The result? The client will be pleased and will notice your work.

Receiving feedback

Getting a testimonial, feedback, or a review after a job well done is important. After your client approves your work, you want to gather feedback. You can then keep track of what others are saying about your work and share on your website or marketing materials. When you post them on your website, other prospective clients can see them, which can help build trust and establish a rapport with them. Check out Chapter 9, where we explain how to get testimonials and feedback and how you can use them to your advantage.

Part VI
The Part of Tens

The 5th Wave   By Rich Tennant

In this part . . .

Every *For Dummies* book has this part, chockfull of fun and quick tidbits. Here we include a chapter on ten reasons you should regularly audition (and pointers to help make those auditions worthwhile) and a chapter on ten ways to get ready for voice-acting jobs. Even if you don't have a voice-acting business, these tips and insight can help you prepare for what lies ahead — whatever way you choose to do voice acting.

Chapter 22

Ten Reasons You Should Regularly Audition

In This Chapter

▶ Keeping you fit as a voice actor

▶ Focusing on getting work

▶ Eyeing industry trends

*M*any voice actors believe that auditioning is their real job, and getting the gig is gravy. What most people don't tell you is that auditioning also helps you to keep your voice in shape, your skills sharp, and your name (and voice) out there for prospective customers to see.

Auditioning is the chief means for professional voice actors to acquire work. Even though some of the work out there may come to you without having to audition, those opportunities to work are few and far between. Having a wide variety of venues through which to promote your voice and submit auditions is very important. Whether you audition in the marketplace (and online), at agencies, or by some other means, auditioning, and auditioning regularly, is the lifeblood of your voice acting business.

The best way to keep in vocal shape — mentally, physically, and artistically — is to audition every business day. Getting behind the mic, reading copy in your car, or even practicing silly voices around the house can do a tremendous service to you and your voice acting career. If you're still not convinced, here are ten reasons why you should audition regularly.

Keeps You in Good Form

Each time you audition, you're conditioning yourself and keeping in shape for your next job. If you stop auditioning, you cease to challenge yourself and the potential to fall into a lazy, apathetic slump may become a very real consequence of failing to "work out" or continue refining your skills.

Just as your body needs to get up and exercise to keep in good shape, you, as a voice actor, need to continuously engage with the written word and interpret direction. Auditioning regularly helps you remain consistent in your ability to read well and work with copy. For example, if you haven't read for a while, you may stumble a bit when reading aloud.

Lifting words off the printed page can also help you with eye coordination. Each opportunity presents you with a fresh piece of copy crafted for voice actors to read and engages you intellectually as well as physically with regard to voice production.

Provides You with a Diverse Array of Copy to Experiment with and Interpret

You may already be picking up everything that comes across your path and reading it aloud. If you don't, the copy you receive with each audition serves as a way to get your voice-over vitamins as it were. You need to experiment with a lot of different scripts. Some scripts may require you to be an announcer, while others have you play different roles, such as narrator, spokesperson, or even instructor. Each role, as we discuss in Chapter 4, requires something special from you as a voice actor, so make sure you read for many different roles throughout the course of your day.

Stimulates Your Voice and Mind

When you audition, the words on your script don't just leap out of your mouth; you must deliver them with purpose and conviction. When you do, you get to explore different parts of your voice you never knew were there and engage different parts of your brain.

Auditioning is no time to go on auto-pilot or to default into reading mode. Let each piece of copy take you on a trip to a faraway place, introduce you to people you've never met, and show you things about yourself that you didn't yet know.

Gives You a Platform to Strut Your Stuff

Auditioning gives you an opportunity to be bold with your choices and stand out from the crowd. When you audition, remember that you have been asked to submit a response based upon either an online profile, your demo, or, if you are fortunate enough, your reputation. In an audition, the floor is yours both virtually and literally to show your skills and abilities. Give it all you have.

Exponentially Improves Your Job Prospects

When you audition, prospective clients (and possibly potential agents) see your name and hear your voice. They have a chance, albeit brief, to get to know you. Even if potential clients don't hire you for a particular job, they may keep you in mind for something more suitable to your voice and specific talents. So you always want to do your best in auditioning because you never know who is listening.

Generates Networking Opportunities

Auditioning affords you face time of sorts with people in a position to work with you. As a result, you can develop new friendships and make new business contacts. You can meet anyone from the casting director to an agent to a recording engineer and voice director. You never know who is waiting in the wings. When auditioning online, you can connect with people in other ways. The bottom line, though, is that it takes showing up (either in person or in the virtual world) to meet people, so show up!

Introduces You to New Areas of Interest

Random pieces of copy that come your way can introduce you to topics or concepts you may find particularly useful to you at some time in your voice acting career. When you audition regularly, you're bound to encounter a plethora of content and pick up some interesting facts along the way. Most voice actors, by virtue of their profession, tend to collect tidbits of information. These tidbits make for good small talk at networking events or parties.

Furthermore, reading about topics in audition copy and then following up on what you read to discover more about the topic can lead you down roads you never knew you'd explore and make you better for it.

Helps You Spot Industry Trends

Some people love to watch television commercials and movie trailers, and listen to audiobooks to see what the trends are in voice casting. Auditioning can also help you identify trends. If you see a number of auditions that ask for similar artistic direction, voice ages, accents, or character archetypes, you may be spotting a trend. Isn't it neat to see this happening before the voice-over is even recorded and aired for all to hear? This sort of research can be helpful for you and also provide ideas for how you can serve a particular niche or demographic with your voice.

Validates the Need for Voice Acting

Auditioning also reinforces the importance of voice acting. Even though technology has improved greatly, a real live human voice can still achieve all the goals producers need for voice acting work. In fact, voice-overs are needed for almost every conceivable application. The need for a custom read of a script isn't going anywhere. There's nothing quite like hearing someone deliver a well-thought-out performance with heart and soul. As long as clients have work, custom voice-over recordings will never go out of style.

Renews Your Faith that Work Exists

Every time you audition is yet more proof that the voice-over work is out there. Many people become discouraged if they don't book a job after so many auditions (the threshold is different for everyone), but each and every audition that you do, see, or hear about goes to show that there is no shortage of work. When auditioning, keep in mind that there is a job for every voice and a voice for every job. Keep auditioning regularly and when the right opportunity comes along, you'll be positioned well to receive it.

Chapter 23

Ten (or So) Tips to Prepare for Voice Acting Jobs

In This Chapter

▶ Hiring a voice coach

▶ Focusing on your goals and expectations

*S*uccess is when preparation meets opportunity. So with that in mind, consider what you can do to prepare for future opportunities. But first, ask yourself:

✔ Would an aspiring singer perform in a recital before taking any lessons?

✔ Would an entrepreneur go to a banker asking for money without a business plan?

✔ Would an agent want to receive a demo CD from a voice actor who doesn't have any training?

You get the point. It pays to prepare. And, whether it's recording your first demo or wanting to do your first audition without any training or direction, the advice still applies. This chapter gives you ten (or so) tips to help you be ready for voice-over work.

Whatever you put into something is what you will get out of it. Define what you need to do in order to make progress as a voice actor. Discover everything you can about the industry. Knowledge is power, and you'll want to have spent plenty of time researching and evaluating opportunities before jumping in the voice-over pool.

Invest in Regular Vocal Training

To be better at anything you do, you need training from experienced people who know what they're doing. Acquiring knowledge and skill is a primary goal. In order to prepare yourself for a voice acting job, you need to spend time and, more than likely, some money for instruction. That training can come from classes and even this book. In fact, many voice coaches are clear that they won't produce voice-over demos for students until they have studied and are ready to do so. (The next section discusses how a coach can help you get ready for voice acting work.)

Work with a Voice Coach

You can get specific training and instruction from a coach. Studying with a coach affords you access to the trained, objective ears of someone with extensive industry experience. A coach knows what needs to be done in order to prepare you for a career in voice acting.

A coach also has connections. When you're just starting out, training is important, but so is getting to know other people in the business. Your coach can facilitate some wonderful networking opportunities for you as well as send you to auditions or recommend you to others for work. Refer to Chapter 3 for advice on finding a voice coach.

Practice, Practice, Practice

To improve your skills and be ready to record a voice-over demo (and get hired), you need to practice. After you practice, you need to practice some more. You can't expect to perfect your voice-over work if you don't take the time to fine-tune your skills. Practicing is the only way to do that.

Hold off on making a voice-over demo that you promote to agents and prospective clients until you've practiced and are ready. You want to make an excellent first impression with agents, producers, and potential clients, and if you haven't practiced and can show you know what you're doing, you may fall flat on your face.

Have Self-Confidence

Confidence, and more specifically self-confidence, is important for any professional, especially someone in voice acting, because the tool you're using to serve people is your voice, which is part of you. Beauty is in the eye of the beholder, and the same goes for what someone thinks is a perfect take or casting in voice acting. Your role as voice actor is to do your best and let your voice shine.

Having confidence isn't necessarily limited to being confident in your vocal abilities. It also means that you stand firm on how much you charge for a voice-over recording. Like most freelance work, fees for voice acting can vary from professional to professional. You may have the perfect voice for a client, but if you're quoting lower than your norm just to get attention to win someone over, you then become the person with the perfect voice who charges the least amount of money when you could have been the person with the perfect voice whose services were well-priced and well-paid for. Don't sell yourself short! Getting someone to pay you what you want them to pay you is a lot harder if you get in the door at a reduced price. (Refer to Chapter 15 for all topics related to quoting rates and getting paid.)

Avoid Being Too Hard on Yourself

Voice actors are often creating voices and sometimes, they even hear them in their heads! Most people can relate to being their own worst critic, perhaps even having an inner critic that picks them apart. Although you need to self-evaluate what you can do to improve, you also want to avoid going too far and expecting perfection. You can be too hard on yourself when you're struggling to grasp a concept, when you're auditioning, and even in the midst of a job.

To separate yourself from your inner critic, you can do the following:

- ✔ **Ignore the voice.** Doing so is difficult, but doable. Tune that voice out by being objective about your performance, using facts and not emotion to determine how closely you matched the requirements.

- ✔ **Walk away from your computer.** Just get away for a little bit and come back with a set of fresh ears to re-listen to your recording and/or audition.

- ✔ **Take some deep breaths and relax.** Try to stop being anxious. Trust that if you're right for the job, you'll get it.

After you do get hired for a job, you need to be careful how you interpret feedback during a session. Interpreting feedback as criticism may be a natural response, but doing so isn't the healthiest response. The director is only trying to communicate his vision through your voice by doing business with you. He doesn't have anything personal against you.

Be Selective

The voice-over auditioning and hiring process is subjective. Obviously you won't get every job you audition for, nor will you be the only business person who can fulfill those needs. Hence you also want to be selective with the opportunities you pursue.

Wise professionals realize that there is a voice for every project and a project for every voice. They know they aren't going to win them all, but they have faith and conviction that they'll win the jobs they are perfect for without having to compromise.

When deciding what kind of work you want to do, listen to both your head and your heart. By focusing on opportunities that you are comfortable with, you'll enjoy your work more and also reap greater rewards if you book the job. (Check out Chapter 14 for more advice.)

Set Achievable Goals and Realistic Expectations

When you set out to have a voice acting career, you need to make sure you set realistic goals and expectations. If you're new to voice acting, make sure you first understand the nature of the business (Chapter 2 can give you some insight). If you're the owner of that business, you're solely responsible for growing your business, educating yourself, and becoming established in the voice acting field.

When you work in voice acting, you only get out of it what you put into it. As a result, make sure you determine your goals regarding training, practice, studio, time, and effort, and what you realistically expect to attain. If you're brand new, your goals and expectations should be different than someone who has been in the field for five years.

Voice actors who set out to use an online marketplace are guaranteed access to concrete opportunities. Although the marketplace may not be able to promise you that you'll get work, it does promise you the opportunity to present yourself for work opportunities to clients directly. In other words, you're receiving concrete opportunities, not concrete work.

Listen to Demos of Established Voice Actors

To be prepared for work in voice acting (and before you record your own demo), you need to know what a great voice-over demos sounds like. You don't have to look too far! You can listen online at marketplace websites, such as www.voices.com.

You can search through the demos and explore a wide array of examples. You can listen to demos in a variety of categories, languages, voice ages, and more. You can also easily look up demos by keyword.

When listening to demos, tune your ear to how the voice actor has presented herself, the contents of the demo, how long it runs, and whether the voice actor included production (such as effects on the voice, music, or sound effects). You can pause on spots that catch your attention and study what it is about those moments that interest you.

Take Advantage of Every Free Resource You Can

Many free resources are available that you can tap into for more help in perfecting your voice acting. These different elements range from interpretation to performance. They can help you create the presence you're aiming to achieve in order to make a killer demo and be ready for a voice acting job.

For starters, look online for free resources. You may find articles and free podcasts by searching for them in your favorite search engine. You can also listen to voice-overs for free on www.youtube.com.

Index

• W •